*PALGRAVE GREAT **DEBATES IN LAW***

D1448493

# PALGRAVE *GREAT* **DEBATES *IN LAW***

**Series editor**
**Jonathan Herring**
**Professor of Law**
**University of Oxford**

Company Law
*Lorraine Talbot*

Contract Law
*Jonathan Morgan*

Criminal Law
*Jonathan Herring*

Employment Law
*Simon Honeyball*

Equity and Trusts
*Alastair Hudson*

Family Law
*Jonathan Herring, Rebecca Probert & Stephen Gilmore*

Jurisprudence
*Nicholas J McBride & Sandy Steel*

Medical Law and Ethics
*Imogen Goold & Jonathan Herring*

Property Law
*David Cowan, Lorna Fox O'Mahony & Neil Cobb*

If you would like to comment on this book, or on any other law text
published by Palgrave, please write to lawfeedback@palgrave.com.

PALGRAVE GREAT **DEBATES IN LAW**

# GREAT DEBATES IN
# EQUITY AND TRUSTS

ALASTAIR HUDSON

Professor of Equity and Finance Law,
University of Southampton, National Teaching Fellow

 macmillan education  palgrave

© Alastair Hudson 2014

All rights reserved. No reproduction, copy or transmission of this publication may be made without written permission.

Crown Copyright material is licensed under the Open Government Licence v2.0.

No portion of this publication may be reproduced, copied or transmitted save with written permission or in accordance with the provisions of the Copyright, Designs and Patents Act 1988, or under the terms of any licence permitting limited copying issued by the Copyright Licensing Agency, Saffron House, 6–10 Kirby Street, London EC1N 8TS.

Any person who does any unauthorized act in relation to this publication may be liable to criminal prosecution and civil claims for damages.

The author has asserted his right to be identified as the author of this work in accordance with the Copyright, Designs and Patents Act 1988.

First published 2014 by PALGRAVE

Palgrave in the UK is an imprint of Macmillan Publishers Limited, registered in England, company number 785998, of 4 Crinan Street, London N1 9XW.

Palgrave Macmillan in the US is a division of St Martin's Press LLC, 175 Fifth Avenue, New York, NY 10010.

Palgrave is a global imprint of the above companies and is represented throughout the world.

Palgrave® and Macmillan® are registered trademarks in the United States, the United Kingdom, Europe and other countries.

ISBN: 978–1–137–01570–9 paperback

This book is printed on paper suitable for recycling and made from fully managed and sustained forest sources. Logging, pulping and manufacturing processes are expected to conform to the environmental regulations of the country of origin.

A catalogue record for this book is available from the British Library.

Typeset by Cambrian Typesetters, Camberley, Surrey

Printed and bound in Great Britain by
The Lavenham Press Ltd, Suffolk

MIX
Paper from
responsible sources
FSC
www.fsc.org
FSC® C010693

*for Huxley*

# CONTENTS

# PREFACE

## BRINGING EQUITY AND TRUSTS TO LIFE

The aim of this book is to surround the ordinary study of equity and trusts law with the deeper questions which arise from legal practice and from a deeper analysis of the journal literature and the judgments. Those deeper questions really do bring even the most unlikely areas of trusts law to life. For example, have you considered the link between the beneficiary principle and international terrorism? Or the disagreeable way in which resulting trusts may unthinkingly treat women worse than men? Or the implausibility of rules created to supervise soft fruit markets in the early nineteenth century being applied to international financial instruments in the twenty-first century? Have you examined Aristotle's view of equity closely, or really thought about what a 'conscience' might be in psychological terms, or uncovered the salacious history of the Emperor Justinian before he became the poster boy for Oxford restitution scholars? And, more importantly, have you considered how each of these issues tells us something profound about the nature of equity and alternative ways of organising our law? Each of these new dimensions to the subject sheds very new light on even the oldest rules.

The great debates about equity and trusts raise complex, technical questions which are necessary for legal practice, as well as high-minded philosophical questions about the very nature of law. The debates which are considered in this book are often international in nature (considering how trusts are used differently in different jurisdictions), and they are also often political (considering how trusts treat women, and how trusts contribute both to tax avoidance and to funding international criminal organisations). There is more to equity and trusts than a mere series of rules. And, perhaps it may be interesting to note, there is a surer path to success in coursework and in examinations if you can bring some of these perspectives to bear on your study of the substantive law.

This book will bring equity and trusts to life by exploring the key debates between judges, practitioners, academics and policymakers in this field. Trusts law is a practical subject: trusts are used as tools by practitioners to achieve their clients' goals, both in England and Wales and internationally. The practical uses of trusts, and the debates among practitioners and policymakers about international trusts law, are at the forefront of this field. Traditional subjects on undergraduate trusts law syllabuses (such as the beneficiary principle) become much more vital when we realise that they are central to the political arguments about the use of trusts in international tax avoidance structures. Other subjects on the syllabus come to life when we understand them in terms of the differences of opinion between different commentators. It is often easier to understand the law as expressed in arguments between people with different points of view than it is to learn abstract rules. Hence we shall be considering this field through the lens of the great debates contained within it. Equity and trusts, as a legal field, is not just a series of rules; rather, it is also a zone of passionate debate between judges, practitioners and commentators. This field is alive in the real world. This book explores that life.

The idea for a *Great Debates* series is an excellent one. It is intended to unpick the debates which are found in both of those places, in an attractively-written way. As such, this book might appeal to students looking for a short-cut to a first class mark by giving them a greater insight into the law; more joyously, it will certainly appeal to serious students who want to understand equity and trusts at a deeper level.

## CECI N'EST PAS UN TEXTBOOK

It is important to point out at the beginning, however, that this is not a textbook. The subheading – 'ceci n'est pas un textbook' – is a reference to a painting by surrealist artist René Magritte which depicted a pipe under the words *'ceci n'est pas une pipe'* ('this is not a pipe'). In the terms of that painting, the initial surprise is that something which is clearly a painting of a pipe is described as being 'not a pipe'. However, of course, it was not a pipe: it was merely *a painting* of a pipe. Similarly, this book resembles a textbook, but it is not textbook in the truest sense.

This book analyses the debates which underlie the law, together with brief explanations of those principles, but it is not a textbook more generally than that. This book does not intend to explain all of the legal principles from scratch. A textbook would promise to explain all of the principles relevant to an understanding of the entire field from the ground upwards. This book does not purport to do all of that. Rather, in this book, each chapter summarises the legal principles briefly where they are appropriate to the discussion, but it does not promise a systematic analysis of the entire subject. Instead, the purpose of this book is to examine the principal debates which arise within the field so as to help you to understand the subject better.

The book you are reading is supported by podcasts and videos accessible via <www.alastairhudson.com>.

## ASKING DEEPER, MORE RELEVANT QUESTIONS ABOUT EQUITY AND TRUSTS

It has always seemed to me that any law student will discover more about themselves and their own attitudes to law as a whole through studying equity and trusts than any other compulsory course on the curriculum. That is because equity occupies such contested ground between positivism and natural law theory: that is, between a desire for strict, predictable rules on the one hand, and a desire for morally defensible judgments in individual cases on the other. Both equity and trusts law have many rigid rules, as well as containing wide-ranging, discretionary principles. There is a tension here between a utilitarian preference for order and a utopian preference for justice. Is law concerned with doing what is socially desirable, or with doing what is right? Fascinatingly, because this is a legal subject, these philosophical problems are then played out in specific cases in the real world. You, as a student of equity and trusts, will learn as much about how you feel about law as a result of considering these problems as you will from the study of almost any other subject.

The aim of this book is to identify the key debates among practitioners, academics and judges. Consequently, each chapter of this book identifies three or four key 'debates' within each topic, places them in context, and surveys the arguments. By conceiving of the law as being composed of arguments between people with differing viewpoints, it is possible to understand equity and trusts at a deeper level than simply treating it as a series of discrete rules. Ultimately, my goal is to communicate just a little of the love and enthusiasm I have for this subject to you.

I am very grateful indeed to Jonathan Herring (the series editor) and Rob Gibson (at Palgrave) for inviting me to make this contribution to the estimable 'Great Debates' series. I am very grateful also to Nicola Cattini at Palgrave and to David Stott. It seemed to me that it was such a marvellous idea that, other commitments notwithstanding, it did not occur to me to do anything other than jump at the chance to write the book which you now hold in your hands.

*Alastair Hudson*
New Year's Day 2014

# TABLE OF CASES

# TABLE OF LEGISLATION

# INTRODUCTION

## THE CORE DEBATE ABOUT EQUITY AND TRUSTS

This book is about 'Equity' and about 'Trusts', and not simply about 'Trusts Law'. Consequently, the very title of this book takes a side in one of the key debates about this subject: is trusts law a technical area in its own right, or can it only be understood properly as part of the more general field of equity? And why do some commentators criticise the very idea of equity? The explanation as to why this book considers equity *and* trusts law together will take most of the rest of this book to explore, but we can summarise it here. In short, it is because the trust can be understood as a coherent whole – spanning both express trusts and trusts implied by law – only if it is understood as being predicated on a philosophical construct of equity which is in turn based on ensuring the conscionable behaviour of the defendant who will consequently act as trustee.[1] If trusts law is understood simply as a series of discrete rules disconnected from their roots then many of the principles will make little coherent sense.

In short, this problem of coherence is important. One of the key discussions about equity revolves around whether or not it is comprised of so many unrelated, discretionary principles that the law which it generates is incoherent or unpredictable. If the individual judgments of courts of equity and the statutory provisions are examined one at a time from close up, then they may seem to be an incoherent mass of contradictory rules. This viewpoint is predicated on one view of equity that judges simply exercise their discretion randomly on a case-by-case basis without reference to precedent or rules. (It is worth noting that this viewpoint does not explain how trusts law operates by reference to clear rules about the creation of trusts, certainty in express trusts, and so forth.)

However, it is suggested that if trusts law is examined in the context of its place within equity more generally, then the ways in which the many equitable doctrines interact will become comprehensible. The effect will be a coherent pattern across the whole of equity. For example, much can be learned about the technique behind constructive trusts if one also understands equity as having given rise to injunctions and to the doctrine of confidence, because their open-textured methodologies are similar. However, if one examines different types of constructive trusts in isolation from one another, then it may seem that the law

---

[1] As established in the leading case of *Westdeutsche Landesbank v Islington* [1996] AC 669.

relating to constructive trusts is unstructured, arbitrary and disconnected from the rest of English law. It is all a question of perspective. Those commentators who are determined to see equity as being incoherent will tend to consider those judgments in one way; whereas commentators who are comfortable with equity as it is currently organised will tend to view those judgments in another way. To misappropriate Shakespeare, nothing is either coherent or incoherent, but rather thinking makes it seem so.[2]

The principal reason why this conception of this legal field seems so complicated is that much of trusts law has hardened, in practice, into strict rules which can resemble the prescriptive rules of contract law to an untutored eye. So, trusts law can appear to be similar to the common law on occasion. For example, in Chapter 4 we shall consider how the rules governing certainties in the creation of express trusts seem to resemble the sort of rigidity which is associated with common law doctrines. To some people. Another reason why this seems unsatisfactory to some people is that lawyers who prefer their law to be rigid and codified dislike the seemingly open-textured idea of 'conscience' and the moral relativism that is bound up in philosophical ideas of equity.[3] To put it crudely, those lawyers feel that equity depends on the moral beliefs of whichever person you happen to be talking to at any given moment.

Two concepts require some explanation. That an idea is 'open-textured' means that it appears to be capable of many interpretations. This is true of a word like 'nice'. It is not easy to know in the abstract what 'nice' might mean, although by examining its application from case-to-case one can build up a picture of its meaning. The same may be true of the idea of 'conscience', as is discussed in Chapter 1. The idea of 'moral relativism' is the idea that there is no single 'correct' morality which everyone ought to follow, but rather that in a society there may be several different moral views which are all perfectly valid in their own way, even if they contradict one another. In tolerant societies, within acceptable limits, it is usually possible to accommodate different moral views about different issues. Some lawyers dislike moral relativism because it seems contrary to the idea that there should be something called 'the Law' (with a capital letter) which is fixed and permanent and dependable.

Equity is, in truth, neither of these things. It is difficult to argue successfully that equity is entirely one thing or entirely another thing. That is a part of its charm. Its principles may be expressed as rules in some circumstances and as general moral prescriptions in others. Equity is, in practice, much larger than trusts law: it encompasses the principles governing all injunctions, specific performance, rescission and so forth, as well as trusts law. Trusts law is only a part of equity. And

---

[2] The coherence or incoherence of constructive trusts is considered in Ch. 8.

[3] As is discussed in Ch. 1, the central principle of the law of trusts is that the trustee is dependent on the circumstances having affected their conscience: *Westdeutsche Landesbank v Islington* [1996] AC 669. Also considered in that discussion is the fact that the principles of equity are predicated on the idea of 'conscience' in *Earl of Oxford's Case* (1615) Ch Rep 1.

yet the structure of law school curricula in England and Wales requires that students are taught trusts law to acquire a qualifying law degree for entry into the legal professions, but not that they study the rest of equity. Consequently, it is easy in universities to see equity as being restricted to trusts law, and trusts law as constituting almost the whole of equity.

So, our first big debate – conducted throughout Part 1 of this book – concerns the very nature of equity itself, and whether trusts law should be considered to be something distinct from it.

## META-THEMES AND SPECIFIC DEBATES

This book will, following the established template for books in the *Great Debates* series, divide each chapter into three or four specific debates about a given topic in an effort to shed light on the underlying nature of that topic. By looking at a question from two sides (in the form of a debate), it will become possible to understand what is said to be at stake in that area. The text will therefore contain many questions.

However, this book will also run a series of 'meta-themes' across the entirety of the book. Those meta-themes are debates about the underpinnings of the entire subject (as opposed to discrete topics within the subject) which surface time-and-again as one considers equity and trusts. Part 1, being Chapters 1–3, of this book will set out those meta-themes; Part 2, being Chapters 4–11, will comment on them as appropriate in particular contexts; and then Part 3, being Chapters 12–14 will aim to draw them together by way of conclusion. The study of equity and trusts is undoubtedly deepened if one is able to look across the fences between particular topics and identify the circumstances in which there is coherence, positivist thinking, moral obscurity, and so forth. Some areas of equity and trusts display different characteristics from others, and consequently those meta-themes will help us to examine those differences.

## THE NATURE OF THE 'DEBATES' ABOUT EQUITY AND TRUSTS

The idea of a 'debate' suggests two or more people discussing a specific proposition, with those people being divided into opposing groups. Usually, a debate takes place in one room at one time – as with the mannered performances at a university debating society, for example. Sometimes, of course, debates may take place in the form of articles which disagree with one another – famously the scientist, novelist and politician C.P. Snow and the literature academic F.R. Leavis debated the differences between the arts and the sciences in a series of articles and lectures in the 1950s. Typically, then, a debate happens between people taking different sides on an issue at the same and in opposition to one another. The most common misuse of the word 'debate' is that deployed by politicians, usually when they disingenuously call for 'a genuine debate' about an issue, when they fully intend to force through their own sectional interest whatever anyone else might think or say.

The type of debate which will take place in this book is something slightly different again. Some of the debates considered in this book have been conducted between commentators (whether judges, academics or others) in their published works or judgments, where they have made reference to one another's arguments in their own pronouncements. Other 'debates' have taken place across the centuries, with very old arguments being unearthed by a modern scholar or by a modern judgment. An example of this kind of debate is the discussion rekindled by the decision of the Court of Appeal in *Sinclair v Versailles* over the question whether bribes received by a fiduciary should give rise a proprietary or a personal outcome. The Court of Appeal restarted a debate (which many commentators had thought settled 20 years earlier by the Privy Council) by returning to a judgment which was nearly 120 years old.

Therefore, the 'debates' in equity and trusts may involve arguments taking place across the centuries. In truth, many of the 'debates' set out in this book are synthetic constructs drawn from different centuries so as to present a different understanding of what equity is and what trusts are; some other debates are current and conscious disagreements between judges and academics where the debate is carried on consciously.

## THE ASSUMPTIONS ABOUT YOUR KNOWLEDGE WHICH ARE MADE IN THIS BOOK

This book is required to proceed on the basis that you already know about the basics of equity and trusts law; or else that you are aware that there is an extensive literature considering those principles, cases and statutes. It will not explain each of these principles from the beginning, nor will it explore every case, article or statute. Instead, the remit of this book is to identify some of the 'great debates' within equity and trusts law, and to present them to you in an easily digestible format in not more than 120,000 words. Those parameters were set by the publishers because the aim of this series of books is to provide short accounts of the debates. It is also assumed that you would necessarily prefer to have a short book than a long one. That is an idea with which I can sympathise: before making a great commitment of time in reading a book, we all require a little reassurance that that investment will be profitable in some way. It is also underpins my objective in writing this book: that is, to connect you with the possibilities and the joys which await you if you leave the beaten track of the current case law principles and strike out into the trees to see what else is out there.

Consequently, I shall make occasional cross-reference to other textbooks, including my own, for those who want to have the core principles explained to them again, or who want to understand how those principles are traditionally understood within the equity and trusts canon. There will be some situations in which an explanation of the law will be required to explain the debate; however, that cannot be the case on every occasion. Generally, I shall summarise the law in a sentence or two where the discussion requires it; but there will be no extensive textbook treatment of the principles here. Instead, this book is intended to take you by the hand and shine a light down several of the pathways which you could follow in studying equity and trusts, and in taking your undergraduate studies or your later research in new and interesting directions.

## THE TRUE NATURE OF THE ACADEMIC DEBATES

There is a type of legal scholarship which prizes the detailed dissection of abstruse points of law above all else. Such scholars often prize the process of trying to organise the law into (what they perceive to be) a practical and reasoned order. In this regard those scholars resemble biologists assembling what are known as 'taxonomies' of the various species of plant and animal on our planet: that is, classifying them and putting them into some sort of order. Although, as we discuss in Chapter 8, a biologist's taxonomy is very different from a legal taxonomy because a biologist observes categories that exist in nature, as opposed to creating them ideologically in law. Indeed, the word 'taxonomy' has become rather fashionable amongst some legal scholars who see structure and order as being the defining qualities of a decent legal system.

However, the field of equity and trusts offers a great challenge to such legal scholars because it is famous for its unruly sprawl of doctrines. On this account, equity is sometimes said to be messy, unprincipled and possibly even unsuitable for a modern legal system. This is not a view with which I can agree. Instead, it seems to me that equity does something which is incredibly human: on Aristotle's account, what equity does is to consider whether the strict application of a legal rule would be unjust in the particular circumstances of a given case.[4] At the deepest, philosophical root, then, what equity is doing is to examine particular circumstances and to apply principles which are different from the strict legal rules so as to achieve a just result. Aristotle discussed equity after he had set out his own complex understanding of a philosophy of justice: in his opinion, equity was superior to any formal system of justice because it would achieve the right result in any particular circumstance. As Aristotle was aware, mistakes will be made in creating laws simply because there will always be factual circumstances which the legislator will not have anticipated.

At this juncture, a reader who is already aware of the principles of trusts law will be remembering that any study of trusts law typically begins with a consideration of the three certainties. So it is an odd thing to suggest that equity is about

---

[4] Aristotle's *Nicomachean Ethics*.

flexibility and a philosophy of unpicking detailed rules, when the first equitable principles which one generally studies are to do with achieving certainty. This is an excellent observation. In truth, as it appears in English civil law, equity (and the law of trusts which is a part of it) is a combination of open-textured principles which permits enormous flexibility, and also detailed rules as to how those principles will operate in practice. The practice of the law of trusts has been an activity of very practically-minded lawyers who were seeking to achieve particular results for their clients. The body of law which has grown out of it is no less practical and pragmatic. Therefore, we shall see that there is always a tension between a desire for certainty on the part of some judges on the one hand, and a desire for flexibility on the part of other judges on the other hand. Between the academic commentators who are discussed in this book we shall also observe similar sorts of different view.

Let us not fool ourselves. These are questions about which people disagree. Sometimes, they are questions about which people disagree quite aggressively. I once chaired a conference of academics at which there were puerile boos and catcalls, as well as a large amount of applause and laughter, at the forthright views of one of the speakers. (I shall not mention the names either of the speaker, nor of those in the audience who were behaving like farmyard animals in booing the speaker, so as to preserve the good name of all involved.) My point is that people – whether judges, academics or practitioners – do take passionate points of view regarding these questions. Consequently, I would encourage you to develop your own opinions. Nothing can beat reading the primary sources and the secondary commentaries for yourself. However, the aim of this book is to put those debates into context for you, and hopefully to light a number of paths down which you may choose to walk.

# PART ONE

# THE SOURCES AND NATURE OF EQUITY

# 1

# THE NATURE OF EQUITY

## INTRODUCTION

### THE NATURE OF EQUITY IN ITS ESSENCE

Equity is the means by which English law achieves fair outcomes in situations in which the formal rules of statute or the common law would otherwise be unfair. More precisely, equity is concerned with ensuring good 'conscience'. At one level, that is a perfectly accurate summary of the original purpose and role of equity within English law. However, equity's offspring over the centuries have frequently developed to such an extent that they exhibit some of the characteristics of idealised common law doctrines: such as rigidity and a tight observance of precedent. The best example of this tendency is the express trust (discussed in Chapters 4, 5 and 6) because express trusts are predicated on requirements of 'certainty', rules governing their perpetuity, and the minimum requirements of the rights of beneficiaries before an express trust may be valid. Nevertheless, there are still many equitable doctrines which appear to operate on very general principles which give ostensibly wide discretion to judges: such as constructive trusts, proprietary estoppel, injunctions and so forth.

That equity contains so many disparate doctrines, with such ostensibly different motivations and effects, means that it is worthy of study in itself. There is something fascinating in the complex interplay of the many different doctrines which fit inside English equity. To some commentators (in particular the Oxford School, identified in Chapter 3) this is unfathomable. For them, law must be ordered and clear both in its structure and in its operation. Within the traditional philosophy of equity, however, is an understanding that life and the world are simply not like this. There is something in the philosophy of Aristotle, as well as in twenty-first-century judgments in courts of equity, which recognises that human beings will generate such complex or unexpected problems that no system of rule-making can anticipate all of them in advance. Moreover, to be able to deliver appropriate judgments, it is often useful to give judges the ability to sculpt precise remedies and responses which achieve the best outcome for the parties and which appear to those judges to be just. Equity makes that possible. These differences in the understanding of equity in general, as well as trusts law in particular, are laid out in Part 1 *'The Sources and Nature of Equity'* in this book, before specific areas of trusts law and equity are explored more closely in Parts 2 and 3.

## UNDERSTANDING EQUITY; UNDERSTANDING YOURSELF

Ultimately, whether you think equity is simply messy or whether you think it is an essential part of creating a just legal system, probably tells you a lot about your personal attitude to law and to jurisprudence. Whether you are an enthusiast for ordered, 'positivist' explanations of law, or whether you are more at home with moral, 'natural law' understandings of law, or whether you see law as having a sociological role in society, is one of the key debates about any human being's attitude to law. Those questions are applied most clearly in the debates about equity and trusts law. As a student of law, your response to these debates should tell you a lot about your own attitudes and beliefs as a legal thinker.

## WHAT ARE THE GREAT DEBATES ABOUT EQUITY AND TRUSTS?

The great debates about equity and trusts fall into different categories. The most vital debates about equity arise specifically in relation to the *practical* uses of trusts. So, in this book we shall consider the political importance of trusts law, the ways in which international trusts law is used to avoid tax, and whether or not traditional rules like 'the beneficiary principle' should be abandoned so as to 'free up' trusts.

A second category of debate about trusts relates to the *academic debates* about the nature of the subject itself. In Chapter 3, we begin to examine the ways in which the traditional model of equity is being challenged by some academics who prefer a rigid 'taxonomy' of legal rules which prevent judges having too much discretion. They base their ideas on ancient Roman ideas, instead of the ancient Greek ideas which provide the foundations for the traditional model of equity.

A third form of debate surrounds *specific legal rules*. Some of the longest-standing debates revolve around the way in which English law should confront people who take bribes and then make a profit from the investment of those bribes. There is also a complex debate around the nature of the trusts which are imposed when lenders advance money to borrowers on the basis that the loan money is only to be used for specified purposes: these are so-called *'Quistclose* trusts'. Both of these particular debates see trusts lawyers (whether practitioners, scholars or judges) debating the minutiae of legal doctrine and precedent in a way which may seem to be at odds with the model of equity which is understood as being based on pure judicial discretion.

There are other technical debates which are far more high-flown in nature: such as the debate about the ownership of the home (which is conducted in Chapter 9, this book's longest chapter). There is self-evidently something essential to the operation of society (especially one in which divorce and relationship breakdown are so common) about the way in which ownership of the home is decided by equity and trusts law. There are also debates as to the circumstances in which people who

10

interfere with trusts will be taken to have been dishonest in so doing, so that they may be fixed with liability for any losses which result. These sorts of debates are more obviously sociological, political and philosophical in nature than the abstract, technical debates about *Quistclose* trusts and so forth would appear to be on their face. Nevertheless, even those ostensibly abstract debates have core philosophical and other concepts at their heart.

## WHAT'S IN A NAME?

One question which may have occupied the academics at your university (or which they may have answered unthinkingly) is: What should this subject be called? Should it be called 'trusts law', or 'equity and trusts law' or 'equity'?

It is compulsory (if you want to acquire a so-called 'qualifying law degree' in England and Wales for the purposes of professional accreditation) that you study trusts law.[1] This supposes that trusts law can be separated off from equity and considered to be a discrete topic. Of course, it is possible to do so; just as it is possible to separate off the law relating to injunctions from the rest of equity, or the law relating to specific performance, and so forth.

However, even though it is theoretically possible to separate off these topics from the main body of equity, there is nevertheless something lost when we insist on looking at the law on trusts separately from the law on injunctions, or separately from the law on proprietary estoppel. They grew in the same soil from the same seed, and so they are best understood as having a common root. That is why this book is called *Great Debates in Equity & Trusts* as opposed to *Great Debates in Trusts Law*. Many of the (wilful) misunderstandings of trusts law result from a refusal to understand that trusts are creatures of equity, and that the nature of equity (in its own terms) flows from a central goal of preventing unconscionable behaviour and from preventing unconscionable profit being taken from such behaviour. The central concept of equity in English law is therefore 'conscience', as is explored below. What that concept involves is significant in understanding the viability of equity as it is understood by its supporters. Its denigrators dislike that sort of 'big picture' thinking and prefer hard-and-fast rules instead.

As a result, there is something very important in the choice of name in itself. In consequence, some people have even tried to argue that trusts law would be better understood for the future not as part of equity but rather as part of contract law! This debate is considered in Chapter 6. However, before exploring the 'debates' about the nature and purpose of equity, we must first address the question 'What *is* equity?' in greater detail.

---

[1] The reason for this is simple: the academic member of the relevant professional committee was a member of the Oxford School (discussed in Ch. 3) which was antipathetic to the idea of equity (but not the practical importance of trusts law).

# Debate 1

## How should we understand the nature of equity?

### TO BEGIN AT THE BEGINNING

To begin at the beginning, we need to attempt a definition of 'equity'.[2] That word means different things in different contexts outside the legal context. To an economist, 'equity' means fairness and equality: that is, a form of egalitarianism which stands in opposition to leaving individuals to the whims of the free market. To a financier, 'equity' means share capital as opposed to debt. To a philosopher like Aristotle, 'equity' is a counter-balance to formal systems of justice, whereby one can reach just conclusions in individual circumstances by correcting mistakes made in that formal system of justice, where the formal system (usually in the form of legislation) will have been creating rules for the universal case and not for specific cases.[3]

### A legal definition of equity

To an English or Welsh lawyer, however, 'equity is the means by which a system of law balances out the need for certainty in rule-making with the need to achieve fair results in individual circumstances' by reference to a concept of good conscience.[4] At first blush, this legal model of equity is similar to Aristotle's model of equity. Significantly, however, Aristotle's model of equity was concerned with correcting oversights by the legislators: i.e. equity on Aristotle's model would operate to ensure fair outcomes in individual situations, if the legislators had not anticipated that particular unfairness being caused by their general rule. As the point was made in Aristotle's *Nicomachean Ethics*:

> '[W]hen the law states a general rule, and a case arises under this that is exceptional, then it is right, where the legislator owing to the generality of his language has erred in not covering that case, to correct the omission by a ruling such as the legislator himself would have given if he had been present there, and as he would have enacted if he had been aware of the circumstances.'[5]

So, the purpose of equity on Aristotle's model is to rectify legislation when it would lead to an unjust outcome because the legislator has in effect made a mistake by not anticipating that particular set of circumstances. By contrast, equity in English law is concerned with a much broader range of circumstances than merely legislative oversights. For example, the law of trusts, the law on injunctions, specific performance and so forth extend far beyond spotting mistakes in legislation, but all are part of equity in English law.

---

[2] For a textbook explanation of the relevant principles in this area, see Alastair Hudson, *Equity & Trusts* (Routledge, 2014), section 1.1.

[3] Aristotle, *The Nicomachean Ethics*, Thomson (tr.) (Penguin, 1955).

[4] A.S. Hudson, *Equity & Trusts*, section 1.1.

[5] Aristotle, above n 3, 198, para 1137a17, x.

An expression which was commonly used in the English case law to describe the way in which equity functions is that equity 'mitigates the rigour of the common law' so that the letter of the law is not applied in so strict a way that it may cause injustice in individual cases. Thus, in the *Earl of Oxford's Case* it was held by Lord Chancellor Ellesmere that the role of equity is 'to soften and mollify the extremity of the law' and also to 'correct men's consciences for frauds, breach of trusts, wrongs and oppressions'.[6] This identifies the general purpose behind equity: to stand as a moral force which both ensures that the harshness of the common law is softened and that people who are acting unconscionably (particularly through breach of trust, fraud, wrongs and other oppressions) are prevented from doing so (or at least they are prevented from taking a benefit from their actions while others suffer harm as a result). Thus, English equity operates on a more generally moral basis than Aristotle's model of equity.

## THE THREE DIFFERENT FORMS OF EQUITY

As Hudson puts it, there are three different, basic ways of understanding equity's role as part of the English legal system:[7]

'First, equity can be understood as the means by which English law ensures that the strict application of a common law or a statutory rule does not result in any unfairness when applied in a specific case. To this extent equity is a form of natural justice, which means that it has a moral basis ... Secondly, equity can be considered, in its formal sense, as constituting the collection of substantive principles developed over the centuries by the Courts of Equity, principally the Court of Chancery, to judge people's consciences.[8] In this sense, equity should be understood as being a code of technical, substantive rules and not simply as a reservoir of general, moral principles. ... Thirdly, equity can be understood as comprising the procedural rules and forms of action developed by the Courts of Chancery over the centuries under the authority of the Lord Chancellor.'

Each of these models of equity is considered in turn below.

### 1. The moral dimension to equity

*The moral basis to equity in the early authorities*

It was commonly said in the early cases that equity has a moral purpose. As was outlined above, equity's particular moral purpose was described by Lord Ellesmere in the *Earl of Oxford's Case*[9] as being to:

---

[6] (1615) 1 Ch Rep 1. St German explained that 'equytie is ordeyned ... to temper and myttygate the ygoure of the lawe' (1528–31), quoted in T.F.T. Plucknett and J.L. Barton (eds), 'St German's Doctor and Student' 91 *Selden Society*, London, 1974, 97.

[7] A.S. Hudson, *Equity & Trusts*, section 1.1.

[8] *Earl of Oxford's Case* (1615) 1 Ch Rep 1.

[9] Ibid.

'correct men's consciences for frauds, breach of trusts, wrongs and oppressions ... and to soften and mollify the extremity of the law'.

Similarly, in *Lord Dudley v Lady Dudley*,[10] it was held by Lord Chancellor Cowper that:

'Equity is no part of the law, but a moral virtue which qualifies, moderates and reforms the rigour, hardness and edge of the law.'

Consequently, equity may be understood as the means by which English law ensures that the strict application of a common law or a statutory rule does not result in any unfairness when applied in a specific case. To this extent equity is a form of natural justice, which means that it has a moral basis.[11] This is a moral purpose in that it both prevents a defendant from taking unconscionable advantage of a situation and also in that it prevents the law inadvertently permitting an unconscionable result. Spry, in his excellent book on *Equitable Remedies*, advances the proposition that 'equitable principles have above all a distinctive ethical quality, reflecting as they do the prevention of unconscionable conduct'.[12]

### The methodology behind the morality

The way in which English equity achieves its moral goal is by examining the conscience of the individual defendant.[13] In essence, equity seeks to prevent any benefit accruing to a defendant as a result of some unconscionable conduct, or to compensate any loss suffered by a claimant which results from some unconscionable conduct. In so doing (and in line with the Aristotelian approach to equity), equity seeks to ensure that common law and statutory rules are not manipulated unconscionably. At its broadest, equity appears to imbue the courts with a general discretion to disapply statutory or common law rules whenever good conscience requires it; however, in practice, modern equity is comprised mainly of substantive and procedural principles which permit the courts only a limited amount of discretion. This broad use of equity is rare in modern equitable practice, as we shall consider in this chapter and elsewhere throughout this book. It is common, for example in relation to the award of interlocutory injunctions, for the courts to seek to limit their apparently broad statutory discretion by imposing their own principles on when that power should be activated.[14]

---

[10] (1705) Prec Ch 241, 244.

[11] See J. McGhee, *Snell's Equity* (2005), paras 1-01 and 1-03, identifying the moral base of equity while also considering the need for the legal conceptualisation of such moral notions as being based on specific principles.

[12] I. Spry, *Equitable Remedies*, 6th edn (Law Book Co, 2001), 1.

[13] *Earl of Oxford's Case* (1615) 1 Ch Rep 1.

[14] See, e.g., *Jaggard v Sawyer* [1995] 1 WLR 269, [1995] 2 All ER 189, discussed in Hudson, *Equity & Trusts*, section 27.1.1, where the Court of Appeal preferred to apply precedent closely rather than consider themselves to have a broad discretion to act as they saw fit under the terms of the Supreme Court Act 1981, s 50, which purported to permit them to grant interim injunctions in general terms.

## 2. Equity as a code of substantive rules

Secondly, equity operates, in a formal sense, as a collection of *substantive* principles which have been developed over the centuries by the Court of Chancery to judge individuals' consciences. In this sense, equity is a body of technical, substantive rules as well as being a code of moral principles. The tendency to think of equity solely in terms of general principles, as opposed to technical devices and strict case law rules, was criticised by Vice-Chancellor Megarry in *Re Montagu's Settlement*.[15] Therefore, as discussed in Chapter 2 and in Chapters 12–14 of this book, the trust operates as a system of technical rules which are predicated on the doctrine of precedent (as opposed to simple judicial discretion).

## 3. Equity as a code of procedural devices

Thirdly, equity may be understood as comprising the *procedural* rules and forms of action developed by the Courts of Chancery over the centuries under the authority of the Lord Chancellor.[16] It should be noted that these second and third aspects of equity differ from the apparent breadth of the first in that they constitute technical rules of law rather than abstract philosophical principles.

# Debate 2

## What is the idea of a 'conscience' in equity?

### THE EARLIEST FORMS OF CONSCIENCE

In the earliest judgments, the courts of equity were considered to be courts of conscience and the Lord Chancellor was considered to be the 'keeper of the King's [or the Queen's] conscience'. The Lord Chancellors were for centuries all clerics: therefore, their protection of the monarch's conscience was in part a religious, priestly role. This usage of the term 'conscience' was not a casual one. If one were to inquire into the history of the British Isles in the sixteenth and seventeenth centuries in particular, one would find the idea of conscience being discussed frequently. The constant see-sawing between monarchs with different religious convictions – between Catholic and Protestant – was accompanied by purges and killings of people of one religion by adherents to the other. For example, King James I was born a Catholic but converted to Protestantism, and was responsible for the killing of many Catholics when on the throne. All of this came in the wake of Henry VIII's having broken with the Catholic Church in Rome when he established the Protestant Church of England. The upshot for ordinary people in England was a constant crisis of conscience, as they sought to maintain their faith in the face of oppression by adherents to the alternative faith. For example, in Tristam Hunt's collection of letters, speeches and documents from the mid-seventeenth century,

---

[15] [1987] Ch 264.
[16] The main equitable principles are considered in section 1.4 of Hudson, *Equity & Trusts*.

titled *The English Civil War*, the word 'conscience' rings like a bell from different people's accounts of their own travails.

Therefore, there is no surprise that the idea of conscience should make its presence felt in the jurisprudence. However, the concept of conscience which was used even at that time was a combination (as was so much thought at that time) of a sublime, religious conscience and a secular, psychological conscience. Thus, a defendant would be judged in practice for acting unconscionably in the sense of breaching moral principles established in equity, although those moral principles at that time would have had their foundation in religious ideas. As Lord Selborne put it:

> 'The courts of Equity in England are, and always have been, courts of conscience, operating in personam and not in rem; and in the exercise of this personal jurisdiction they have always been accustomed to compel the performance of contracts and trusts as to subjects which were not ... within their jurisdiction.'[17]

The reference to the courts operating '*in personam*' is important. In this particular context, that a court uses conscience '*in personam*' means that the court examines the situation of the individual defendant to decide whether or not that person had acted unconscionably. This is methodologically similar to the Aristotelian model of equity, which requires consideration of the individual circumstances of a case to see whether or not justice requires the formal rule to be set aside. In the twenty-first century, the idea of conscience is a moral and a psychological one exclusively.

## WHAT IS A CONSCIENCE?

The critics of the idea of conscience in equity have generally not thought through what a conscience is. In this short discussion, we shall consider two forms of conscience: the psychological conscience, and the use of conscience in literature. First, however, we shall consider the real meaning of the word 'conscience'.

### The meaning of a conscience

The word 'conscience' is a combination of 'con', meaning 'with'; and 'science', meaning 'knowledge'. The earliest definitions of the word 'conscience' had the following idea: it is knowledge of oneself *with oneself*. Significantly, conscience is not simply subjective knowledge of oneself; rather, it recognises the existence of a conscious self and another self within one's mind. This is exactly how the conscience is experienced. The conscience is not something that can be controlled by the conscious mind. Instead, when the conscience is disturbed, it will nag at the conscious mind, disturb sleep, and not be controlled. The conscience is inside the mind but it is outside the control of the conscious mind. In this sense, it is possible to have knowledge of oneself with oneself.

---

[17] *Ewing v Orr Ewing (No 1)* (1883) 9 App Cas 34, 40.

An analogy with the theory of aesthetics may be useful. In the aesthetic theory asserted by Theodor Adorno, there is no such thing as subjectivity:[18] Adorno asserts that one's reaction to artworks is culturally controlled. One is educated to like and not to like different types of artwork and other cultural objects. Therefore, your subjectivity is really objective programming when it comes to aesthetics. Similarly, Adorno argues that there is no such thing as objectivity: instead, there is simply a sufficient critical mass of subjective opinions that they appear to constitute an objective opinion when taken together.

Adorno has a penetrating insight into the way in which people accept artworks which appears to describe the conscience very neatly: it is privately-situated but objectively-constituted. For Adorno, the appreciation of the artwork takes place within an individual's mind, but the set of beliefs and opinions which create the appreciation of the artwork are formed objectively. That an artwork is located in an art gallery, prominently displayed and surrounded by security guards and other, gawping viewers, means that we tend to accept that work as being 'art'. Other work, like the street paintings by Banksy, are treated as being a different kind of 'art' as a result of the counter-cultural hoop-la which attends them.

In the same way, the conscience is an aggregation of objective moral opinions which the individual has assimilated through life. From birth, her parents will have educated her as to right and wrong; her schooling will have continued that education as to morals and as to ways of behaving; and throughout life the media and society continue to present ideas of right and wrong. Throughout her life she will have absorbed messages about right and wrong consciously and subconsciously. The individual conscience is generated out of a subjective reaction to all of those messages over time. Thus, the conscience is something which resides inside the individual mind, but it is not right to think of it as being entirely subjective in the sense of being formed entirely out of unique, subjective opinions. Instead, the contents of the conscience are made up of stimuli which are received from outside the individual. One forms one's conscience in reaction to the outside world, and not entirely from within one's own mind. One can only truly know how one's conscience will react to a circumstance when the outside world confronts you with that circumstance. Will you stand your ground? Will you tell the truth? Will you be true to your beliefs? Or will you turn and run, or lie, or indulge in a little hypocrisy without being troubled by it? The conscience is formed by a series of collisions with the outside world and gestated within individual minds. Importantly, then, the conscience is in part objective. Consequently, if a person has a conscience which purports to permit actions or omissions which are contrary to the ordinary mores of society, then it is entirely appropriate for the law to sit in judgment over that individual. If the conscience is in part objective, it is appropriate for a court to comment on what ought or ought not to have been in that conscience or in a person's actions.

---

[18] T. Adorno, 'Subject and object', in A. Arato (ed.), *The Essential Frankfurt School Reader* (Continuum, 1978).

It is because the conscience is properly understood as being 'privately-situated but objectively-constituted' that it is possible for the conscience to form the organising principle of equity.

## The psychological conscience

The Freudian understanding of the conscience considers that the conscience is something which sits outside the conscious mind, just as the etymological understanding of the word indicates that the 'con-science' is something outside the conscious mind. In *Civilisation and its Discontents*,[19] Sigmund Freud explained the formation of the conscience in the following terms, as the individual assimilates social messages about how to act, even when that is in contravention of the individual's instincts and base desires:

> 'Every renunciation of instinct now becomes a dynamic source of conscience and every fresh renunciation increases the latter's severity and intolerance. ... [I]nstinctual renunciation (imposed on us from without) creates conscience, which then demands further instinctual renunciation.'

Thus, in the Freudian model, conscience is the conditioned belief that membership of society requires the suppression of a variety of instinctual drives. Just because we desire a friend's iPod, we do not take it because we have been conditioned to believe that stealing is wrong. Just because we desire a friend's partner, we do not try to seduce them because we have been conditioned to believe that that is wrong. If we transgress what we have been conditioned to believe is wrong, then our conscience will warn us in advance and it will nag at us afterwards, causing feelings of remorse, shame and regret. And so, in Freudian terms, the conscience plays an important role in forcing us to control our instinctual, base desires so as to live a civilised life. Importantly, this privately-located conscience is formed in reaction to social messages about what is acceptable and what is unacceptable behaviour.

## Conscience in literature

There is a long history of the conscience being portrayed in literature and in drama as occupying a human form outside the mind of the principal character. There is nothing new in this idea that the conscience is both within the individual mind and yet that it is something separate from the ego. This device is useful for writers because it enables the principal character to enter into a dialogue with their own conscience. Most famously in Shakespeare's *King Lear*, the King has a Fool who capers around him singing songs and making often lewd jokes. The role of the Fool is to question the King's decision to reject his virtuous daughter in favour of the other daughters who flatter him at first and then reject him later. The Fool was part of a device which was common in European theatre to hold up the principal character to examination precisely by asking them barbed questions, making jokes at

---

[19] S. Freud, *Civilisation and its Discontents* (1930) in *The Penguin Freud Library*, vol. 12 (Penguin, 1991), 321.

their expense, and sparing them no quarter, in exactly the same way that a real conscience spares the conscious mind no quarter. The Fool was in truth the King's conscience, given human form for dramatic purposes.

Perhaps the clearest image of a conscience appears in Luigi Pirandello's play, *Each in His Own Way*. The character Diego challenges the other characters, who are talking about taking confession and consequently claiming that their consciences will be clear after they have done so. As Diego says: 'But what is conscience? It is the voice of others inside you.'[20] This identifies the source of the conscience. It is not simply something subjective inside a person; rather, it is the voices, opinions and attitudes of other people (family, church, school, society) as they have lodged within a person. The Catholic confession is in itself the classical objectification of the conscience: one is observed by a god, and one makes admission of one's sins to a priest and thus to that god. As Cardinal Newman put it, 'the conscience is the aboriginal vicar of Christ'. In other words, having filled a person's mind with the teachings and demands of the religious faith, those teachings will have filled the conscience so that the individual will always obey (or react to) that conditioning throughout life. The conscience is 'aboriginal' in the sense that it will go wherever the individual goes and keep that conditioning within that individual's mind.[21] The conscience is necessarily socially constructed in this way. Therefore, the behaviour of the individual can be measured against the expectations of the community.

As the old proverb has it, 'A guilty conscience needs no accuser' because someone with a guilty conscience has an accuser inside their own mind already. To quote another proverb, 'A guilty conscience sleeps in thunder' because the conscience will keep a person awake at night. There is wisdom in these old homilies.

The conscience comes to us unbidden. It is comprised of many attitudes and beliefs which have been implanted in us by other people, together with some which we have assembled ourselves in reaction to the outside world. Understanding the conscience in these terms is central to understanding why it is such a good basis for equity.

## UNCONSCIONABILITY AS A TECHNICAL CONCEPT

There is an approach in a large part of the academic literature which treats the concept of 'unconscionability' as being a purely technical concept. That is, those commentators do not concern themselves with the psychological or theoretical notion of the conscience. Instead, they examine the cases in which the concept of unconscionability has been used, and try to erect consequentialist models of the different types of unconscionability which have arisen in the cases. This approach to the idea of unconscionability is considered in detail in Chapter 8.

---

[20] L. Pirandello, *Each in His Own Way* (Firth tr.), *Pirandello – Collected Plays*, vol. 3 (Calder, 1992), 71, spoken by Diego in Act 1. Also rendered in other versions as 'Don't you see that blessed conscience of yours is nothing but other people inside you!' (see, e.g., N. Williams, *The Wimbledon Poisoner* (Faber & Faber).

[21] Or, as Mencka described the conscience (in another context): 'Conscience: the inner voice which warns us that someone may be looking.' H.L. Mencka, 'A Little Book in C Major'.

## Debate 3

# Is equity uniquely disorganised, and why might that matter?

## LAW: WHAT IS IT GOOD FOR?

What is law for? Is its role simply to create a modicum of order in society, or is it a series of rules by which people are meant to live? Or is law supposed to achieve justice? If law is supposed to create order out of the chaos that would otherwise exist, then it requires hard-and-fast rules. However, law is not simply about identifying the line between acts which are criminal and acts which are not criminal. Rather, on many occasions, law presents models to people (as with contract law or trusts law) whereby the state promises to support contracts or the creation of trusts if they are created in the ways set out in those laws. In this sense, law produces order and predictability, but without the need to give commands to society as the criminal law does.[22] In this sense, our private law creates models by which people are encouraged to live (in creating their contracts and so forth), and thus establishes a moral order.

Alternatively, if law was intended to achieve justice, then that would involve plenty of hard-and-fast rules so that people would know where they stood and what their rights and obligations were, but it would also involve some latitude for the judges to be able to mould the appropriate response to difficult sets of circumstances. For example, when judging in divorce proceedings, the way in which the children of the marriage are to be cared for must be decided as part of a subtle assessment of their needs and of their parents' situation. Consequently, hard-and-fast rules can only get the court so far because those children may have medical problems, or their parents may live in different countries, and so forth. The judge needs to do what is right by reference to a series of high-level principles, such as the welfare of the child being paramount (as under s. 1 of the Children Act 1989). Therefore, an appropriate law in that context requires a different approach from the hard-and-fast rules of contract or criminal law; it requires law that is orientated around high-level principles and which gives discretion to the judiciary to sculpt the precise remedy which is suitable for the circumstances.

There are also many circumstances in between in which a *blend* of strict rules and discretionary justice may be needed to achieve the best outcomes both for the litigants and for society at large. This is where equity becomes significant, not only because it offers a different sort of rulemaking from the common law, but also because equity is itself comprised of firm rules as well as discretionary principles which will be applicable in different circumstances. Equity is probably best understood as being a blend of strict rules and discretionary principles. One of the principal attributes of English law is its flexibility: knowing when to be firm and when to permit discretion to enter into the mix. At one end of the spectrum, commercial

---

[22] The positivist model of law, considered below, conceives of law as being the sovereign body in society, and in that capacity as giving commands to society's members.

law requires strict rules so that it provides predictability for its participants; whereas, at the other end of the spectrum, child law requires that the court identifies a precise solution which will ensure the welfare of the children involved. Whereas much of the debate about law is concerned with absolutist arguments – my idea is right, and your idea is wrong – in truth what any legal system requires are different legal models which are suitable for their own particular contexts.

## THE EXAMPLE OF CONSTRUCTIVE TRUSTS

In the light of this recognition that there may be benefits behind different types of rules in different situations, we should identify one theme which runs through much of the scholarly criticism of equity: the suggestion being that equity is simply too conceptually messy to be useful. So, as is discussed in Chapter 8, one of the principal objections which Professor Peter Birks (of the Oxford Restitution School) raised against constructive trusts is that they are doctrinally disordered and that one cannot know what it is that gives rise to a constructive trust. As Birks complained, the label 'constructive trust' does not tell us how that thing came into being, but rather merely tells us what that thing is called. His suggestion was that constructive trusts arise almost at random and are simply grouped under the same collective noun: 'constructive trust'.

However, this attitude is almost wilfully blind to the approach taken by judges like Lord Browne-Wilkinson in *Westdeutsche Landesbank v Islington*[23] to the effect that a constructive trust arises whenever the defendant has knowingly acted unconscionably in relation to property. (This principle is explored in the next Chapter.) The defendant is construed to be a trustee of that property by virtue of knowingly dealing unconscionably with it. The categories of unconscionability may arise *sui generis* or by reference to earlier authority. Because the defendant is 'construed' to be a trustee means that they are, by definition, a 'constructive trustee'. Their 'constructive' nature stems from their having been 'construed' to be such.

This is an important theme for this book and for this topic as envisaged by scholars in the UK. The explanations advanced by judges and equity traditionalists for the operation of equity in its current form – that it is based on an idea of equity which can be observed from the older authorities via the doctrine of precedent – are simply ignored by those who need their law to be orderly and arranged in a taxonomy. It is as though they cannot see any other form of legal principle as being in truth a law at all.

For some lawyers, neatness is everything. For lawyers of that type, law is only law in a real sense if it is bolted to a central organising framework so that everyone (judges, lawyers and litigants) can know where they stand without needing to go to court. One of the principal questions for this book will be whether there is only one sort of law, or whether there are several sorts of law (even just within equity) each of which is appropriate to its context.

---

[23] [1996] AC 669.

The US President Robert Kennedy made a very perceptive remark to the effect that 20 per cent of people would always disagree with everything he said, no matter what was at issue. For Kennedy the problem was that no matter how reasonable he considered his policies to be, he would always encounter opposition from some people. Human beings are an odd lot, with very different viewpoints on the same question. If you don't believe me, try sitting more than three people down in front of a television with a remote control and a pile of different DVDs, and watch disharmony reign when you ask them to agree what to watch. It is because some people will always disagree that we need rules. However, it is because some people will always disagree about what the rules mean that we need to empower our judges to reach the right conclusions. It is also because some people will always be perverse enough to act in unexpected ways that we need to build a tolerable amount of flexibility and fairness into our laws to accommodate the surprises that they will spring on us. In part, this is why we need equity.

## CONCLUSIONS: SOME THEMES FOR THE REST OF THIS BOOK

### EQUITY, DEBATES AND BINARY DISTINCTIONS

Equity and trusts law conforms very neatly to this idea of a two-person debate precisely because it is comprised of a series of binary distinctions,[24] as well as a number of binary differences in view. This is helpful in a book which aims to consider the 'great debates' in that field.

Central to the organisation of English private law (that is, the substantive law which relates to everything except public law and the criminal law) is the distinction between the common law on the one hand and equity on the other. In class I have often sought to attribute personalities to the common law and to equity so as to bring this distinction sharply into focus for students.

### The personalities of equity and of common law

The distinction between the personalities of equity and the common law operates as follows. When listing the range of remedies which are available at common law and in equity, it was easy to identify the very few remedies available in a common law court (principally damages, and personal restitution by way of money had and received) when compared to the huge range of remedies available in equity (from injunctions, rescission, specific performance and so forth, through to the various forms of trust implied by law if one wanted to stretch a point). As a result, I personified the common law as being bluff and uncomplicated, but also as being slow and unimaginative: sticking doggedly to the one remedy (damages) which it knew

---

[24] A binary distinction being a distinction that falls into two parts, just as a debate involves two competing points of view.

well. By contrast, equity was nimble and quick: positively giddy with excitement at the new remedies it could create when justice demanded it.

While the common law might be indifferent to the suffering of many and content to stick with the old ways, equity would be pained that anyone should suffer uncompensated harm and would be concerned to hear the parties' stories and to suit the remedy to meet the case. It is easy to see how we might attribute personalities to these type of law: equity is both imaginative and also keen to avoid harm to any individual; while the common law is bluff and indifferent to individual suffering provided that it is for the common good. In this sense, equity may appear to be predicated on a moral base, whereas the common law is utilitarian.[25]

### Some (imagined) differences between common lawyers and equity specialists

In other contexts, the personalities might change slightly. In constructing a hypothetical archetype of each type of lawyer, I would imagine the minutiae of their domestic circumstances so as to shine a light on their scholarly attributes. When discussing the modern common lawyer (of the Oxford Restitution School, discussed in Chapter 3, for example), I would stress their need for neatness. I would imagine what their houses might be like. I would paint a picture of the home of the quintessential common lawyer. Their taste in architecture would tend towards the modern: all clean lines in the manner of the architect Frank Lloyd Wright; windows occupying an entire wall to allow in light; and all of their possessions concealed in floor-to-ceiling cupboards (concealed behind smooth, blond wood doors) which ran the length of the walls and opened at a slight pressure on the appropriate point on the door (but without obtruding door handles). The effect would be a minimalist room entirely free of clutter: very like an Ikea advert in which every object had been tidied out of sight. Each cupboard would contain objects of a certain type, everything would be in its place, so that each storage space obeyed a guiding taxonomy. Stationery in one section; books on another wall; outdoor clothing separated off from indoor clothing; and so forth. Everything put away in perfect order and hidden from sight. This personality would be reflected in the conceptual order demanded by the common lawyer in their scholarly work.

By contrast, the equity specialist would be passionate, quixotic and positively flirtatious with the possibilities of life. In Larkin's phrase, the equity specialist would live an 'unfenced existence'. The quintessential equity specialist would hold strong, central beliefs, but otherwise would meet life with an open mind and would relish colour, discord and noise. Excited dogs, playful children and saucepans of tagliatelle bolognese would vie for dominance of the senses as you entered the living-rooms of their colourful homes. Their houses would be painted in many bright colours. The bookcases would overflow with books; bric-a-brac and children's toys would be thrown into wooden boxes at all angles. The coffee table

---

[25] Where 'utilitarian' refers to a philosophy which is concerned with doing the best for society generally, even at the cost of some discomfort to some individuals.

in the sunny living-room would be hidden under cups, magazines and mess; and all would be vibrant and bright. There would seem to be little order to the outsider, although the equity specialist would claim to know where everything was in the precarious piles of stuff. A keener eye might spot a series of different projects which had been begun and then discarded on different tables in different rooms in the house.

While the common lawyer would listen calmly to the precise progressions of Bach; the equity specialist would wriggle to the cut-up surprises of Stockhausen or improvised jazz. Both would see beauty in what they heard. That point is very important: both of them would find beauty in their very different ways of living their lives, in different ways of thinking about law, and in their different musical tastes. The common lawyer would find the clean order to be beautiful but would see no value in any other way of living. The equity specialist would value the colour and noise and vibrancy. The equity specialist, being less dogmatic by nature than the common lawyer, might see value in the common lawyer's lifestyle but would shrug ruefully and admit that it would not be possible for them.

I always undercut these observations with the idea that, in truth, neither species of lawyer tends to conform to type in reality. In the real world, common lawyers frequently have kitchens which look as though they have waged war in them rather than cooked meals. This is often the result of the hours spent crafting their taxonomies and prodding at the cracks in arguments in their messy studies, which means that there is little time left for the bourgeois preoccupations of tidying up. All that time spent in a study overflowing with books and papers means that the kitchen rarely gets tidied and the lawn is never mowed. Equity specialists often yearn for order in reality, and have their books marshalled onto shelves in carefully constructed sequences. Their minds often need to be ordered and precise so as to sift the ostensibly formless precedents which occupy their working hours. Precisely because their scholarship involves finding order in these discretionary doctrines, they may well crave order in the rest of their lives. Their wardrobes are frequently comprised of subtle variations on the same theme and carefully segregated into groups. For example, people often remark on how tidy my office at the university is. They also say that it looks 'like a home' (because I have filled it with my own furniture, pictures and favourite objects). In truth, my study at home – where I do my real work – is full of books, mp3 and DVD players, notebooks, computers, tablet computers, memory sticks, treasured objects, and boxes and boxes of ideas.

People are people, after all: full of contradictions, and yet constantly striving to imagine a better world for themselves and everyone else.

### A different perspective

The novelist Charles Palliser took a different approach from the one set out above to the different personalities of the common lawyer and the equity specialist in his novel *Quincunx*.[26] In the atmospheric opening to that novel, one lawyer visits

---

[26] C. Palliser, *Quincunx* (Canongate, 1989).

another lawyer at home on a dark, autumn night. We are told that 'Law, embodied in the person of a small, pale-faced gentleman of about forty years of age with a large head, mounts the steps and rings the bell'. Interestingly, it is Law that dances attendance on Equity: 'Equity is some fifteen years the elder, with a high-coloured complexion, a lofty nose and a face most remarkable for a pair of black bushy eyebrows'. It is Equity who is superior in every sense in this novel. (Interestingly, though, these descriptions are almost the inverse of my own, as set out above.) Equity occupies a traditional home with an established practice. Equity is traditional and slow-moving. By contrast, in Palliser's novel, it is Law who is younger and slighter. Also, different from the culture of English legal academia, it is not the common lawyers who are commanding, superior and dogmatic.

What is interesting nevertheless is the way in which these different legal codes take on personalities of their own in both accounts in Palliser's novel. I can still remember the thrill of excitement as I read the opening to this novel in the somewhat battered and neglected copy held in the bookshop at the Museum of London. What is important for present purposes is the way in which private law is possessed of a binary distinction between the two codes. Many of the debates about the nature of equity fall into place if they are understood as being conducted between different personality types.

## A JURISPRUDENTIAL DISTINCTION: POSITIVISM AND NATURAL LAW

Among the other binary divisions is the division between positivism and natural law in jurisprudence. This is a useful model for understanding the distinction between common law and equity. The distinction between positivism and natural law is really a debate between two competing understandings of the nature of law itself.

Typically, positivists (such as Bentham and Austin, in their stereotypes) conceive of law as a series of commands which are given to the people by a 'sovereign'. People are obliged to obey laws which have been created by the appropriate mechanisms for creating laws in any given jurisdiction. By contrast, natural law theorists (such as Aquinas and Finnis) emphasise the importance of a central store of moral precepts from which laws are born. In the USA, for example, this is identified in the US Constitution, which was created in the wake of the revolutionary war which unseated the British. That Constitution creates a set of principles which are taken to infuse both social life and all of that country's laws. All laws fall to be interpreted in accordance with the Constitution. It is important to note, however, that much American law can also be understood as operating on a positivist basis, because those laws are created by reference to a series of rules about the proper creation of law.

Equally, many positivist laws contain moral standards. Sometimes those moral statements are the florid excesses of legislators appealing rhetorically to the people, or sometimes those moral statements are intended to be high-level principles by reference to which those laws are to be interpreted. For example, the law of the

European Union typically contains statements of principle in its Regulations and Directives, even when those laws create clear standards for the way in which financial regulations are to be created in Member States.

Equity and trusts law is an interesting amalgam of these two philosophies. At first glance, equity appears to be a natural law code which works outwards from a central concept of good conscience, as outlined above. In relation to doctrines such as injunctions, the courts are free to order behaviour in parallel with that central concept of good conscience. However, as emerges in the next chapter, from within equity there came trusts law, which is predicated on strict rules such as the three certainties and the beneficiary principle which govern the validity of a trust in the first place, among other rules. Therefore, the offspring of equity will often demonstrate positivist tendencies such as a close adherence to the doctrine of precedent, clear 'tests' governing the validity of equitable doctrines, and a limitation of the sort of discretion which is commonly assumed to be at the heart of equity. Consequently, it is a difficult question to know whether equity is based on natural law, or whether equity (or rather some of its key doctrines) can be better understood as operating in a positivist fashion in many circumstances.

## EQUITY AND FREUDIAN PSYCHOANALYSIS

A parallel to this division between the common law and equity may be found in Freudian psychoanalysis: that is, the distinction between the ego and the id, the conscious and the unconscious mind. In the Freudian system, to summarise enormously, the conscious mind is represented by the ego. The conscious mind therefore engages all of the thoughts and decisions that we would wish to have as members of a civilised society. However, in *Civilisation and Its Discontents*, Sigmund Freud maintained that this conscious compliance with what we know we are supposed to think and how we are supposed to act, leads to a repression of many instinctual desires and drives.[27] In consequence, we do not steal an object we find attractive, we are polite to acquaintances we otherwise find irritating enough to subject to an assault, and so forth. Nevertheless, this means that these repressed emotions can cause a build-up of psychiatric problems which can only be resolved and assuaged by identifying their root causes and talking them through. The wellspring for these instinctive desires is the 'id'. The id arises in the unconscious mind. A large amount of advertising is directed at appealing to the id, because that accesses the emotional side of human beings and their 'true' desires. You cannot sell chocolate to a conscious mind, because we know in our conscious mind that it is fatty, sugary and unhealthy; but you can sell the idea of the taste of chocolate in luxurious, eroticised surroundings to a person's instinctual desire for pleasure. Consequently, adult human beings may be seen standing near shops selling confectionery while muttering to themselves or hopping from foot-to-foot: they

---

[27] S. Freud, *Civilisation and its Discontents* (Penguin, 1930).

are struggling with their instinctive desire for pleasure and their conscious knowledge that they should not eat unhealthy, non-nutritious food.

E.M. Delafield's wry narrator in *The Diary of an English Provincial Lady* put it most succinctly when she said:[28]

> 'Query here suggests itself, as often before: Is it utterly impossible to combine the amenities of civilisation with even the minimum of honesty required to satisfy the voice of conscience?'

She was being forced, out of social embarrassment, to stand on a damp lawn in the evening in entirely unsuitable shoes to watch some awful fireworks and listen to the inane ramblings of an old man who was boring her about something or other. She wanted to stay indoors in the warm and keep her feet dry. She also wanted not to have to listen to this man who had attached himself to her for the evening. But politeness – something she had been conditioned to practise in her upbringing – prevented her from doing any of that. It was her conscience that told her that she must tolerate these annoyances (and the cold that she knew she would develop in the coming days as a result), even though it was not what she wanted to do at all.

Clearly, there needs to be a resolution of these conscious, civilised thoughts and the flow of unconscious, instinctive drives: that resolution takes place in the 'super-ego' in the Freudian scheme. Importantly, then, the human psyche is presented in this model – which is now a commonplace in ordinary conversation, in tabloid newspaper gossip columns, in film and so on – as a reconciliation of two very different types of thought in a synthesised personality. The conscious mind and the instinctual drives become reconciled in some way.

It could be said that, in this analogy, the common law (and statute) constitutes the ego: an ordered, premeditated system of rules which was deliberately formulated so as to achieve specific goals, both in the ordering of the law and in the ordering of society. The common law is generally considered to be reasoned and predictable. (A study of the law of tort might cause us to question this analysis, but that question is for another time.) The common law is said to be an orderly structure of rules which judges simply need to apply to factual circumstances. By contrast, equity is akin to the id. Its roots are emotional, being concerned with 'justice' in some fashion, and are based on the seemingly psychological idea of the 'conscience'. To a common lawyer, the equitable approach appears to be entirely emotional and based on identifying how one might want to treat the litigants if there were no rules in existence at all. In that sense, the id constituted by equity threatens to destabilise the carefully ordered universe of the ego.

What is most satisfying about this analogy is that the Freudian system reconciles the distinction between the ego and the id in the super-ego: that is, a zone in which conscious thought and unconscious impulse resolve themselves in the individual's particular psyche. In this way, the common law and equity resolve

---

28 E.M. Delafield, *The Diary of a Provincial Lady*, 1930 (Virago Modern Classics), 73.

themselves into a form of private law which both applies positivist rules to situations in accordance with legal procedure and technique, and which also seeks to achieve fair outcomes by reference to general moral principles. The outcome is a synthesised balance between order for the general case and justice in exceptional circumstances. In that sense, English private law may be understood as a well-balanced synthesis of equity and the common law, just as a well-balanced mind synthesises the ego with the id and develops a healthy super-ego.

# 2

# THE NATURE OF TRUSTS LAW

## INTRODUCTION

This chapter considers the nature of the trust and the nature of trusts *law* in consequence. The purpose of this chapter is to establish some key themes which will run through the debates in Part 2 (Chapters 4–11) of this book: those debates relate to particular aspects of trusts law. The previous chapter considered the nature of equity and conceived of trusts law as being a part of equity. Within that discussion, however, was a suggestion that there is something about trusts law which is paradoxical or awkward to categorise as a result of trusts law being both a part of equity and yet being comprised of some detailed rules which seem at odds with the caricature of equity as a zone of discretionary principles. Unpacking that aspect of trusts law is the underlying goal of this chapter.

Trusts fall into two broad categories: *express trusts* and *trusts implied by law*. Express trusts are created intentionally by a settlor. Before an express trust can be valid, it must comply with the formal requirements which are analysed in Chapters 4, 5 and 6 of this book. By contrast, trusts implied by law arise by operation of law (that is, without the need for any settlor's intention) where it is appropriate for that to happen. Trusts implied by law are analysed in Chapters 7–11 of this book.[1]

Express trusts have a long pedigree as the means by which the landed classes in England and Wales organised the ownership and maintenance of their real and personal property down the generations. (That historical context is outlined below.) In consequence, the rules of express trusts law were created with that context in mind. However, in the modern era, express trusts continue to be important for those purposes, and in particular for 'asset management', principally in the form of tax avoidance by corporations and wealthy private individuals. Consequently, the rules governing express trusts have tended to become more rigid than one might expect from an equitable doctrine: they are certainly more

---

[1] It should be recalled that this book is not strictly-speaking a textbook, and therefore the reader who wants an explanation of all of the basic principles (beyond the summary which is presented below) is referred to Alastair Hudson, *Understanding Equity & Trusts* (Routledge, 2014) or *Equity & Trusts* (Routledge, 2014).

rigid than the critics of equity would normally suggest in their caricatures of equity. There is also an important political and social context behind the use of these devices: they have an odd relationship with the different genders (in particular, their role as protectors of women, purportedly, at one time), and their role in tax avoidance has made them particularly controversial during this period of economic austerity which exists at the time of writing.

By contrast, trusts implied by law (principally constructive trusts and resulting trusts) are a much more dynamic form of trust which at times are characterised by comparatively strict rules and at others are characterised by ostensibly broad moral principles which govern their creation. Much of the case law in this area revolves around litigators pushing at the boundaries of when a trust implied by law will arise. Many of the leading cases have involved large financial institutions or other large corporations, primarily because the litigation is complex and therefore expensive. Trusts implied by law will enable the recovery of loss or protection against a counterparty's insolvency (and so forth) in situations in which the common law or express trusts law offer no recourse. Because these areas of equity involve both the application of general principles and also cross-reference to earlier authorities which also applied general principles, there is always scope for wide-ranging development of this area of law as new cases come forward. This means that our discussion of trusts implied by law in Chapters 7–11 of this book will continue the theme which was raised in Chapter 1, as to whether equity is really best understood as an open-textured zone of general principles, or whether it is better understood (at least on occasion) as a litany of detailed rules operating strictly by reference to a doctrine of precedent.

## THE IMPORTANT DISTINCTION BETWEEN 'IS' AND 'OUGHT' IN TRUSTS LAW

Before we embark on our discussion of express trusts law, however, it is important to be aware of the tendentious and tetchy nature of the debate which takes place between some of the commentators in this area. There is one particularly significant line to be drawn when entering into discussions about trusts law, because many commentators hop across it sometimes unconsciously, sometimes accidentally, and sometimes in simple bad faith. That line is the line between 'is' and 'ought'.[2]

There are arguments about what the law 'is'. That is, the arguments concern the precise rule which applies in a given situation. In some circumstances (as is true of most common law systems) there are competing authorities which can claim to be of equivalent weight in terms of precedent and authority in trusts law. In those situations it may be difficult to know what the law 'is'. In other situations, a general rule may be well understood, but a sub-rule which permits deviation from the general rule may be acknowledged in some circumstances. For example, if a rule requires that all hats worn at an event must be 'entirely black',

---

[2] An idea explored by D. Hume, *An Enquiry Concerning Human Understanding*, 1748.

then it would be a 'sub-rule' which excused the wearing of a white hat if, for example, a pigeon had, with a large white splattering, befouled a hat which had previously been entirely black, as its wearer had crossed the car park on their way to the event. The sub-rule would be the rule that the hat will be treated as being 'entirely black' if the spoiling of its blackness was the result of an accident such as white bird mess falling on it. A sub-rule, in this sense, adapts the main rule in a particular context.[3]

At one level, establishing sub-rules in certain circumstances is the central business of equity. For example, when a 'secret trust' is upheld so as to give effect to the settlor's intention even though it had not been mentioned in the settlor's will, that breaches a rule in the Wills Act 1837 by establishing a sub-rule so as to benefit the person whom the settlor had intended to benefit. A secret trust works, broadly, as follows. According to statute, only people named in the will may take a benefit from property held on the terms of the will. However, it happened frequently that married men who had had mistresses and illegitimate children would leave property in their will to a close friend with instructions that that property should in reality be paid clandestinely to the settlor's mistress without his wife's knowledge. Courts of equity would find that even though this arrangement breached the Wills Act, it would be wrong to allow the friend to keep the money as though it was entirely his own, and so deny the mistress and children who were intended to benefit from that arrangement under the so-called 'secret trust'. Therefore, the sub-rule established to give effect to secret trusts cut against the main rule in the statute so as to prevent the friend's taking an unconscionable benefit from the situation after the settlor's death. Thus, the secret trust operated as a sub-rule which eluded the main rule in the Wills Act in appropriate circumstances.

However, it is perfectly possible for principles of equity (such as the rule in *Morice v Bishop of Durham*[4] that a gift cannot be completed by means of inferring the existence of a trust) to be subverted in their turn by other equitable sub-rules (such as the principle in *Re Rose*,[5] which permits the inference of a transfer of an equitable interest if the transferor had done everything necessary for them to do to transfer the property by way of a gift). Therefore, when principles of equity are occasionally subverted by further equitable sub-principles, we must simply accept that as part of the way of the world. Equity may appear to subvert the common law, but other equitable principles may in turn subvert equitable rules so as to achieve just outcomes.

In these situations, identifying what the law 'is' may be complicated in circumstances in which it is unclear how the sub-rule is to operate in relation to the main rule. Anyone who has studied English law for more than a few days will have become used to the way in which we no sooner encounter a rule, than there

---

[3] That is, as opposed to being merely an interpretation of the main rule in some context.
[4] (1805) 10 Ves 522.
[5] [1952] Ch 499.

is an exception lurking around the corner which qualifies that rule, or a strange interpretation applied to that rule by a judge who was determined to reach a particular outcome in the interests of justice.

Significantly, there are also very many arguments in trusts law about what the law 'ought' to be. This is something very different from what the law 'is'. It is common for professors of trusts law (and related subjects) to think that they know better than the judges what the law ought to be. (Indeed this tendency is not limited to professors of trusts law.) Consequently, those professors, who have spent decades studying the law of trusts closely, will tend to be dismissive of any judgment which contravenes their preferences for the field of trusts law. They are tempted to describe such a judgment as being 'wrong'.[6] (They are far more likely to do this in conversation or in the seminar room than in their writings.) They will tend to dismiss that judgment, and either to marginalise it by moving it to the footnotes of their writings, or to give it an undue centrality of place in those writings so that they can attack its deficiencies in a display of their own intellectual pyrotechnics.[7] It must, however, be observed that a professor of trusts law may very well be displacing what the law 'is' with what they think the law 'ought' to be in so doing. This is the case no matter how cogent their argument, no matter how profound their knowledge, and no matter how pure their motives. Professors of trusts law do not make the law – even if they sometimes think that the world would be a better place if they did.

Indeed, if the law in a common law system can be understood as being a conversation between the participants in that system then we may expect these sorts of differences of opinion to arise frequently. But that does not displace the simple truth that, under the doctrine of precedent, no academic argument becomes the law unless it is given expression by a judge at an appropriate place in the judicial hierarchy. Therefore, what an academic wishes the law to be is not necessarily what the law 'is'.

Therefore, in considering equity and trusts law, we must be on our guard to categorise arguments according to whether they constitute what the law 'is', or simply represent an argument as to what the law 'ought' to be in the opinion of that author. Many outcomes in academic arguments are dictated by beginning with propositions as to what the law 'is' which are in truth expressions of what the lecturer thinks the law 'ought' to be, in defiance of the doctrine of precedent. Criticisms of the law often come from a refusal to accept the whole of conception of equity as it was set out in the first chapter of this book. That is not to say that competing arguments cannot be right: far from it. Rather, it is to acknowledge that we must begin with an understanding of what the law actually is, and where it has

---

[6] The more time you spend with a certain breed of professor of trusts law, the more you will encounter this phenomenon.

[7] Professors of law often imagine, fondly enough, that their every idea is accompanied by literal as well as intellectual fireworks.

come from, before we can hope to criticise that law coherently or to propose better ways forward.

## DEFINING WHAT A TRUST IS

To begin at the beginning of trusts law, we must identify the most authoritative, modern statement of the nature of a trust in English law.[8] That is the decision of the House of Lords in *Westdeutsche Landesbank v Islington,*[9] and in particular the judgment of Lord Browne-Wilkinson. His Lordship sought to uncover the core values behind the trust with the first of his 'Relevant Principles of Trust Law':

> '(i) Equity operates on the conscience of the owner of the legal interest. In the case of a trust, the conscience of the legal owner requires him to carry out the purposes for which the property was vested in him (express or implied trust) or which the law imposes on him by reason of his unconscionable conduct (constructive trust).'[10]

Therefore, the root of the trust concept is that a person will be deemed to be a trustee when good conscience requires it. In relation to express trusts, a trustee (or trustees) will be required by conscience to obey the terms of the trusteeship which was imposed on them by the settlor. In relation to trusts implied by law, it is knowledge of some factor which should affect the trustees' conscience which invokes the authority of the courts of equity to acknowledge the existence of a resulting trust or a constructive trust in any given set of circumstances.[11] In particular, a constructive trust arises when someone deals unconscionably with property, as is discussed in Chapter 8.

While some commentators have tried (erroneously) to say that conscience has played no part in the history of trusts law, Lord Browne-Wilkinson was simply re-stating the history of trusts law as a part of equity and identifying the centrality of this idea of conscience in both fields. Because trusts law was part of equity meant that it was a standard of conscience which created the equitable obligations which govern the trustees' legal title in the trust property. It is conscience which binds an express trustee to observe the terms of the trust as established by the settlor, and it is conscience which causes the 'operation of law' which in turn calls a constructive trust into existence. In that sense, as discussed in Chapter 1, the trust has a moral root in the principles of equity.

---

[8] For a textbook explanation of the relevant principles in this area, see Hudson, *Equity & Trusts*, above n 1, section 2.1.

[9] [1996] AC 669.

[10] [1996] 2 All E.R. 961, 988.

[11] As is discussed in Ch. 7, it is less clear how 'conscience' relates to resulting trusts in all cases, except to the extent that anyone who becomes a trustee is bound by the equitable requirement of good conscience to obey their fiduciary duties.

# Debate **1**

## Are trusts used *in practice* in a way that prioritises form over substance?

### INTRODUCTION

It is a core concept of equity that substance must take priority over form.[12] That is, the courts will give effect to the real nature of a document or arrangement, as opposed simply to following any label which the parties may have purported to attach to it. So, if a document claims that a transaction is to be analysed as *x*, even though the true intention of the parties is *y*, then a court of equity should ignore a label which claims that the transaction is doing *x* and instead should recognise (and order) that the transaction is really doing *y*. Consequently, if a document is labelled as being a 'lease' (by the words 'this is a lease' having been written across the top of it in thick black ink), the court may nevertheless decide that it is in truth a 'licence' because the arrangement bears all the hallmarks of a licence.[13]

Nevertheless, the practical uses of trusts law by lawyers, accountants, bankers and others *in the real world* may often have the effect that apparently artificial devices (which label *y* as really being *x*) are often entirely effective for trusts law, tax law and other purposes. There is nothing unusual in this from the perspective of English law more generally. Lots of fictitious and artificial devices function perfectly well. After all, even though companies cannot function without human beings to make their contracts, look after their affairs and restock their photocopiers, we nevertheless accept that companies are 'separate legal persons' who create contracts in their own names, own their own property and so forth.[14] The very idea of a company is both central to the operation of modern capitalism and yet predicated on the idea that an intangible 'person' actually operates itself.[15] So, there is a clear example of an artificial device being given legal effect because it is convenient to do so. Therefore, trusts law is not unique in this regard when it alters the apparent ownership of property, although the apparent artificiality of these techniques does appear to operate contrary to equitable principles which require that equity (and therefore the trust) operates on the basis of substance and not form.

### THE NATURE OF AN EXPRESS TRUST

A definition of the term 'trust', particularly in relation to an express trust, might run as follows: a trust is created where the absolute owner of property (the settlor) passes the legal title in that property to a person (the trustee) to hold that property

---

[12] E.g. *Street v Mountford* [1985] AC 809.

[13] Ibid.

[14] *Salomon v A Salomon & Co. Ltd* [1897] AC 22.

[15] See Alastair Hudson, *Understanding Company Law* (Routledge, 2011) for an explanation of how company law achieves this, esp. Ch. 2.

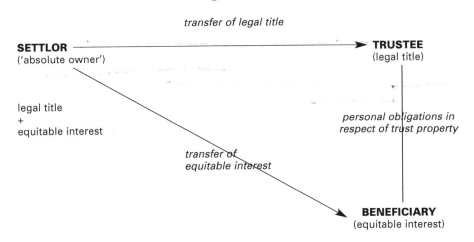

*transfer of legal title*

**SETTLOR** ————————————————————————▶ **TRUSTEE**
('absolute owner')                                                      (legal title)

legal title
+
equitable interest

*personal obligations in*
*respect of trust property*

*transfer of*
*equitable interest*

**BENEFICIARY**
(equitable interest)

Figure 2.1 The magic triangle of express trusts

on trust for the benefit of another person (the beneficiary) in accordance with terms set out by the settlor. There are three legal capacities to bear in mind in the creation of a trust: the settlor, the trustee, and the beneficiary. These three capacities form the 'magic triangle' of express trusts. See Figure 2.1 above.

There is something beautiful in the simplicity of the structure of the express trust. The settlor creates the trust but then, in the capacity of settlor, plays no further, direct part in its operation. The intentions of the settlor are revealed through the trust instrument (if there is one), or through the recollections of the parties otherwise as to the intentions of the settlor as they were communicated to the trustee(s). Thus the settlor retains a profound influence over the functioning of the trust without having any tangible role in their capacity as settlor in it. The trustee takes no direct benefit from the trust (beyond that sanctioned by the settlor in advance). Rather, the trustee works solely and selflessly for the benefit of the beneficiary. The beneficiary is therefore both a volunteer (in the sense that she takes her benefit without having given any consideration for it), a rightholder (in that only she has *locus standi* to sue the trustee in the event of any breach of trust) and a supplicant (in that, in the vernacular sense of the word 'trust', she is required to repose confidence and trust in the trustee to obey their duties under the terms of the trust).[16]

Thomas and Hudson define the trust in the following way in *The Law of Trusts*:[17]

'The essence of a trust is the imposition of an equitable obligation on a person who is the legal owner of property (a trustee) which requires that person to act in good

---

[16] Where trusts law reverses the traditional concept of 'trust' is in creating obligations over the trustee which make the trustee personally liable for any loss caused by a breach of trust: in that sense, the person who is doing the trusting becomes powerful as a result of the operation of trusts law: R.B.M. Cotterrell, 'Trusting in law: legal and moral concepts of trust' (1993) 46(2) CLP 75.

[17] G.W. Thomas and A.S. Hudson, *The Law of Trusts*, 2nd edn (Oxford University Press, 2010), 1.01.

conscience when dealing with that property in favour of any person (the benefici-ary) who has a beneficial interest recognized by equity in the property. The trustee is said to 'hold the property on trust' for the beneficiary. There are four significant elements to the trust: that it is equitable, that it provides the beneficiary with rights in property, that it also imposes obligations on the trustee, and that those obliga-tions are fiduciary in nature.'

These elements of the trust are considered in this chapter. Some of them have been questioned by academics who want to remodel trusts law, and by practitioners who want to achieve tax-efficient results for their clients. First, however, we should turn to the practical uses of the trust which manipulate these features so as to achieve commercial objectives.

## PLAYING TRICKS WITH TRUSTS LAW: THE PRACTICAL USES OF TRUSTS

The principal use of the trust in the modern world is for avoidance of various kinds: tax avoidance, regulatory avoidance and so forth. This is one of the core paradoxes in the use of trusts: whereas the express trust is based on concepts of good conscience, its principal use in modern practice is to avoid tax and other regulatory oversight. The 'tricks' referred to in the heading above are the creation of clever devices which minimise liability to tax and so on.

The trust plays a useful trick in that it takes the settlor's absolute ownership of property and creates new property rights out of it, creating a division between the legal title of the trustees and the equitable interests of the beneficiaries. The nature and the extent of those equitable interests is at the discretion of the settlor (as they are guided by their legal advisers). The endless flexibility of the trust is one of its key attractions for professional tax advisers and their clients, as well as for people with other objectives in mind. The trust can be fixed between a number of benefi-ciaries, or it can be bare, or it can be discretionary, or it can be contingent. The trust can be resident in England and Wales, or it can be resident overseas, or it can move its residence between jurisdictions depending on the composition of the trustees. The identity of the trustees can be altered, and the interests of the objects of a discretionary trust can be altered by the use of the trustees' powers. Different people may become beneficiaries at different times, depending on the decisions of the trustees in accordance with their powers or the passage of time, or following the death of other beneficiaries, or whatever else. In essence, anything that is not illegal is possible. Even the residence of the trust for legal purposes can be altered simply by changing the composition of the trustees so that a majority of the trustees are resident in one jurisdiction rather than another (with a more benign tax code). The settlor (and their advisers) can sculpt any arrangement they please, so long as it is not in pursuit of illegal goals or anything of that sort. As the legal historian Maitland put it, the trust is English law's greatest gift to jurisprudence, precisely because it is such a marvellously useful and flexible tool.[18]

---

[18] F.W. Maitland, *Equity*, 2nd edn (Cambridge University Press, 1936).

## Sometimes form wins out over substance

The amalgamation of all of these techniques (and the many others which are commonly used by trusts law practitioners) means that trusts can be adapted for an infinite number of circumstances and objectives. At first blush, this may seem to conflict with one of the basic principles of equity: that the court should look to the substance and not to the form of arrangements. If we consider cases like *Street v Mountford*[19] in the law on leases, we see the House of Lords was keen to invoke the equitable idea that even though a transaction may be described as 'a licence' in the document which solemnised it, the court would recognise that it was in truth 'a lease' (with all of the additional statutory protections that that classification invoked) because that court would look at the substance of the arrangement (i.e. its real nature when the circumstances were analysed closely) as opposed merely to its form (i.e. the label which one of the parties had hung on it). Nevertheless, this is how trusts law functions in practice.

## Using trusts (artificially) to manage your assets

Let us take an example to illustrate the inherent flexibility of the trust. A trust may be used to make it appear that the house which Glenda occupies is actually owned by her trustee, Derek, such that she has a right to occupy it only if the trustee permits her to do so. Other people (such as her adult children, some of her friends, or even a charity) may appear to have rights of occupation which muddy the tax position when Glenda dies, so as to minimise the liability to tax of the trust and her adult children who ultimately will go into occupation. In truth, Glenda will have been the settlor and, on advice from her solicitors, she will have constructed a discretionary trust more than seven years before she was expected to die, which identified other members of her family, her friends and a charity (which might have been added to improve the tax analysis in the opinion of those solicitors) as being the objects of that trust. It was Glenda's house and in practice Glenda still lives there alone; she treats the house as though it is hers, although there is a show of having the trustee exercise powers which permit Glenda to do that. All of this is simply a device to manage Glenda's assets in a tax-efficient way using trusts, and also to manage the succession to her property in a way which is overseen by her trustee so as to prevent discord and conflict (she hopes) among her children and friends after her passing. The details of the tax analysis are unimportant for our purposes. For our purposes, it is important to note two things: the trust can achieve a clever outcome if it is constructed correctly, and its self-evident artificiality need not be any obstacle to its effectiveness in practice.

## Using trusts to manage liability to tax and business assets

Take the example of a successful hedge fund manager in London. She takes advice on setting up a trust to manage her assets. She is advised to create a trust

---

[19] [1985] AC 809.

offshore[20] to hold her assets, but in a way which does not identify her as being the sole equitable owner of those assets, such that she does not have to declare any taxable profits in the UK. So, the trust could be notionally resident in the Cook Islands, because its trustees are employees of the investment bank which sold the advice to the settlor that her trust should be organised in the Cook Islands for tax purposes.[21] The settlor may be living in London and investing in UK companies, but the trust which holds her assets is legally resident in the Cook Islands.

In practice, many of these trusts (no matter how much counsel in Lincoln's Inn in London might advise to the contrary) are actually managed from an office in London (where the adviser meets the settlor in practice to take instructions further to their contract of retainer, before e-mailing those instructions to the employee in the Cook Islands who then copies and pastes them into a memorandum which records that a meeting of the trustees took place in the Cook Islands). A better-run trust would at least have everyone talk on a conference telephone call which is initiated by the employee of the accountancy firm, solicitors' firm, or bank in the Cook Islands which is notionally the trustee: that would make it appear that management of the trust was taking place in the Cook Islands, as opposed to this being a complete fiction. A better-run trust yet would actually have all of the relevant people travel to the Cook Islands for an annual (at least) meeting of the trustees. It may be the case that while all those professionals are physically present on the Cook Islands, the business of several different trusts would be conducted over the space of a couple of days. Again, the aim would be make it appear as if the trust were genuinely operated from that territory.

This pretence has the effect that the trust can claim to be operated in the Cook Islands (because that is notionally where the trustees meet) and to be resident there both for trusts law and tax law purposes. So little tax would be payable in the Cook Islands that the arrangement would be effectively tax free for the wealthy client at home in London. Consequently, an investor who put money into this trust would suffer only a very small cost in terms of fees and tax on the trust's profits. This is clearly a useful fiction for tax avoidance purposes. The residence of the trust in the Cook Islands is a useful fiction. Tax advisers are constantly involved in a merry dance with Her Majesty's Revenue and Customs as to the genuine residence of these sorts of trusts, whether these trusts are actually managed outside the UK and so forth. Often the work of a trusts law practitioner is to know exactly how far one can go with these sorts of arrangements before the tax authorities will seek to interfere. (The international trusts law context is considered in detail in Chapter 5.)

---

[20] By creating it 'offshore' we mean that it is intended to be resident outside the UK for tax purposes. The residence of a trust will ordinarily be governed by the residence of the majority of its trustees.

[21] The Cook Islands are beautiful islands which lie hundreds of miles off the coast of New Zealand. That territory has a surprisingly welcoming tax regime.

## Debate 2

## How do equity and the trust fit into ethical theory?

The ethical project which Aristotle suggests for equity raises a number of questions about how equity fits into ethical theory. The principal question in terms of ethical theory is whether equity and trusts law are 'deontological' or 'consequentialist'? This division will arise frequently in this book.

A *deontological* way of thinking establishes an objective set of moral duties, and of reasoning outwards from those central principles. Equity thus purportedly operates deontologically by reference to high-level principles such as 'conscience'. A deontological method answers any specific case by going back to its central principle and asking: Has there been good conscience in this instance? (Or whatever the principle happens to be.)

A *consequentialist* way of thinking considers each case on its own merits and then, working backwards from the cases which have been considered, begins to assemble a moral understanding of how one should behave. So, consequentialist ethics are derived from the moral decisions which have been made in individual cases. In this sense, it is the cases which create the moral principles. Or, more precisely, the moral code is an aggregation of the decisions which we observe having been made on a case-by-case basis. There is no moral principle set out in advance. Rather, the principles emerge from confrontation with circumstance.

Of course any sensible moral code will blend these two ways of thinking, although some people may claim to stick doggedly to one approach or the other. If one has no sense of what one believes (that people should be free; that people should avoid doing harm to one another; or whatever) then dealing with the world, and dealing with the difficult ethical and moral questions which arise in the world, can be very difficult. Therefore, world religions tend to set out a litany of moral statements which adherents are expected to follow. From within the Jewish tradition, the Ten Commandments (such as, 'Thou shalt not kill') constitute one of the best-known moral codes in the Western world. The prohibition on killing is not so much a religious principle as a moral principle which is core to most human societies. The question is then how to apply those moral principles to individual cases. Suppose a person killed another in self-defence. This is the most obvious challenge to the rule that one must not kill. Is the need to defend oneself a defence to the breach of the rule against killing?

Immediately, the abstract moral principle meets a challenge, and the society learns more about itself and its rules when the answer to that challenge is reached: do we punish the killer who acted in self-defence regardless of the duress under which they found themselves, or do we absolve them of guilt because the circumstances were so extreme? The former decision marks the society out as a strict one which intends to impose its rules strictly, regardless of the circumstances; whereas the latter decision requires a significant qualification to the rule against killing. Is the rule against killing extended to killing animals as well as humans? If so, then that society is self-evidently vegetarian; whereas, if not, that society clearly has both a blind-spot of some sort in relation to harm caused to animals, and probably a carnivorous diet.

Therefore, the deontological methodology ('killing is wrong') quickly incorporates individual cases into the definition and development of its moral principles. Even though deontology begins with abstract principles, we lawyers know that any abstract rule (no matter how clearly it is drafted) will always be susceptible to important alteration or qualification by judges in individual cases, or by the extent to which society chooses to ignore it in practice. So, the law on murder is treated much more seriously than the laws against parking illegally or driving over the speed limit because murder is taken to be more serious than parking unlawfully. The latter category of laws are punished less severely and are less likely to be investigated or enforced by the police than murder. Moreover, murder takes place much less often than breaches of the speed limits on our roads. This suggests that there is some 'relativism' in both the enforcement of the law and in the observance of the law: people tend not to kill each other as often as they park unlawfully. That means that deontological principles like 'You must obey the law' actually operate differently in different contexts in practice.

Thus even deontological methodologies use consequentialist practices to help to define what the principles mean in practice. That is, individual cases (and decisions by judges in legal practice, for our purposes) will shape the precise meaning or definition of those principles. So already, we might be catching hold of the idea that even if equity is comprised of a central moral principle about acting in good conscience, individual cases will be demonstrating to us what the judges think that principle means in different situations.

However, just as deontological methodologies often use consequentialist practices to define their terms, so consequentialist methodologies also resort to deontological principles to help people understand what the rules are and what that tells them about the nature of their society. Suppose the creation of a primitive human society entirely without any previous knowledge of law or morality. (Most philosophical discussions start with this sort of abstract, implausible example, but bear with it.) In that society Alf sets up home in a cave, puts some fruit in the cave to eat later, and then goes out to hunt. In the meantime, Bernard goes into that cave, eats all the fruit and sets up home for himself. The human society is required to make a decision: should Alf be entitled to keep his cave and his fruit, or should Bernard be entitled to take both the cave and the fruit?

The moral content of the decision will be important. The other people could decide that they all want to be protected from one another, and so they agree to establish a rule that you do not take another person's food or cave, or else the tribe will punish you. Alternatively, the people could come to the same decision on the basis that Alf had worked hard cleaning the cave, had discovered the fruit growing on a remote hilltop to the benefit of everyone in the tribe, and was the most skilled hunter and was therefore often absent from the village acquiring food for everyone else as well as himself. Alf may be thought to deserve his cave and fruit on the basis of his good work. Thus, an ethical principle of 'desert' may emerge, i.e. that property law is built on Alf's deserving to keep his fruit and his cave. From that understanding of the rules being based on an idea of deserving conduct there may emerge an idea of rules which protect property which one has earned. Differently again, Bernard may be thought to be a lazy bully (who never works nor helps anyone else) who does not deserve anything he has not earned for himself, and thus an ethical principle of punishing laziness may emerge.

Alternatively, the decision may be that Alf *needs* his cave and his fruit because he and his family have been sick, and to help the tribe they need to have food and shelter so as to recover. The morality underpinning this decision would be a combination of protection of the weak and also an understanding of the long-term needs of the tribe. Those tribe members will die without food and shelter, especially if they are sick. Many other decisions with many other motivating factors might emerge. Clearly, each decision will tell the tribe something about its own morality. That morality will emerge through a chain of decisions relating to Alf's cave, setting aside land to grow crops, burial rituals, rules against murder and assault, and so on.

What is important about this primitive human society is that it is both creating rules on a case-by-case basis (realising as each problem arises that a rule is necessary) and developing a moral sense of itself. So, if the tribe praises hard work then its morality will be predicated on deserving actions. Whereas, if the tribe prioritised the protection of need (whether individual needs or the long-term needs of the tribe) then its morality would have a different basis akin to a rudimentary welfare state. As that society evolved so as to attain a level of self-knowledge, it is likely that the tribe would describe itself as being based on hard work and desert, or the protection of the weak through communal action, or whatever. It is likely, as the tribe becomes self-aware, that it will use that understanding (as well as the memory of earlier decisions) to help it to make future decisions. Suppose that Zena had stolen food from Sheila while Sheila was tending the tribe's crops. The tribe might decide as follows:

> 'If we protected Alf in the past because of his hard work, then we should protect Sheila today because she has tended the crops on her own for many weeks. Zena must not be allowed to steal from Sheila's cave while Sheila is working. Sheila deserves protection due to her hard work. That is how we treat our people.'

This judgment would clearly be based on consequentialist principles: the decision in relation to Alf would govern the decision in relation to Zena and Sheila. The judgment that was given against Bernard (and any punishment of Bernard) would be replicated in relation to Zena. However, the rule might develop in a different direction if Zena argued that she stole food because she was starving. If Zena could demonstrate that Sheila eats all the crops she grows (without sharing them with anyone else), that she excludes the other women from the field by violence and that she is fat as a result, then the tribe might agree that it was acceptable in this instance for Zena to take food from Sheila. A different idea of Sheila's level of desert might develop, and thus the morality might change to being one that prizes both hard work but also fairness in the distribution of access to the land and its crops.

However, in the judgment itself there is also a sense that this tribe treats its people in a particular way: that is a deontological development because the tribe would be developing an understanding of the general principle which binds their decisions together. This tribe may understand that it prides both hard work and also fairness in the distribution of social goods like food. Without a central principle, all of the rules might seem a little arbitrary over time. So, a society will often use deontological thinking to develop their consequentialism, or to make it easier to understand the common thread in their consequentialist rules so as to assist in making judgments in the future.

This is what textbook writers do and it is what judges do when they use the doctrine of precedent: from earlier decisions, a principle is discerned which may be applied consistently in the future. Only the salient facts from the earlier decisions are used, so that they may inform future decision-making.

In exactly this way, equity is probably best thought of as a synthesis of deontological and consequentialist modes of thought. Equity has always had an idea of 'conscience', from the *Earl of Oxford's Case* in 1615, through decisions of judges like Lord Jessel in *Re Hallett's Estate*[22] and the court in *Re Diplock*,[23] judges like Megarry V-C and Scott J in the twentieth century, and into the leading judgment of Lord Browne-Wilkinson in *Westdeutsche Landesbank v Islington*[24] and beyond. Therefore, a deontological principle existed all along. However, the doctrine of precedent that is used in equity, just as it is used in the common law, has had the result that our understanding of what 'good conscience' and 'unconscionability' mean in various contexts (in relation to express trusts law, constructive trusts law, estoppel, injunctions, and so on) has been shaped by the ways in which judges in earlier cases have used that concept. Therefore, the moral basis of equity and trusts is neither entirely deontological nor entirely consequentialist. Instead, it is a blend of those two things.

That will be the central message of this book, in effect. For all the debates between the commentators which tend to argue that the position must either be black or white, the best solutions in practice and in theory are usually some shade of grey in between. Trusts law is a particularly significant marriage of the deontological and the consequentialist: it contains underlying principles, but it also expresses a close adherence to precedent in the development and application of its rules.

22 (1880) 13 Ch D 696.
23 [1948] Ch 465.
24 [1996] AC 669.

# Debate 3

## Is the trust really a part of property law or should it be part of contract law?

### INTRODUCTION

To be entirely honest with you, dear reader, there is a tendency among some academics in all fields to make arguments out of sheer wickedness or cussedness. Such people occasionally argue things in which they do not really believe because they like 'to stir the pot'; or because they feel their discipline has fallen into cosy habits which should be questioned; or because they want to re-imagine their discipline out of a need to feel 'radical' or 'progressive'; or because they think someone arguing something heretical is 'cool' and they want to jump on the bandwagon. Otherwise, their discipline might drift along unchanged for the 40 years or so of their academic career, which can be boring for some people, even if it is reassuring for others.

An example of just such an argument (although the motivations for making it are less clear) is the one which was briefly fashionable at the end of the twentieth century. It went as follows: 'Trusts are not really part of property law; instead, they create merely personal obligations on the part of trustees towards their beneficiaries.' Moreover, it was said, the sorts of obligations which trustees owe to their beneficiaries are best understood as being contractual in nature, as opposed to being in some way equitable or fiduciary in nature.

Before we start to analyse these arguments – which may tell us something interesting about the nature of modern express trusts law – it is useful to point out from the very beginning that they are not a correct account of what trusts law *is*, even if their proponents do believe that they might be a better account of what trusts law *ought to be*. (It is this writer's opinion that they are not correct on either count.) Trusts do grant proprietary rights to beneficiaries and the trustees become the legal owners of the trust property; and the obligations of the trustees are undoubtedly fiduciary in nature, and the rights of the beneficiaries are equitable in nature. That much is settled law. Nevertheless, these heresies are worth considering.

### IS THE TRUST A PROPERTY RELATIONSHIP?

The trust is, in essence, a property relationship. Without property being on held on trust by the owners of the legal title for the benefit of beneficiaries there would be no trust. Any relationship not conforming to that pattern is something other than a trust; by extension only a relationship conforming to that pattern falls to be described as a trust. It is important to state these matters plainly because, as will emerge below, there are forces abroad who would suggest that the trust is something other than a property relationship.

The trust is, however, a hybrid property relationship: if it were not, it would simply be a matter of outright ownership at common law. This hybrid relationship operates at two levels. At the first, the one which generates the most confusion, is the matrix of obligations which the trustee owes to the beneficiary. In that sense, the trust is comprised both of proprietary rights and of ostensibly personal obligations between trustee and beneficiary. At the second level, the trust enables two (or more) people to have rights in property simultaneously: the trustee has the legal title and the beneficiary the equitable title. It is this feature which marks the trust out from common law property relationships and from contracts.

The questions asked of the law of trusts have simply continued to become more and more complicated because much of the property developed and used in the modern world is itself more complicated: such as dematerialised securities in ordinary companies,[25] money held in electronic bank accounts,[26] and book debts.[27] Nevertheless, the trust from its earliest beginnings was a property relationship.

## THAT ALL TRUSTEES ARE FIDUCIARIES – BAR NONE

At this point the position of the trustee is evidently more complex than that of the bare trustee. A bare trustee who is required simply to maintain property for safe-keeping – whether as a nominee over land or even the depositary in relation to collective investment schemes[28] – does not have to balance the competing claims of beneficiaries with claims against the same property, albeit that their rights have different incidents and extents. Indeed some would go so far as to say that the bare trustee is not a fiduciary at all, because her obligations are similar, in effect, to those of a bailee of property required to mind it for its true owner.[29] It is said that it is only when a trustee is charged with some discretion or some power in relation to the trust property that she is properly considered to be a fiduciary in relation to it.[30]

This view is incorrect. The bare trustee is a fiduciary. My reasoning is as follows: it is suggested that it is far from controversial. In this context there are two forms of fiduciary duty. First, there are *active* fiduciary duties which police the manner in which trustees and others carry out their express powers. Secondly, however, there are *latent* fiduciary duties which apply equally to a bare trustee as to a trustee charged with some power. Such latent fiduciary duties are only evident when the bare trustee performs some act which, while perhaps not even mentioned in the express terms of her trusteeship, nevertheless offends against fiduciary law. Examples of such latent fiduciary duties are the rule against self-dealing, the rule against making secret profits from the fiduciary office and so forth. These rules apply to a bare trustee as to any other type of trustee. If the bare trustee behaves properly then no mention of them need be made. However, that does not mean

---

[25] E.g. *Hunter v Moss* [1994] 1 WLR 452.

[26] E.g. *MacJordan Construction Ltd v Brookmount Erostin Ltd* [1992] BCLC 350.

[27] E.g. *Agnew v IRC (The Brumark)* [2001] 2 AC 710.

[28] A.S. Hudson, The Law on Investment Entities (Sweet & Maxwell, 2000), 206.

[29] J. Penner, 'Exemptions' in *Breach of Trust*, P. Birks and A. Pretto (eds) (Hart Publishing, 2002), 245, 14n.

[30] *Ibid.*

that they do not apply to such a bare trustee. A little like the station platform which slips from view as our train pulls away: just because we cannot see it, it does not mean that it is not always there.

So, if a bare trustee uses the trust property to make a profit for herself (for example, by renting out a house which is held on trust and then keeping the rents for herself in a way that is not permitted by the terms of the trust instrument), then the understanding of the bare trusteeship as being fiduciary means that the trustee is obliged to account to the beneficiaries for those unauthorised profits.[31] All trusts are fiduciary in nature, it is just that the fiduciary aspects can be latent while the trustee is performing her duties properly.

## THE CONTRACTARIAN ANALYSIS: ARE TRUSTS REALLY CONTRACTS?

The trust is said by some commentators ('the contractarians')[32] to revolve around the contractual retainer between the settlor and the trustee. Their argument is that there is nothing special about the trust and that it should instead be considered to be a part of contract law precisely because, they argue, there will be some contract between settlor and the professionals who will act as trustees which entitles those professionals to be paid an hourly rate for their advice, and so on. Their underlying goal is to make the trust more commercially useful (they think) by allowing it to be interpreted under contract law rules which are familiar to commercial people. In particular, Professor Langbein is determined that every trust is part of a contract and therefore that there is no need to consider the nature of the trust in isolation from the contractual matrix of which (he considers) it forms a part.[33]

Therefore, the imposition of duties on the trustee by the settlor has led some commentators to suggest that the essence of the express trust is the relationship between settlor and trustee, and not that between trustee and beneficiary.[34] The question really is whether an express trust is concerned to effect the intentions of the settlor, or whether it is concerned merely to police the conscience of the legal owner of property (i.e. the trustee). Under the former analysis we might say that the trust is concerned with a form of contract between trustee and settlor, whereby the trustee is required to observe the wishes of the settlor and nothing else. This would mean, for example, that the beneficiary would not be entitled to terminate the trust nor to deal with the property in any way which conflicted with the wishes of the settlor: however, under English trusts law the beneficiaries can terminate the trust and call for delivery of the trust property.[35] Alternatively, to focus on the latter approach is to accept that the settlor has no further part to play in the trust, and that there is no objection to the beneficiary exercising proprietary rights to deal with the trust, so acting contrary to the wishes of the settlor if necessary. This

---

[31] *Boardman v Phipps* [1967] 2 AC 46.
[32] E.g. J. Langbein, 'The contractarian basis of the law of trusts' (1995) 105 *Yale Law Journal* 625.
[33] Ibid, 625.
[34] Ibid.
[35] *Saunders v Vautier* (1841) 4 Beav 115.

latter approach treats the trust as a combination of the beneficiary's property rights and obligations borne by the trustee in favour of the beneficiary; whereas the former approach treats the trust as being comprised simply of contractual obligations borne by the trustee to the settlor.

Before continuing any further with this analysis, it is worth pointing out that this fundamental assertion is wrong. Many trusts are not bound up with a contract. It is suggested at the outset that this argument cannot hope to describe constructive, resulting or implied trusts, and therefore requires a dismantling of any all-embracing definition of a trust. As outlined below, it also fails to provide a complete analysis of even express trusts, given that there are express trusts which are recognised as having come into existence without the conscious action of the parties,[36] let alone the formation of a contract between settlor and trustee. Express trusts may arise in English trusts law without the parties knowing they are creating a trust, let alone requiring the existence of a contract between settlor and trustees. Therefore, this theory is bunkum from the very beginning. However, its larger objective is worth some consideration.

In relation to commercial practice, it will commonly be the case that there will indeed be a commercial contract which uses a trust as a device to hold security for payment or a contract for services whereby some person will be limiting their liability and identifying their fee in return for acting as trustee. To that extent, the Court of Appeal has held that this contract ought to limit even trustees' liability for breach of trust if the terms of the trustee's contract for services require that – even where the trustee has been guilty of gross negligence.[37] However, many express trusts arise without a contract, for example in will trusts and in situations like *Paul v Constance*[38] or *Re Kayford*[39] where the parties create something akin to a trust but which they may not necessarily have described as a trust themselves – these sorts of trusts may occur naturally in the wild in great profusion but the parties to them are unlikely to have enough money at stake to reach the Chancery courts. Nevertheless, these unconscious express trusts have been analysed by the courts as being express trusts even though the parties had no notion that they were creating such a thing.[40] Therefore, express trusts can arise in English law without the existence of a contract; trusts implied by law necessarily arise by operation of law and not as a result of any act of the parties.

Thus, the contractarian thesis can be rebutted on the basis that beneficiaries own the trust fund in equity in the English position,[41] and that the settlor drops out of the picture in the English context.[42] However, the principal reason for saying that trusts are not capable of being subsumed within the box labelled

---

[36] E.g. *Re Kayford* [1975] 1 WLR 279.
[37] *Armitage v Nurse* [1998] Ch 241.
[38] [1977] 1 WLR 527.
[39] [1975] 1 WLR 279.
[40] *Paul v Constance* [1977] 1 WLR 527.
[41] *Saunders v Vautier* (1841) 4 Beav 115.
[42] *Paul v Paul* (1882) 20 Ch D 742.

'contract' is that trusts necessarily create fiduciary duties whereas contracts do not necessarily create fiduciary duties (except in relation to partnership and agency contracts). Contracts are means of allocating risks between the contracting parties. Trusts necessarily create property rights in the beneficiary and fiduciary duties in the trustee. This is so even if the trustee is merely a bare trustee.

# 3

# THE UNJUST ENRICHMENT INSURGENCY

## INTRODUCTION

A key theme in the debates about equity, especially in relation to trusts implied by law such as constructive trusts and in relation to tracing, has been the development of an entirely new way of explaining how many of the doctrines which are currently part of equity (and part of contract law and tort law) should be organised and understood. This has ignited debates about the organisation of 'private law' – that is, everything that is not criminal law nor public law. That new way of thinking has taken many different names over the years: 'the law of restitution', 'the law of restitution of unjust enrichment', 'the law of unjustified enrichment', and 'the law of unjust enrichment'. The changes in name reflect two things: the evolution of that way of thinking among its adherents, and also disagreements between its adherents as to the way in which it should operate. In this book it will be referred to as 'unjust enrichment' for ease of reference, with many of the subdivisions of opinion being considered separately. It is given such prominence in this book because its feasibility and its structure have been such a large part of the academic debates about equity and trusts in the last three decades.

### THE PURPOSE OF THIS CHAPTER

The purpose of this chapter is to identify some of the key themes which will run through this book about the impact of 'unjust enrichment' thinking on equity and trusts. This is a development in the academic literature which has generated (literally) furious debate, and which has spilled over into some of the most significant judgments in this field over the last 20 years.

### THE ROOTS OF UNJUST ENRICHMENT THINKING

Simply put, unjust enrichment thinking began in 1939 in the USA with the statutory *Restatement of Restitution*, which prioritised dealing with unjust enrichment as being the central basis for awarding a range of different remedies. This way of thinking was advocated for England and Wales by Robert Goff and Gareth Jones (later Lord Goff of Chieveley and Professor Gareth Jones of the University of Cambridge) in the first edition of their book *The Law of Restitution*, published in 1966. This book collected together a range of hitherto well-understood aspects of contract law and equity (such as undue influence, duress, rescission and so forth), and suggested that they could respond to a central concept of unjust enrichment. It was said that all of the pre-existing doctrines which were collected into that book were concerned with achieving restitution for the claimant, and that that was a bonding principle among them. Otherwise, that book was a scholarly description of existing English law principles which was marketed to practitioners in the main in a handsome, hardback treatise.

The unjust enrichment field received a boost in its scholarly arm in the late 1980s with the publication of the first edition of Professor Peter Birks's *Introduction to the Law of Restitution*, which sought to explain the underpinnings of the field as he understood it. Birks was Regius Professor of Civil Law at the University of Oxford and collected around him a group of motivated young scholars whose imaginations were fired by the idea of reorganising English private law on this model. Birks himself was an evangelist for the changes which he was advocating, speaking regularly to audiences of judges, practitioners and academics about his theories, and generating a large output of scholarly essays and articles on the topic. His presence on the professional accreditation committee for the law degrees even led to 'restitution' being added to the list of fields which law students must study to receive a qualifying law degree in England and Wales.

Birks's model of unjust enrichment was more dogmatic than that suggested by Goff and Jones. In his judgments, Lord Goff demonstrated an affection for 'justice' in the broadest sense: not a weak-willed, indulgent justice, but rather a reasoned sense of right and wrong. Examples of this tendency in this book are the judgments in *Tinsley v Milligan* (discussed in Chapter 7) and in *Westdeutsche Landesbank v Islington*, considered below. In essence, Lord Goff was in the grand equitable tradition in many senses: looking for a just, principled result and not simply an arbitrary one which followed the law obediently. By contrast, Birks had no truck with ideas of 'justice' in the general sense of that word. The concept of '*unjust* enrichment' in his scheme meant a list of unjust factors which were set out in advance in a rigid taxonomy,[1] such that the law would not respond to injustice in general terms but rather only where there were 'unjust factors' of the sort which appeared on that list. That list, as set out below, involved traditional doctrines of English law like mistake, duress and so forth. There was certainly not to be any general principle in Birks's scheme of the sort that is found in equity. The idea of 'conscience' as an organising principle was an anathema to Birks because he considered it to be so vague and unprogrammatic. Equity tradition-alists would argue that Birks had simply not considered or not understood their

---

[1] Where a 'taxonomy', as was explained in Ch. 1, is the sort of ordering commonly undertaken by biolo-gists to organise living things into different categories and subcategories for a better understanding of their natures.

way of thinking about ideas like conscience – ways which were outlined in Chapter 1.

The discussion of unjust enrichment in this chapter is necessarily truncated because it compresses millions of words generated by Birks and his followers into a few key propositions which are discussed here. The key authors in the unjust enrichment movement were research students of Birks in their younger days or academics at the University of Oxford. Consequently, they are referred to in this book as the 'Oxford Restitution School'. One of the clearest accounts of restitution is set out by Professor Graham Virgo, of the University of Cambridge, in his book *Principles of the Law of Restitution*.

Birks's theory is explained in this chapter as having gone through three phases which are important for equity and trusts. First, the period before the decision in *Westdeutsche Landesbank v Islington*,[2] where Birks argued that restitution in cases involving property disputes should be achieved by a radically restructured and expanded version of the resulting trust. This theory was explicitly rejected by the House of Lords in *Westdeutsche Landesbank v Islington*. The second phase sought to re-explain how property law should deal with situations in which property is taken from a person without their consent. This did not really solidify into a new theory. In the meantime, other members of the Oxford Restitution School had been advocating that other areas of equity (such as resulting trust, tracing and subrogation) should be reorganised on unjust enrichment lines. At the edges, the concept was becoming frayed because there were so many disagreements over points of detail as to how unjust enrichment should work. The third phase saw Birks attempting to construct a new methodology in the years before his untimely death, in a smaller book titled *Unjust Enrichment* in which he argued that all forms of unjust enrichment should coalesce around a central principle which requires action in any situation which is 'analogous to a mistake'. Given that mistake was the clearest example of unjust enrichment, Birks began, in effect, to work outwards from that central principle.

It is ironic, perhaps, that this last phase of the project had begun to establish a central organising principle which seemed to be of the same methodological type as equity.[3] It is ironic because equity had been the target of so much of the Oxford Restitution School's critique; and yet to explain the principles underpinning unjust enrichment, it had become necessary to retreat into the use of a single, central principle to explain the theory, as opposed to relying on a neat taxonomy of the various forms of action without using a deontological method. Perhaps that development in itself suggests that in the modern world, it is necessary to use general principles (whether or not as a root for detailed rules) to cope with the rapid pace of social change when making laws which are intended to stand the test of time. The significance of unjust enrichment thinking has waned in the decided

---

[2] [1996] AC 669.

[3] Methodological in the sense that it relied on having a central principle at all (as opposed to a taxonomy of claims), and not in the sense that it had adopted a moral central principle like 'conscience'.

cases. No longer do judges worry about whether a doctrine is part of unjust enrichment, or property law, or equity (as Lord Millett did in *Foskett v McKeown*[4]). Instead, it appears that the idea of unjust enrichment is increasingly being treated as being a subset of equity: that is, the idea of something being 'unjust' is simply taken to be akin now to its being 'unconscionable'. That was exactly not what Birks had intended.

These developments are traced through this chapter. The aim, ultimately, is to identify some of the key themes which run through this book from the unjust enrichment theories.

## Debate 1

## What was the Birksian model of unjust enrichment?

### A DESIRE FOR ORDER

It is supposed that restitution is neater than equity, where the latter has a large historical baggage which includes, in side pockets and under flaps, many fragmentary doctrines. Birks[5] approved Professor Beatson's project of displacing equity with a law of restitution.[6] Similarly, side-projects like the development of a unitary law of tracing are intended to remove the need to trace specifically in equity, thus permitting an ability to trace generally.[7] So, what is at issue in this debate is the very existence of equity.

The Oxford Restitution School are classically interested in something called 'taxonomy'. That means, like biologists codifying the different types of butterfly and moth into categories, they insist on law being reduced to rigid categories so that the ability of the courts to use their discretion is reduced by the requirements of that code. This is not 'order' in the sense of people being allowed to go about their lives in a peaceful society with some reassurance that things are predictable; instead, this sort of ordering requires that all of the circumstances giving rise to rights and obligations must be codified in the form of complex tables, and that the remedies which are available must necessarily follow from the type of claim that is brought. The upshot is a sort of law-making which resembles a bus timetable: one has only to identify the type of claim, ask whether or not its prerequisites have been satisfied, and then look up the remedy which results, much as one would identify when the bus would reach the Cowley Road. There is not much philosophy here. As was mentioned before, the idea of this orderliness and rigid predictability is taken to be a good in itself.

---

[4] [2001] 1 AC 102.
[5] P. Birks, *Private Law* (Oxford University Press, 2000), 261.
[6] J. Beatson, *Use and Abuse of Unjust Enrichment* (Clarendon Press, 1991), 244 *et seq.*
[7] E.g. P. Birks, 'Establishing a proprietary base' [1995] *RLR* 83.

## THE ROMAN ROOTS OF UNJUST ENRICHMENT IN BIRKS'S THOUGHT

The Emperor Justinian is the hero of much of Birks's restitution theory.[8] Justinian had introduced a code of law which divided between 'actions, people, and things': in essence, it is said, a comparator to our procedural rules, law of obligations, and property law respectively. In this spirit of orderliness, and to emulate *Justinian's Institutes* in Roman law, Birks suggested the following reorganisation of English private law into three new categories, namely:

- *Consent* – which would encompass contract law, express trusts law, and any other legal construct built on agreement.
- *Wrongs* – which would encompass torts, breach of contract, breach of trust, and so forth.
- *Unjust enrichment* – which would comprise restitution of unjust enrichment, as considered below.

The aim was to introduce order (and possibly a minimalist elegance) to the law. What Birks was seeking to do, therefore, was to reorganise the current actions and remedies in English law into a new taxonomic framework. This is an interesting conceptual reorganisation of English law, which omits equity entirely; although one cannot help but wonder whether the entirety of English law needed reorganisation if one's key quest was to introduce greater tidiness.

There is a tremendous irony in the fact that Justinian was far from being the paragon of good order and legal virtue which Birks and others like to think. First, Justinian's *Pandects* were an important source of equity on which Professor Story relied in his *Equity Jurisprudence*.[9] Indeed, Roman law used the concept of *aequitas* to achieve equity in many cases. It should be remembered that the Romans borrowed largely from the Greeks, and equity was important in Aristotle's *Ethics*.

Secondly, and far more salaciously, Justinian was an absolute rotter. What we know about the Emperor Justinian comes primarily from the historian Procopius. And what we know most clearly about Justinian the man and Justinian the emperor, we know from Procopius's book *The Secret History*. While some have sought to argue that *The Secret History* is so shocking that it cannot be true[10] (thus ignoring the general bad behaviour of Roman emperors, like Caligula), Procopius is accepted by all historians as being the principal authority on Justinian's wars against the Persians, the Vandals and the Ostrogoths (in his multi-volume *History of the Wars*). Therefore, Procopius has a large amount of historical credibility. In *The Secret History*, Justinian and his wife Theodora are revealed to be corrupt, lascivious and deeply wicked. Justinian is accused of ordering murder, the seizure of

---

[8] See P. Birks and G. McLeod (trs), *Justinian's Institutes* (Duckworth, 1987); P. Birks, 'Definition and division: a meditation on *Institutes* 313' in Birks (ed.), *The Classification of Obligations* (Clarendon Press, 1997).

[9] J. Story, *Commentaries on Equity Jurisprudence*, 2nd edn (Little and Brown, 1839).

[10] Even though Procopius acknowledges in his introduction that what is about to relate may appear to future generations to be incredible and unconvincing, despite its being true.

villages, the burning of cities, and of stealing other people's property, while ruining the Roman state. Far from being an upholder of the law, Justinian received bribes from wealthy murderers not to prosecute them, as well as bribes to decide land disputes in a particular way. He amended the criminal law on a whim, and used new offences to hold men guilty (without even needing any accuser) of crimes like pederasty so that they could be punished (by castration and so forth) and be paraded through the streets. All of this is, clearly, in the worst traditions of the Roman empire operating under the yoke of half-mad emperors who considered themselves to be demi-gods.

Most interestingly, for a man who is lauded for the order he supposedly brought to the law, Procopius tells us:

'The maintenance of established institutions meant nothing to [Justinian]: endless innovations were his constant preoccupation. In a word, he was a great destroyer of well-established institutions.[11] ... No law or contract retained any force on the secure basis of the established order, but everything turned to growing violence and confusion, and the government was indistinguishable from a tyranny – not, however, a stable tyranny but one that changed every day and was forever starting afresh.'[12]

Justinian's proclivity for seizing land is, in particular, at odds with the sort of orderly property law which Justinian's *Institutes* are supposed to inspire in our own legal system. This sounds like the stereotype of discretion-wielding equity judges which Birks advances, albeit with less actual tyranny. We are told that 'chaos' was the key feature of Justinian's early political ambitions. Procopius describes him as being 'dissembling, crafty, hypocritical, secretive by temperament, two-faced ...', and so it goes on.[13] Even worse than that, perhaps, we are told that he wore a 'mullet' hairstyle.

Worst of all, for the Birksian project, we are told that:

'[Justinian's] judicial decisions were made not in accordance with the laws he himself had enacted but as he was led by the prospect of a bigger and more splendid promise of monetary advantage.'[14]

The book continues in this vein with a series of shocking and lewd revelations about the lives of Justinian and Theodora. In short, far from being the epitome of orderliness and juridical good sense which Birks would seek to have us believe, Justinian was an evil and corrupt demagogue, whose use of law was entirely predicated on his own personal advantage[15] and whim. He was quixotic and cruel. At the very least, equity specialists seek to apply their doctrines in good conscience,

---

[11] Procopius, *The Secret History*, revised trans. Williamson and Sarris (Penguin Classics, 2007), 27.
[12] Ibid, 31.
[13] Ibid, 35.
[14] Ibid, 56.
[15] The extent of his preparedness to accept bribes 'without a blush' and to disapply laws when bribed to do so, is explained as being at the heart of his administration of the law: ibid, 60.

which is a million miles away from behaviour of this sort. As the French essayist Michel de Montaigne put it:

> 'I hardly agree, therefore, with the opinion of that man [Justinian] who tried to curb the authority of his judges by a multitude of laws, thus cutting their meat up for them. He did not understand that there is as much liberty and latitude in the interpretation as in the making of them.'[16]

What this shows, it is suggested, is that having a system of rules which appears to be orderly on paper is only a part of the story. What is more important than that is to have those laws administered fairly and ethically. However, rigid systems of rules rarely work effectively: particularly not when measured against the complexities of the modern world. A moral code is a useful way of ensuring that rigid codes of laws work fairly in practice. As was suggested in Chapter 1, a blend of structure and discretion is likely to ensure the fairest outcome to individual cases, while achieving that amount of order that is necessary for any modern society to operate properly.

## THE ORGANISATION OF UNJUST ENRICHMENT BASED ON *MOSES v MACFERLAN*

As we have seen from the references back to Roman law which Birks made on several occasions, unjust enrichment thinking is always concerned to establish an historical pedigree for itself, as opposed to appearing to be a theory which has arisen out of thin air. The case of *Moses v Macferlan*[17] is generally taken to be a *fons origio* for unjust enrichment by restitution scholars, even though at no stage in the judgment does the court use the words 'restitution', 'unjust' or 'enrichment'. Instead, remarkably enough, the court refers exclusively to 'equitable' concepts. Nevertheless, the case is said to create a pattern by reference to which restitutionary ideas may be identified.

That case related to an action for 'money had and received'. In *Moses v Macferlan*, Lord Mansfield CJ held:

> 'The action for money had and received, an equitable action to recover money which the defendant ought not in justice to keep ... lies for money paid by mistake; or upon a consideration which happens to fail; or for money got through imposition (express or implied); or extortion; or oppression; or an undue advantage taken of the plaintiff's situation, contrary to laws made for the protection of persons under those circumstances. In one word, the gist of this kind of action is, that the defendant, upon the circumstances of the case, is obliged by the ties of natural justice and equity to refund the money.'

Unjust enrichment scholars use the list of actions in that passage (mistake, failure of consideration and so forth) as constituting the basis for their taxonomy. Significantly, however, this action is described as being 'equitable', and as arising

---

[16] M. de Montaigne, 'On experience' in *Essays* (J. Cohen, trs.) (Penguin, 1958).
[17] (1760) 2 Burr 1005.

on the basis of 'natural justice and equity' as opposed to a taxonomic list of actions. Therefore, even the foundational case is actually adhering closely to equity and its traditional methodology, as opposed to the Birksian scheme. It is the bedrock of restitution's taxonomy, and yet it is a decision predicated clearly on equity. It is only if you fail to read what the judge actually said in *Moses v Macferlan* that you can kid yourself that it has something to do with unjust enrichment.

One of the most significant modern judgments which is used to establish unjust enrichment as part of English law is the case of *Fibrosa Spolka Akcyjna v Fairbairn Lawson Combe Barbour Ltd*, in which Lord Wright held that:

> 'It is clear that any civilised system of law is bound to provide remedies for cases of what has been called unjust enrichment or unjust benefit, that is to prevent a man from retaining the money of or some benefit derived from another which it is against conscience that he should keep.'[18]

Significantly for unjust enrichment thinking, this judgment mentioned the concept of unjust enrichment and found that it was necessary in any civilised system of law; but significantly for equitable thinking, this judgment also bases itself on whether or not the defendant is acting in good conscience. Therefore, this judgment is equivocal at best as to whether this is unjust enrichment based on a taxonomy, or simply a general notion of justice which operates on the basis of conscionability as equity has always required.

As is considered below, the presence of unjust enrichment in English law was confirmed by the House of Lords in 1991.[19] What is remarkable is that many legal historians have started to pretend that this notion of unjust enrichment has always been a part of English law; instead of recognising that it can only have been part of English law since 1991, and arguably part of English legal-scholarly culture since 1966.[20]

## THE COMPONENT PARTS OF 'RESTITUTION OF UNJUST ENRICHMENT'

The classic three-step test in the traditional restitution model operated as follows:

1. there must have been an enrichment taken by the defendant;
2. that enrichment must have been made at the claimant's expense; and
3. that enrichment must have arisen as a result of some unjust factor.

It is said that restitution is concerned to reverse an enrichment of the defendant where that enrichment has been made as a result of some unjust factor. Reversal is

---

[18] [1943] AC 32, 61.

[19] *Lipkin Gorman v Karpnale* [1991] 2 AC 548.

[20] See, e.g., D. Ibbetson, *A Historical Introduction to the Law of Obligations* (Oxford University Press, 1999), which mounts a detailed and entirely convincing account of the roots of the law of obligations, complete with a remarkable depth of footnote referencing, before collapsing in the final chapter into an unsubstantiated claim that unjust enrichment thinking has always been part of English law, without footnotes to support those claims. Unjust enrichment simply has not been a part of English law before the late 20th century. Whereas Equity has been a part of English law for many centuries.

achieved by the 'subtraction' of the enrichment from the defendant. In short, the claimant is entitled to say: 'You have made an enrichment at my expense, so give me that enrichment.' The form of the enrichment may therefore either be the acquisition of a specific piece of property, or it may be the acquisition of some cash value. The problem for restitution lawyers is therefore whether the remedy ought to be personal or proprietary.

The unjust factors are to be identified from a list of unjust factors and are *not* to be identified by the courts when they consider it to be appropriate by reference to some general moral principle. So, you might ask: Do we have a complete list of the unjust factors? The answer is: no. Birks and Chambers took the view that there were 43 unjust factors.[21] However, each unjust enrichment scholar has their own view as to the number of unjust factors there are. One account suggests that there is only one unjust factor, which is to be identified by reference to a general principle.[22]

The nature of the restitutionary response to a finding of unjust enrichment was complex. In essence, the earliest unjust enrichment thinking was not interested in 'compensation' nor in 'remedies', but rather in 'subtraction of the unjust enrichment' from the defendant. The approach of restitution lawyers was centred around the development of responses which require a defendant to give up an enrichment received at the plaintiff's expense. The appropriate response was one which required the defendant to give up to another an enrichment received at the other's expense or its value in money. Birks declares his central concern to be with 'the second sense of "restitution" ... that is, with gains to be given up, not with losses to be made good'.[23]

On this model, the law of restitution creates a new right, rather than giving effect *ex post facto* to a pre-existing right. That right is generated by the receipt of the unjust enrichment with the effect of depriving the defendant of the value received at the plaintiff's expense. In Birks's terms: 'Restitution is that active or creative response at the moment of enrichment.'[24] That means that the rights would come into existence only at the date of the court order prospectively, which was an idea that was rejected by the House of Lords in *Westdeutsche Landesbank v Islington* in relation to constructive and resulting trusts, as is considered below.

In *Orakpo v Manson Investments Ltd*, it had been held by Lord Diplock that 'there is no general doctrine of unjust enrichment in English law'.[25] However, in the House of Lords in *Lipkin Gorman v Karpnale*,[26] it was held by Lord Goff (author of *The Law of Restitution*, remember), when considering the liability of a casino for

---

[21] P. Birks and R. Chambers, *Restitution Research Resource* (Mansfield Press, 1997).
[22] S. Meier and R. Zimmerman (1999) 115 *LQR* 556.
[23] P. Birks, *Introduction to the Law of Restitution* (Oxford, 1989), 11.
[24] Ibid, 14.
[25] [1978] AC 95, 104.
[26] [1991] 2 AC 548.

receiving money from a solicitor which he had taken from accounts which were held on trust for the firm's clients, that:

> 'I accept that the solicitors' claim [for money had and received] in the present case is founded upon the unjust enrichment of the club, and can only succeed if, in accordance with the principles of the law of restitution, the club was indeed unjustly enriched at the expense of the solicitors.'

At this moment, it became clear that unjust enrichment in some form was a part of English law. The question, as will be discussed in various places later in this book, is how it interacts with equity.

### 'Unjust' is a word with a purely technical meaning

One of the more difficult aspects of the restitution project is its determined amorality and its equally determined refusal to explain what its philosophical underpinnings are. A claim for unjust enrichment begins with an enrichment, and then requires there to be one of the 'unjust factors' on the list of unjust factors in play at the time. While one might expect that a theory of *'unjust* enrichment' has at its heart a moral project, in truth its goals are entirely positivist and so not concerned with morals. Birks was clear on this point: '"Unjust" here is technical. An enrichment is unjust if the circumstances are such that the law requires its recipient to make restitution.'[27] The project is entirely positivist and intended to create order. What restitution lawyers require is rationality. As Birks put it: 'We are not all as brave as Cranmer but like him we know it is better to burn than to live in a world which has abandoned rationality.'[28]

Nevertheless, this is deeply problematic. Not only have we arbitrarily selected one judgment by one judge (in *Moses v Macferlan*) as establishing the basis for this new area of law (which will eradicate hundreds of years of authority at a stroke), but we are not even going to state the basis on which we are intending to do so. A need for order is all that we have by way of a philosophy. In fact this is an entirely Nietzschean project, with Birks as its superman. As Nietzsche told us in *The Will to Power*:

> 'It is the powerful who made the names of things into law, and among the powerful it is the greatest artists in abstraction who created the categories.'[29]

The unjust enrichment project – which seeks to re-write English private law as a vast taxonomic project and which sets about lobbying judges to that effect – is about dominating the discourse of private law and about subjugating it to a new model in this obscure philosophy. As Nietzsche points out, creating the categories is not only an act of power, but rather it is also an act of abstract creation. Deciding which forms of unjust factor go onto the list and which do not is a creative act in

---

[27] P. Birks, 'Rights, wrongs and remedies' (2000) *OJLS*, 1, 6.

[28] Ibid, 8.

[29] F. Nietzsche, *The Will to Power*, para. 513.

itself. It is based on value judgments just as much as any other model of law. Thus, the creation of unjust enrichment theory is in fact a creative act based on value judgments about the nature of law, even though it purports to be an entirely amoral taxonomic project.

Birks's theory has gone through various iterations: each of them is considered in turn below as they apply to equity and trusts.

## Mark 1: the restitutionary resulting trust

The central idea of 'subtraction of the unjust enrichment' from the defendant led to two possible models. First, cases of personal restitution (where no specific property was to be recovered) involved the use of money had and received at common law. That meant that the defendant would account in cash terms for the amount of the enrichment. Secondly, cases of proprietary restitution, where property was to be recovered so as to achieve subtraction of the unjust enrichment by holding the property constituting the enrichment on resulting trust for the claimant.[30] Birks's model of the resulting trust (as considered in Chapter 7) is that the property held on resulting trust 'jumps back' to the beneficial owner. On this model, the property at issue would jump back to the claimant in the unjust enrichment action.

Importantly, in _Westdeutsche Landesbank v Islington_ this theory was rejected.[31] In that case, a local authority had entered into an interest rate swap with a bank lasting for 10 years. Five years into the transaction it became clear that it was beyond the powers of a local authority to enter into an interest rate swap, and therefore the interest rate swap contract was void _ab initio_. If Birks's theory had been correct, the amount paid under the interest rate swap would have been held on resulting trust for the bank by the local authority from the moment of the court's order. Lord Browne-Wilkinson rejected this idea because it would mean that a trust could take effect over uncertain property: which money exactly would be held on the terms of this resulting trust? It would be impossible to prove the existence of such a resulting trust in an insolvency – because the trust would come into effect too late at the date of the court's judgment when seeking to subtract the enrichment from the defendant – especially where the property had been mixed with other property. (It was held more generally that no property claim was supportable because there was no identifiable property in the hands of the defendant which could be held on trust, that the defendant's conscience had not been affected before the time at which the money had been spent (because neither party had known at the outset that their arrangement not enforceable under contract law), and because no traceable proceeds of that money remained.) It was held, however, that because the contract was void, the local authority should be required to account for the amount which it had received from the bank. That meant that the

---

[30] P. Birks, 'Restitution and resulting trusts' in Goldstein (ed.), _Equity: Contemporary Legal Developments_ (Jerusalem University, 1992), 335.

[31] W. Swadling, 'A new role for resulting trusts?' (1996) 16 _Legal Studies_ 110.

authority was required to write a cheque equal to the amount which had been paid to it beforehand, albeit that no specific money was to be treated as being held on trust. This claim is known as a claim for 'money had and received' (or, a 'personal claim in restitution', according to Lord Goff). It was fortunate for the bank that the authority was still solvent because it had only a personal claim against the authority and not a claim based on trust.

For Birks, this meant that he was required to go back to the drawing-board with his theory.

## Mark 2: the retention of property rights

The second model of the thesis is contained in a slew of ideas which were developed in the wake of the decision in *Westdeutsche Landesbank v Islington*, but before the publication of *Unjust Enrichment*. Birks began by criticising the judgment in *Westdeutsche Landesbank v Islington*.[32] Other commentators simply claimed that that judgment was part of mainstream unjust enrichment thinking.[33] A key part of 'mark 2' of this thesis was to re-think the way in which property could be recovered by a person who had had it taken from them without their consent or subject to some unjust factor. In essence, the second version of theory took the view that such a person should be deemed not to have parted with any property rights at all. This theory, which was not pursued for over long because it seemed to beg as many questions as it answered, was that property which had not been parted with consensually by its owner (for example, if it had been stolen) should be treated as continuing to be the property of its original owner. Questions remained as to the difference which this made to the existing law if the property was put beyond reach, or was mixed with other property, or was sold to an innocent purchaser, and so forth. It also suggested that the idea of subtracting an enrichment was no longer necessary because ownership was taken not to have passed at all.

It was also important to change the name of the theory from 'the law of restitution' to 'the law of unjust enrichment', because the term 'the law of restitution' merely told us what the law was seeking to achieve (viz. restitution of something to someone) but did not tell us what the basis of claim was. Thus, we did not know if the claim was based on mistake, the smell of garlic or whatever; all we knew was that restitution of some sort was being achieved. This was the sort of inexactitude which Birks had criticised in the law on constructive trusts. By contrast, calling this theory 'the law on unjust enrichment' correctly identified the taking of an unjust enrichment as being the factor which brought the claim into being.[34]

A part of the problem here was that outsiders (such as judges) became suspicious that this theory was insufficiently thought through and insufficiently coherent to form the basis of their judgments. Changing the name of the theory and changing

---

[32] P. Birks, 'Trusts raised to avoid unjust enrichment: the *Westdeutsche* case' [1996] *RLR* 3.

[33] E.g. A. Burrows, *The Law of Restitution*, 2nd edn (Butterworths, 2008), 1, sees *Westdeutsche Landesbank* as a case which advances personal claims in restitution, i.e. money had and received. This does seem a little like being knocked out by a boxer and then claiming to have hurt his fist with your nose.

[34] P. Birks, 'Misnomer' in Cornish et al. (eds), *Restitution, Present and Future* (Hart Publishing, 1998), 1.

the bases on which it operated would be unlikely to encourage judges to adopt the theory. This was disastrous for Birks because the establishment of this doctrine in the common law – i.e. in court judgments – was the principal objective. Nevertheless, the second model of the thesis contained a difficult proposition: for example, the idea that there should be no talk of 'remedies' because each claim necessarily contained its remedy as if in a symbiotic relationship.[35] However, the problem with this proposition was that there are many discretionary doctrines (such as proprietary estoppel), important procedural devices (such as injunctions), and entire legal fields (such as family law) in which the precise nature and shape of the remedy in any individual case is unknown until the court makes its order, sculpting a remedy from the jurisprudential clay available to it.

### Mark 3: analogous to a mistake

Birks had embarked on the third version of his theory before his death. The third version of Birks's scheme provides that the law on unjust enrichment (as it is now to be called) operates in relation to any set of facts which is 'analogous to mistake'.[36] This version of restitution – the last before Birks's untimely death – had moved from taxonomic certainty into metaphysics. It was unclear what was meant by the idea that something must be 'analogous to a mistake': How analogous? In what way? What sort of mistake? Behind Birks lay a veritable bar fight made up of unjust enrichment scholars arguing over the number of unjust factors which could give rise to a right to unjust enrichment, the viability of the so-called 'quadration thesis', what exactly might be meant 'by analogy with mistake'; whether a remedy can achieve restitution or whether restitution is itself the remedy; and other intellectual niceties. Restitution is not neat: rather, it is bedevilled by the uncertainties which are all part and parcel of any properly functioning system of private law – namely, the need to reach the best result on the facts of any given case.

### The retreat from restitution

It seems that there has been a retreat from unjust enrichment, and a restoration of equitable thinking in recent cases. For example, in *Niru Battery v Milestone*,[37] Sedley LJ and Clarke LJ suggested that they considered the defence of change of position as being an equitable doctrine and not a restitutionary doctrine. Similarly in *National Westminster Bank v Somer*[38] it seems that the doctrine of change of position is now to be replaced by a recast, equitable doctrine of estoppel by representation. The loss of change of position to equity-thinking is a profound challenge to the viability of this doctrine.

---

[35] Birks, above n 27.
[36] P. Birks, *Unjust Enrichment*, 2nd edn (Clarendon Press, 2005).
[37] [2003] EWCA Civ 1446.
[38] [2002] QB 1286.

# Debate 2

## What is wrong with conscience?

### THE CRITICISMS OF CONSCIENCE-BASED THINKING

Much of the criticism of equity is predicated on the common lawyer's preference for schemes of rigid rules much like a biologist's taxonomy of plants.[39] There is also a presumption that the phenomenon of a 'conscience' is an entirely random and entirely subjective one which is unique to each individual mind. As was argued in Chapter 1,[40] the conscience is understood in the psychological literature as being something which is privately situated but objectively constituted.[41] That is, the contents of any person's conscience are formed by interaction with the outside world, and therefore its deficiencies are open to criticism and judgment on the basis of what the law considers that a person's conscience *ought to have* contained. Thus, equity is engaged on a deontological, moral project, which it does by reference to the doctrine of precedent and centuries of careful worrying at its core concepts.

### CRIMES AND MISDEMEANOURS

Birks's concerns about a subjective conscience could be illustrated by reference to a scene from Woody Allen's exquisite, tragi-comic film *Crimes and Misdemeanours*. The central character, Judah Rosenthal (played by Martin Landau), is married and has been conducting a long-term adulterous relationship with Dolores Paley (played by Angelica Huston). Dolores has decided that she is no longer prepared to wait in the shadows, and so she tells Judah that she is going to confront his wife and make their affair public knowledge. Judah panics. He does not want to lose his relationship with his wife, nor to ruin his family unit. So, at Judah's request, his shady brother, Jack (played by Jerry Orbach), procures a hit man to kill Dolores. The scene in question is a perfect jurisprudential minefield. Judah conceives of his dilemma as being a choice between destroying the life of his family or destroying his mistress. In his delusional frame of mind, Judah considers that both of those actions are moral equivalents: whatever he does will lead to destruction and pain for someone, so he simply has to choose between his wife and family on the one hand, or his mistress on the other hand.

Clearly, to us, watching the film, Judah's self-serving babble is based on his cowardice and deceitfulness, and the idea that he will have Delores murdered by a paid assassin is abhorrent. We can see that there is no equivalence between killing

---

[39] Except that a biologist's taxonomy of plants is not based on an ideological view of how the world should be, but rather is based on observation of how the natural world actually functions.

[40] A.S. Hudson, *Equity & Trusts*, 7th edn (Routledge, 2012), 10.

[41] See, e.g., S. Freud, *Beyond The Pleasure Principle* (Penguin, 1923) and S. Freud, *Civilisation and its Discontents* (Penguin, 1930); and C.G. Jung, 'Structure of the psyche' (1927) in Storr (ed.), *Essential Jung* (Fontana, 1998).

Delores and causing strife for his family. Oddly, the voice of conscience at this moment is Jack, who points out that 'without law, there is only darkness'. That is a striking commentary on the need for obedience to law in society. Nevertheless, Judah prefers to see his dilemma as being about his own delusional view of 'justice', not law. In his mind, his mistress is acting unreasonably and is out of control. She will wreak havoc on his carefully organised hypocrisies and the equilibrium of his life. He considers that it is just for him to protect himself and the life he really wants. That is how he claims to justify to himself that his final decision to have Delores killed is right.

For Birks this is exactly the risk which is posed by an equity which is based on the idea of conscience. A conscience, he said, is a subjective phenomenon. Judah can only pretend to justify this murder to himself by a subjective form of conscience which purports to excuse murder so as to save his marriage and his family life. In consequence, Birks considers that the use of conscience to answer cases would mean that all cases would be decided according to entirely subjective criteria, which in turn might mean reaching results in some cases which are objectionable to most people in society.[42] Consequently, changing his conception of conscience significantly (from the conscience of the defendant to the conscience of the judge), he considered that if we judge people according to our subjective idea of conscience then each application of that rule will differ depending on the judge. It would be a different matter, and presumably worse in Birks's view, if the judgments were reached according to the individual defendant's own conscience; at least if the judgments differ according to the judge's conscience then that would suggest some level of objectivity outside the desire of the defendant to escape liability. As Lord Seldon was reputed to have said, the phenomenon of allowing too much discretion in courts of equity would be as if each judgment in equity were decided according to the length of the Lord Chancellor's foot – it would be as arbitrary as that.[43]

However, the entire point about *Crimes and Misdemeanours* is that the viewer necessarily recognises that Judah's self-justifications are wrong, and that organising to murder Delores is wrong. We are not fooled by Judah. Instead, we all know what Judah's conscience *should have* told him: that murder is wrong, that you are a lying, fornicating coward, and that you are about to get your just deserts. And that is why conscience can be such a useful principle (if we use it in the right way), precisely because equity can judge what a person's conscience *should have* told them objectively.

The central point, however, must be that Judah's dilemma contains a false dichotomy. While he may well seriously disrupt his family's living arrangements

---

[42] It is interesting that the word 'objectionable' and the word 'objective' share the same root: something is 'objectionable' if it would appear to be unacceptable or wrong to the majority of people.

[43] Lord Chancellors with small feet would be taken to deliver different judgments from Lord Chancellors with larger feet. In the same way, allowing conscience to dictate whether or not someone is liable would depend upon the individual judge.

and relationships if his affair is revealed, that harm is not a moral equivalent to killing another human being. Adultery is a fact of life for many people and nearly one half of all marriages fail. While this is traumatic for the people involved, it is not the same as taking a life. Quite the opposite: the pain of a break-up is often a part of continuing to live life. However, paying for Dolores to be killed is to commit a wrong of an entirely different order of magnitude from causing upset to his children. Objectively speaking, there is no possibility of confusing those two things. It is only in Judah's delusional mental state – in truth, seeing the world through the lens of his cowardice and deceit – that one could possibly see those two choices as being equivalent. We are right to judge and condemn Judah. Birks need not be concerned because the conscience which is used in equity is an objective conception of what the individual defendant ought to have thought, not a subjective expression of what the defendant actually thought. (The problems with allowing subjectivity to intrude into equity are considered in Chapter 10 in relation to the law on dishonest assistance.)

The film *Crimes and Misdemeanours* ends on a quietly sour note: Judah realises, in spite of his agonising earlier in the film, that in fact he is untroubled by the death of Dolores and that he is oddly capable of carrying on with his life as though her death had never happened. This attitude is something which provokes condemnation from the audience: it was monstrous to pay for someone to be killed, but it is also generally taken to be monstrous to show no remorse for it after the event.[44] And yet, many people are able to come to terms with events of which they could not be proud. That is the surprising and subjective element to a conscience. That is precisely why it is not a subjective form of conscience which is deployed by equity, but rather an objective statement of what equity considers that a defendant's conscience should have prompted them to do.

## TWO CHEERS FOR CONSCIENCE

The term 'conscience' itself has been criticised as being incapable of explaining a system of legal rules. It has been considered throughout this book consciously and unconsciously, that is, on the basis that all trusts are predicated on a notion of conscience and that courts of equity are courts of conscience. The feasibility of the notion of conscience as founding a system of rules is considered in greater detail in Chapter 1: briefly put, it is suggested there that our idea of conscience must be concerned both with considering the morality of the defendant's behaviour and also with an understanding that the morality making up an individual's conscience is objectively formulated such that it is susceptible of external sanction through law.

A less temperate attitude to 'conscience' was taken by Birks. First, Birks was suspicious of conscience thinking in any event because (he said) equitable

---

[44] That we are supposed to show remorse after any death of someone close to us is explored in Albert Camus' remarkable novel *L'Etranger*.

concepts such as constructive trusts do not make it clear on what basis the remedy is being awarded.[45] The counter-argument is simply that concepts such as constructive trusts are imposed in any situation in which the defendant has acted unconscionably. Therefore, the breach of good conscience is the trigger for the constructive trust; and we know what good conscience requires by looking consequentially at the cases in which the doctrine has already been invoked. Consequently, its premise is clear but the content of the term 'conscience' requires careful construction, just as the 'justice' comprised in unjust enrichment requires explanation.

Secondly, what Birks says further about 'conscience' is the following, surprising thing. In three essays,[46] Birks has drawn attention to the fact that the leading Nazi, Rheinhard Heydrich (chief of the Gestapo and architect of the vile 'final solution' of the concentration camps) accounted for his actions on the basis that he was acting in line with his own conscience:

> 'For the fulfilment of my task I do fundamentally that for which I can answer to my conscience ... I am completely indifferent whether others gabble about breaking the law'.[47]

Therefore, it is said by Birks, anyone who propounds this notion of conscience is adopting thinking characteristic of Nazis. Of course, that is the very last thing that the proponents of conscience are arguing for. What they *are* arguing for, briefly put, is an acceptance of the proposition that law must be made up of a combination of positivism and natural law: that is, there must be law created through legitimate means and also law which responds to some form of morality. By definition that is the antithesis of the Nazi code, which Professor Fuller and others have argued does not qualify even as 'law' because it lacked the necessary moral worth.[48] All we ask is that the law retain a set of principles (equity, in effect) as a means of distinguishing between right and wrong. As Hedley has pointed out, just because a Nazi once used the word 'conscience' in sense *x*, that does not mean that anyone else who uses that word also means *x*.[49] Birks's argument must mean that anyone who doubts restitution on the basis of an idea of conscience is a fascist.

That is not an idea I intend to dignify with any further consideration. Millions of people died in the Holocaust. It was, axiomatically, one of the most extraordinary acts of bureaucratic evil in the history of humanity (albeit that it was rivalled in terms of numbers killed by Stalin, Mao Tse Tung and Pol Pot, and in genocidal intent by events in countries like Rwanda and Bosnia). Zygmunt Bauman's *Modernity and the Holocaust*[50] identifies the evil as being 'bureaucratic' in the sense

---

[45] Birks, above n 23, 89.
[46] E.g. Birks, above n 32, 10.
[47] Quoted in A.H. Campbell, 'Fascism and legality' (1946) 62 *LQR* 141, 147.
[48] L. Fuller, *The Morality of Law* (Yale University Press, 1964).
[49] S. Hedley, 'The taxonomy of restitution' in A.S. Hudson (ed.), *New Perspectives on Property Law, Obligations and Restitution* (Cavendish, 2004), 151.
[50] Z. Bauman, *Modernity and the Holocaust* (Polity, 1991).

that the Nazis used modern technology (including computers to process lists of human beings and machines capable of killing large numbers of people very quickly with poisonous gas) to achieve genocidal goals which would otherwise have been impossible. What was truly evil about the Holocaust was the determined intention to exterminate the entire race of Jewish people and to decimate the population of Slavs. As Hannah Arendt has made clear,[51] there was a banality to this evil in that it was organised by bureaucrats and carried out by ordinary soldiers who did not question their orders. The technological advances which made the Holocaust possible, as Zygmunt Bauman has explained,[52] were combined with a callous intellectual brutality which relied on a masquerade of 'laws' to justify these actions. They call into question the very idea of what it means to be human, and what it means to be moral in the modern world.

There is no question that the Holocaust was one of the most evil events in human history, and Heydrich was one of the monsters who was responsible for it. To use those events to score a High School debating point about a preference for unjust enrichment thinking over equity thinking is truly revolting.

The Nazis did not have a conscience as any right-thinking person could possibly understand that term. That is precisely the point. Conscience is not decided by reference to subjective factors alone. Instead, as was explained in Chapter 1, it is formulated by reference to objective notions of what a good conscience ought to require. Any right-thinking code of legal principles would recognise Heydrich's conscience as being abhorrent, and would condemn it for being at odds with an objectively correct conscience.

# Debate 3

## Is there nevertheless something worthwhile in traditional equity?

### 'BIRKS' WORKS' AND THE SPIRIT OF EQUITY

It has always struck me as being slightly ironic that one of the more famous examples of the expression 'Birks' works' is actually an album by the jazz pioneer Dizzy Gillespie called 'Birks' Works'. The avant-garde form of jazz known as 'be-bop' was the forerunner of the musical underpinnings of modern hip-hop, with its scope for improvisation, fluidity and looseness in many ways. While it is difficult perhaps to imagine it now, after the initial excitement caused by jazz in the 1920s (displacing what we know think of as classical music, 'lieder' and music hall songs) and its slow transformation into 'traditional jazz' played by large numbers of unimaginative white musicians, there was a renaissance in jazz music in the 1950s, as experimental and hugely talented performers and composers transformed the language of the music. The result was 'be-bop', and Dizzy Gillespie

---

[51] H. Arendt, *The Human Condition*, 2nd edn (Chicago University Press, 1958).
[52] Bauman, above n 50.

was one of its foremost exponents, along with luminaries like Charlie Parker, Charles Mingus and Miles Davis. It is from this form of jazz that many musicologists trace the development (in particular through artists like Herbie Hancock) of the music which became so important in the growth of hip-hop.

Dizzy Gillespie's real name was John Birks. A part of his contribution to jazz was the way in which he improvised a way of playing jazz trumpet which broke all the rules of traditional jazz and yet remained musical. The opening track of the 'Birks' Works' album ('Jordu') does not sound transgressive to modern ears: instead it is an upbeat, melodic instrumental jazz piece. It is certainly not 'disorderly' nor chaotic, even though it broke many of the received rules of the music before that time. It grew out of improvisation and a radical change in the language of jazz.[53] The track flows from one melody into another across its four minutes, with several changes of tempo and chord. To one mindset it is beautiful. It is certainly based on a firm pattern.

Equity is much the same. This is a very important point about the nature of equity. Equity is not entirely chaotic in the way that Birks and the Oxford Restitution School have painted it. Instead, there are clear patterns in the precedents and the uses of equitable doctrines which show the courts of equity are occasionally improvising (by manipulating those doctrines to reach a suitable outcome in particular cases) but always building on well-established principles of equity. This means that the Oxford Restitution School simply do not like those equitable ways of thinking, not that there is no thinking in equity.

There was a review of the seminal jazz band led by Dave Brubeck in *Time* magazine in 1954 which, to my mind, encapsulated the essence of this new movement in jazz and also provides us with an excellent description of equity.[54] The review described their brand of 'cool' jazz in the following terms:

> 'It is tremendously complex, but free. It flows along, improvising constantly but yet it is held together by a firm pattern. ... The essence is the tension between improvisation and order; between freedom and discipline.'

It seems to me that this is an ideal description of equity at its finest. Equity exhibits a tension between order and flexibility. To its denigrators, equity is disorganised, chaotic and unprincipled; to its adherents it exhibits clear patterns in compliance with subtle but meaningful principles. The adherents have simply understood the field better than its denigrators – they have understood the subtlety of its method. As Lord Jessel MR explained in *Re Hallett's Estate*,[55] equity is not beyond child-bearing: it is capable of creating new doctrines and, consequently, capable of meeting new challenges in new ways. This is evident in the growth of doctrines such as

---

[53] The version of 'Jordu' on that album is a version of the standard written by Duke Jordan as interpreted by Gillespie.

[54] The idea that there is an overlap between equity and 'cool' jazz is explored in detail in Hudson, *Equity & Trusts*, Ch. 1.

[55] (1880) 13 Ch D 696.

constructive trusts and proprietary estoppel in recent years, and in the invention of completely new doctrines such as the super-injunction. Each appears to operate entirely freely, but in truth each is bound by clear principles which operate sensibly in practice.

## CONCLUSION

Belief in unjust enrichment law is an article of faith: if one believes that it exists, then one is able to see it everywhere; whereas if one does not believe, then existing legal doctrines have an explanation for everything that it purports to cover. And a part of the reason for believing in it may be that one is simply pre-disposed to need order above all else.

Other people take another approach to the universe. In their view, perhaps the world is just messy and chaotic. While the unjust enrichment taxonomists want to introduce order into the world, many of those who sit as judges are all too aware of the chaos and complexity of the random litany of cases which come before them. The unjust enrichment specialists are like gardeners constantly snipping at their plants and trying to keep them in neat rows and pruned into orderly, boxy shapes. And yet, over the kitchen garden wall in the fields and meadows beyond, there is nature growing wildly. In its unfettered existence, it is vital, chaotic and out of their reach.

Change is the most natural thing in the world. And yet legal taxonomy does not permit change. Psychologically, it demonstrates a need in human beings to impose an understanding on the world around them. It pins ideas to sheets of paper like dead butterflies to biologists' boards. The taxonomist in the humanities is the taxidermist of ideas: permitting no space for new ideas in the display cabinets, he seeks to understand everything and to display it – perfect and immovable forever. If there was only one way of understanding the world then that would make modern society impossible. Modern society is dependent on its diversity.

These competing concepts of rigidity and flexibility, of order and open-texture, of positivism and natural law, of unjust enrichment and equity, are themes which will run throughout this book. They are at the heart of every theoretical debate about the nature of equity and trusts.

# PART TWO

# DOCTRINAL ISSUES WITHIN TRUSTS LAW

# 4

## CERTAINTIES

## INTRODUCTION

The rules which are often known as 'the three certainties' are at the heart of express trusts law. Usually they are one of the first sets of rules which are taught to undergraduate students of trusts law. The basic rule is this: before a valid express trust can be created, three prerequisites must be satisfied.[1] Classically, those prerequisites are understood as follows. First, it must be certain that the settlor intended to create a trust, as opposed to intending to establish some other legal or equitable mechanism (such as a charge or a gift). Secondly, the identity of the property which is to be held on trust must be certain; that is, it is commonly said, the trust fund must be segregated from all other property. Thirdly, the identity of the people who are to be the beneficiaries (or, objects) of the trust must be known with sufficient certainty. These doctrines are known respectively as certainty of intention, certainty of subject matter, and certainty of objects. What is remarkable about them, perhaps, is that they immediately establish the law of trusts as being concerned with the sort of strict rule-making which is often identified with idealised common law doctrines, as opposed to the sort of loose principles which are often associated with equity, as was discussed in Chapter 1.

The first debate which we consider in this chapter is whether the use of certainties at the heart of express trusts law means that the field of trusts law is different in some way from equity as it was discussed in Chapter 1.[2] There are three further debates which relate to the nature of certainty of subject matter, certainty of intention and certainty of objects respectively, as a result of recent case law. The current shape of two of those doctrines has been affected in particular by the litigation which began in the wake of the insolvency of the US investment bank Lehman Brothers on 15 September 2008 (which transformed a short-term banking crisis into a full-blown global panic). That litigation has arguably reshaped many of the classic concepts of trusts law in relation to certainty of intention and certainty of subject matter, so that the courts could achieve short-term goals relating to that

---

[1] For further details of the relevant principles in this area, see Alastair Hudson, *Equity & Trusts*, Ch. 3.
[2] See also ibid, Ch. 7.

particularly significant insolvency. The concept of certainty of objects has always contained some well-concealed debates, and raises complex questions about the types of beneficiaries who may be considered to have the sorts of rights which are sufficient to satisfy the requirements of certainty of objects.

## Debate 1

### Do the rules on certainties demonstrate a paradox at the heart of trusts law?

#### THE CENTRAL PARADOX IN TRUSTS LAW

It is perhaps the central paradox of trusts law that, while the field is based on a purportedly discretionary concept of good conscience, nevertheless the core rules which one encounters in any treatment of the subject are the requirements of certainty. Most discussions of trusts law begin with a discussion of the sorts of open-textured concepts we met in Chapter 1, but then descend very rapidly into the sort of debates which relate to strict rules about the formalities necessary to create a trust. As outlined above, those requirements are that there be certainty of intention, certainty of subject matter and certainty of objects.

#### THE HISTORICAL REASONS FOR THIS HARDENING OF PRINCIPLES INTO RULES

This hardening of 'principle' into 'rules' began in earnest in the mid-nineteenth century.[3] It was the product of the work of judges like Lord Mansfield and Lord Eldon, who had considered equity to be a 'roguish thing' precisely because it seemed to grant judges the discretion to reach whatever conclusion they considered appropriate in any given situation. Whether or not equity was in truth entirely discretionary was much contested, as was discussed in Chapter 1. Similarly, the notion that a discretionary equity was a bad thing was also contested. Nevertheless, it is possible to understand this hardening of the rules of trusts law specifically (as opposed to the principles of equity in general) as being part of the drift among those judges (particularly in the early Victorian period) to introduce greater order and predictability to the law.

A part of that trend towards a tightening in the law may be understood in terms of the social role of the trust in eighteenth- and nineteenth-century England and Wales among the upper classes. That is, the trust was essential to the management of the property of the wealthy and propertied classes. Wealthy aristocratic and bourgeois families had their homes, their chattels, their heirlooms and so forth held on the terms of complex family 'settlements',[4] so that their ownership and use could be settled for generations to come by the patriarchs in those families. With the coming of the Industrial Revolution in the nineteenth century, the new

---

[3] *Knight v Knight* (1840) 3 Beav 148.

[4] A 'settlement' is a particular form of trust: see Hudson, above n 1, Ch. 2.

industrialists also used trusts to manage their new wealth within their families. Any weakening of the trust institution would threaten the security of those families and their property. Therefore, the social significance of trusts law – and a move to make it more predictable and more certain – is central to its operation in practice. In the twentieth century, the use of trusts became a key part of tax avoidance for those same social groups as they sought to organise the holding of their families' property in the most tax-efficient manner. Consequently, given the social importance of the trust, judges began to see the need for a measure of order to be introduced to the law.

We should not forget that this was part of the great scientific age among the Victorians. Amateur biologists, astronomers and so on among the well-to-do were legion. This was the age of the Industrial Revolution and a shift from the agrarian organisation of England (where the ordering of the seasons had dictated much about life) into the creation of the great industrial cities which pulled people from the countryside into a different pattern of dangerous, dirty urban living, working in factories. There was a great re-ordering in society and in intellectual life.

A part of that change in intellectual life was the production of many learned books which attempted to put the common law and equity into some sort of order. Many of those books are still in print: *Chitty on Contracts, Clerk and Lindsell on Tort, Palmer on Company Law* and so forth. In the equity field, significantly, there was *Underhill on Trusts and Trustees, Lewin on Trusts*, and *Snell on Equity*. Their legacy was a work of synthesising all of the case law into comprehensible categories precisely so that those general principles could be understood as having particular expression in the case law (and thus a meaningful doctrine of precedent). Before there was systematic law reporting and before there were orderly textbooks, the work of those early authors was difficult. They had to read centuries of approximate and often clumsy reports of earlier judgments, and they had to try to organise them into some sort of order.[5] A by-product of this scholarly activity was the development of hard-and-fast rules in some circumstances. For example, the rules governing the situations in which a trust may be said to come into existence, and the existence of the three certainties in the old cases.

## THE SOCIAL AND COMMERCIAL IMPORTANCE OF THE TRUST

It is worth spending a little while on the reasons why the trust was so extraordinarily important to the lives of the upper middle class and the aristocracy in England in previous centuries. To occupy a higher social station meant that one did not do anything as vulgar as work. For such people, their wealth, their homes, their heirlooms and so forth, were all held on trust by family retainers (often the family solicitors) acting as trustees. Those trustees were, under the old law, subject to an overriding obligation of 'prudence' in the ways in which they carried out

---

[5] With the advent of the Internet, the work of contemporary textbook writers has also become complicated again, because it is necessary to wade through a larger number of judgments than ever before.

their fiduciary duties as trustees (as is discussed in Chapter 6). Consequently, the most significant form of trust was the express trust, and its role in protecting the wealth of the upper classes was pivotal.

Much of the drama in some of the greatest works of fiction in the English language (such as Charles Dickens' *Bleak House* and Jane Austen's *Pride and Prejudice* or *Sense and Sensibility*) revolves around the main characters having their fortunes dictated by the terms of trust instruments. Jane Austen's heroines are always being thrust out into the world to find husbands, precisely because their fathers are the life tenants under family settlements and, when they die, the rights under those family settlements will pass to other, male cousins and away from their daughters. This means that the male cousins will go into occupation of their houses and the daughters, who had come to think of their grand houses as being their homes, will be thrown out into the street. It is therefore essential for those daughters to find husbands before their fathers die. Hence the stress caused to the mothers in these novels – such as Mrs Bennet in *Pride and Prejudice* – who see the propitious marriage of their daughters to wealthy husbands as being the organising duty of their lives. Because the judiciary was drawn from this same social class, the need for a predictable form of trusts law would have been at the heart of their mission of generating an ordered society.

The organisation of commercial life also depended on contract law and trusts law for a long period of time. Before the development of the company with distinct legal personality in England in 1897,[6] the trust was an important component of the principal commercial vehicle in the expanding British Empire: the joint stock company. Wealthy people would put up property ('the stock') for a company to sell to other people, or to trade in some other way. Those wealthy people would be a 'company', just as a 'company' is a colloquial description for a group of people meeting for dinner or going to the theatre. They would appoint people to work on their behalf to manage the business. These managers would be trustees of the business: obliged to carry on the company's trade, to safeguard the assets and to earn a prudent profit. The wealthy individuals who put up the stock would be the beneficiaries of this arrangement, and they would also enter into a contract of partnership with one another as to the sharing of profits and losses. The company with its own legal personality (created in 1897 by the decision of the House of Lords in *Salomon v A Salomon & Co Ltd*) removed the trust structure, and instead made the company the owner of its own property and enabled it to enter into contracts on its own behalf. The wealthy people who put up the capital became shareholders who bore no personal liability for the losses of the company (unlike partners who would have borne all those losses personally). Nevertheless, the trust had been central to commercial life through much of the eighteenth and nineteenth centuries.

Consequently, it should come as no surprise that the evolution of the express trust took it away from the territory of discretionary principles and into a terrain

---

[6] *Salomon v A Salomon & Co. Ltd* [1897] AC 22.

of stricter rules. Nor should it come as any surprise that cases would arise which required judges to ask whether or not those strict rules would be fair and appropriate in all circumstances. This constant movement between those two poles is the habit of English trusts law and of equity generally.

With the collapse of Lehman Brothers in 2008, we can see another crisis commanding the attention of the judiciary as centuries-old trusts law principles are being adapted to meet the circumstances of that collapse. The cases growing out of the failure of Lehman Brothers illustrated another important function of the express trust in English law: if a person holds property on trust before they go into insolvency, then that trust property will be held sacrosanct on trust so that it is protected from the insolvency. If there were no valid trust in effect, then the property would simply be distributed among all of the unsecured creditors in the insolvency proceedings: that is, the property would be distributed among all of the poor souls who had not protected themselves against the risk of that insolvency. An express trust, on the other hand, elevates the beneficiaries of that trust to the status of secured creditors in the event that the trustees go into insolvency. Consequently, it becomes critical to know whether or not there is a valid trust (and over which property the trust takes effect) in the event of a massive bankruptcy like that of Lehman Brothers. It is that issue of certainty of subject matter which we consider next.

## Debate 2

### Does the doctrine of certainty of subject matter require that the trust fund must always be segregated from other property?

#### INTRODUCTION

The logic of trust law is predicated on the idea that the beneficiary controls the trustee through the courts. Hence the development of the beneficiary principle which requires that there must be an identifiable beneficiary so that there is someone in whose benefit the court can decree performance of the trust.[7] Similarly, the requirements of certainty of the settlor's intention,[8] of the identity of the beneficiaries[9] and of the identity of the subject matter of the trust,[10] are necessary to ensure that the court is able to police the actions of the trustee on behalf of the beneficiary effectively. It is the beneficiary who is really 'Equity's darling'. The roots of the strict liability approach to trustees' liability for breach of trust even where the loss occasioned to the trust fund was only indirectly the fault of the trustees,[11] would appear to be a judicial acceptance of the fact that the wealth and

---

[7] *Morice v Bishop of Durham* (1805) 10 Ves 522.
[8] *Knight v Knight* (1840) 3 Beav 148.
[9] *Re Hay's ST* [1981] 3 All ER 786.
[10] *Re Goldcorp* [1995] 1 AC 74; *Westdeutsche Landesbank v Islington* [1996] 1 AC 669.
[11] *Target Holdings v Redferns* [1996] AC 421.

security of the English upper and middle classes was, in the manner of Jane Austen novels, dependent entirely upon the viability of their trust funds, whether containing land, money or valuable chattels.

## THE BASIS OF THE CERTAINTY OF SUBJECT MATTER RULE

The traditional doctrine of certainty of subject matter provided for a perfectly sensible rule, seen from the perspective of property law: if some property is to be treated differently by the law of trusts from other property, then that trust property must be separately identifiable from all the other property in the world. To use an awkward modern expression, that trust property must be 'ring-fenced' or 'segregated' from other property so that it is possible to know which property is subject to the trust and which property is not. For trustees to know what their obligations are, it must be possible for them to know with certainty which property is subject to their trust powers so that they can deal with it in accordance with their trust duties. Trustees bear obligations to maintain, safeguard and even to invest trust property. To discharge those obligations, it must be certain which property is subject to those obligations. Those are the reasons for the creation of the rule that there must be certainty of subject matter before there can be a valid trust.

It would be meaningless, at one level, to have a law of property if that law did not insist that one person's property is separately identifiable from another person's property. If property law has any meaning at all then it must be as a means of allowing each individual to distinguish between what is 'mine' and what is 'yours', and to be able to protect the rights attaching to the various items of property. Trusts are a part of the law of property because they create ownership rights for the beneficiaries in the form of their equitable interests in the trust fund. Therefore, it is important for those individuals to know which property is held on trust for their benefit. Equally importantly (possibly more importantly in practical terms), the trustees must know which property they are legally responsible for holding and maintaining.

In consequence, *Knight v Knight*,[12] *Morice v Bishop of Durham*[13] and other cases established one of the most important principles in express trusts law: if the courts are ultimately responsible for judging whether or not the trustees have conducted themselves lawfully, then it must be possible for courts (as well as the trustees) to know which property is held on trust, who the beneficiaries are and so forth. It must be possible to say with certainty in whose favour the court shall decree performance of this putative trust.

[12] (1840) 3 Beav 148.
[13] (1805) 10 Ves 522.

## THE PROBLEM OF MONEY AND INVESTMENTS HELD IN ELECTRONIC BANK ACCOUNTS

In some circumstances, it may be that the identity of the trust property is simply an accounting exercise. For example, when 'money' is held in a bank account, what really happens is that an intangible account is created by creating a file in a computer's memory which notionally allocates an amount of value to one partition in that computer's memory which is supposedly separate from all of the other intangible partitions in that computer's memory (or in the memory of other computers). In reality, a bank account is just a book-keeping record or a file in a computer. It could be said that it does not matter which 'property' is held in that account as opposed to being held in another account. The very idea of property being 'held' 'in' an account is misleading. The verb 'hold' and the preposition 'in' both suggest that there is something physical which is physically located within something else that is physical. But, in the case of electronic accounts, both concepts are simply ideas. There is nothing physical. Even the 'money' is in the form of amounts of value attributed to each of the those accounts, and not notes and coins.

Consequently, if there is nothing physical, then it might be said that the idea of certainty of subject matter is meaningless. To separate one amount of electronic money off from another amount of electronic money simply means a change in the amount allocated to one account in the computer's memory and a change in the amount allocated to another account in another computer's memory by the same amount. Things were different before computers. Before computers, and centuries earlier before intangible property, all property was tangible. So, if one wanted a trust to be created over a herd of cows, then the cows held in that herd had to be segregated from the cows held in any other herd. If one wanted a trust to be created over money, then the notes and coins which were to be held on trust needed to be segregated from other notes and coins. However, even those notes and coins were treated as being money owned by the bank once they were deposited in a bank account (*Foley v Hill* (1848)): the bank merely kept an account to show that it owed a debt to the customer equal to the amount of the deposit. Therefore, even trusts over cash would be trusts over intangible debts, as opposed to trusts over tangible notes and coins. It was only if the notes and coins were held physically in a cash box and identified as being the trust property, that there could be a tangible trust over money.

➔ Clearly, the principle of certainty of subject matter is critical in relation to the cows, but is it equally important in relation to amounts allocated to electronic bank accounts or intangible holdings of shares? Is it meaningful to talk of segregating electronic money off from other electronic money? If the electronic accounts are simply records showing that a given amount is owed to a particular customer, then how can it be meaningful to talk of the 'money' in those accounts being segregated from other money? However, if we do not maintain this sort of fiction that 'money' 'held' 'in' an electronic bank is separate from other 'money', then how can our property law operate? The use of electronic money and records in account books is so useful in our daily lives (from the largest corporations to the poorest individual) that the law must find a way to keep up with the pace of change. Consequently, property law has developed the useful fiction that 'money' 'held' 'in' an electronic bank account is different and separate from 'money' 'held' 'in' another electronic bank account. Moreover, we would lose important ideas like the use of trusts to protect 'our' 'money' against the insolvency of the person who is 'holding' it for us if we did anything different.

Those are the parameters of this debate. On the one hand, it is vital to know which property is to be held on the terms of the trust. On the other hand, there may be circumstances in which the idea of certainty of subject matter is merely an idea, and its application may be less important than other considerations, or persisting with the idea may have other useful outcomes. This alternative approach has become significant in recent years, in particular in the wake of the collapse of American investment bank Lehman Brothers. However, before jumping into the Lehman Brothers collapse, we need to understand the case law which had established this rule, and the seemingly heretical line of authorities which questioned the need for it to be quite so strict.

## THE LONG-STANDING DEBATE ABOUT CERTAINTY OF SUBJECT MATTER

### The traditional rule in all its glory

The traditional rule governing certainty of subject matter was a strict one: there cannot be a valid express trust unless the property over which that trust is to take effect is sufficiently certain. Admittedly, this principle was born in a time when most property was tangible property, although we must not overlook the centuries-old existence of intangible property rights like copyright. Nevertheless, the result of the traditional principle is that the trust property must be separately identifiable, or that it must be segregated from other property. Other judgments in recent years, dealing with intangible investments like shares, have doubted whether this rule always needs to be so strict. That is the debate which we shall consider first, as a preface to the issues raised by the Lehman Brothers collapse.

The long-standing debate about certainty of subject matter is most clearly illustrated by comparing the judgments in *Re Goldcorp*[14] and in *Hunter v Moss*.[15] In the former case, the traditional principle was maintained in the insolvency of a dealer in precious metals (gold, bullion and so forth). That dealer was Goldcorp. The customers of Goldcorp had contractual rights to have metal held to their account in Goldcorp's vaults. Therefore, when Goldcorp received an order from a customer, it was contractually obliged to fulfil that order by acquiring the necessary precious metal and storing it in their vaults. In breach of contract, Goldcorp failed to acquire the metal to meet the orders of many of its customers and instead used

[14] [1995] 1 AC 74.
[15] [1994] 1 WLR 452.

their cash to fund its increasingly unsuccessful investment activity. When it fell into insolvency, some customers were fortunate enough to have had metal identified as being held separately for their account by Goldcorp: those customers were found to have trusts over that separately identifiable metal precisely because it was separately identifiable and because their contracts provided that their orders would be held separately for them in this way. Other customers who, as a question of fact, had not had metal segregated to their account, were less fortunate: the lack of segregation meant that there was no trust. The same approach was applied in the older cases of *Re Wait*[16] and in *Re London Wine*.[17] The principle was therefore well-established.

## The challenge to the traditional rule

By contrast, in cases in which the property at issue is intangible and where justice appears to demand that some trust rights are found for the claimant, it has occasionally been found that a trust would exist even though the trust fund had not been segregated from all other property. A good example of this approach was the decision of the Court of Appeal in *Hunter v Moss*.[18] It was this decision which began to weaken the principle in the 1990s. The claimant was employed by the defendant via his company, and his contract of employment provided that a part of the payment for his work would include 50 shares in the company. Those 50 shares were to be taken from the defendant's own holding of 950 shares in the company. The claimant and the defendant fell out and the claimant's employment was terminated, but the claimant was never given his shares. Therefore, the claimant sued the defendant for delivery of the shares. The claimant's argument proceeded on the basis that the defendant must have held 50 shares on trust for the claimant out of his 950 shares. The defendant counter-argued that, because no 50 shares had ever been segregated out of the holding of 950 shares, then there could not be a trust over any 50 shares because there was no certainty of subject matter.

Nevertheless, Dillon LJ held that there was a valid trust. It is important to read the judgment to get a sense of just how vague and unsatisfactory its arguments are in comparison with the admirably clear (if tough) judgment of Lord Mustill in *Re Goldcorp*. Dillon LJ, in essence, sought to demonstrate that the certainty of subject matter rule was not a strict rule that applied in *all* circumstances: so, he noted that in cases of a will, the executors do not know which property is held by the deceased until they start to administer the will, and therefore that that demonstrates that some trusts can come into existence without complete certainty. However, this argument relies on a sleight of hand. The executors *do* know as a question of law which property is held by the deceased: that is, all of the property which the deceased owned at the time of their death. The executors may not know as a question of fact precisely which property was owned by the deceased, but their

[16] [1927] 1 Ch 607.
[17] [1986] PCC 121.
[18] [1994] 1 WLR 452.

first job is to establish that as a matter of law. Any will trust itself does not excuse uncertainty of subject matter: instead, as a question of law, it will apply to any property in which the testator had a proprietary right.

Moreover, Dillon LJ sought to distinguish earlier cases like *Re London Wine* on the basis that they related to the 'appropriation of chattels', whereas *Hunter v Moss* related to a 'declaration of trust'. This argument was also entirely spurious. The issue in *London Wine* had also been whether or not there was a valid trust over property (albeit chattels as opposed to shares). In consequence, although Dillon LJ was very, very careful not to say this, Neuberger J, in the later case of *Re Harvard Securities*,[19] was reluctantly forced to acknowledge that *Hunter v Moss* appeared to have created a test which established a different rule for intangible property than that applied to tangible property.

This is unsatisfactory at many levels. Why must tangible property *always* be treated differently from intangible property? Imagine a truck full of identical microprocessor chips. Each chip has identical memory capacity. None of them is faulty. They have been manufactured by the same manufacturer in the same factory, with identical components down to the most microscopic level. Why should that form of property be treated any differently from the shares in *Hunter v Moss*? In both cases, it cannot matter which unit one acquires in the underlying property because they have identical properties and identical values. By contrast, it would have mattered in *Hunter v Moss* if the defendant had gone into insolvency, because then there would have been more claimants to those shares than there were shares to satisfy those claims. In *Hunter v Moss*, the defendant was solvent throughout, and therefore Dillon LJ had the comparative luxury of deciding which of the two solvent litigants had the better right to property when there were no other claims on that property. By contrast, in *Harvard Securities*, a securities dealer had gone into insolvency and therefore there were more claims to that intangible property (the investments made on behalf of customers) than there was property to satisfy all claims. Nevertheless, Neuberger J felt bound by the earlier decision of Dillon LJ to the effect that there was no need for certainty of subject matter if the property was intangible property comprising identical units (such as shares). If one reads the judgment of Neuberger J, it is clear that he feels constrained by precedent to decide as he does.

### So why did Dillon LJ do it?
So why did Dillon LJ do what he did? He was asked to consider the possibility of a trust being imposed over 50 shares within a holding of 950 shares, in circumstances in which the defendant had employed the claimant and contracted to transfer 50 shares to him out of that holding of 950 shares. The defendant had cleverly argued that there were no 50 shares segregated to the claimant's account at the time when he was sacked from his employment, and therefore that the claimant could not have property rights in any given shares. Clearly, this was an

---

[19] [1997] 2 BCLC 369.

inequitable outcome, because the defendant was therefore able to renege on his clear contractual promise to the claimant. Therefore, an equitable outcome in the most general sense would have awarded shares or their cash value to the claimant in some form. Dillon LJ could have, in theory at least, resorted to the ancient equitable principle that this was simply unconscionable and therefore that the defendant should be required to account to the claimant for 50 shares (perhaps by holding the entire 950 shares on constructive trust for himself and for the claimant in the proportion 900:50). That might have been the sort of approach which we would have expected from an equity purist like Lord Denning, with his general commitment to 'fair' outcomes. However, Dillon LJ appeared to be a traditional common lawyer (in this instance) who was determined to come to the right outcome. Therefore, his Lordship sought to distinguish the earlier cases, because that is what good common lawyers do as opposed to deciding on an entirely discretionary basis.

This case is significant for our purposes because it shows the ways in which a common lawyer might use common law techniques to come to the right outcome in a case. The judgment in *Hunter v Moss* has been roundly criticised by many judges and academics precisely because its arguments are so thin. Simply as a piece of literature, it reads like a person trying to cover up coming to a preferred solution by using arguments which he knows to be thin but which he hopes will convince people for long enough to achieve his desired outcome. If it were performed on stage, his Lordship would speak the passages referred to above much more quickly and in a lower voice than the rest of his judgment, perhaps coughing self-consciously as he did so.

How much more elegant it would have been if Dillon LJ could simply have stepped back and said:

> 'This is unconscionable. You employed this man and these shares were part of his salary, in effect. Now you are using a legal technicality to avoid making a payment which you know that you should, in good conscience, make. Therefore, relying on the ancient equitable principle of conscience, I order that the holding of 950 shares, out of which you accept that payment was to have been made, is held on constructive trust by you for the benefit of the defendant and yourself in the ratio of 900:50.'

Now, one could object to the power of a judge to deal with a defendant's property on that basis, but one could not argue with the internal coherence of the argument. That is, you might not agree with the judge but you would have to acknowledge that his reasoning was easy to understand. One might argue that that type of argument is unattractive, but at least it is clear on what basis the judge is making that award. The equity textbooks would simply record that this was another example of unconscionable behaviour giving rise to a constructive trusts so as to rank alongside theft and fraud: refusing to pay someone the full emoluments of their employment when you know you have those emoluments in your possession and control, would simply be another example of a constructive trust in operation.

However, Dillon LJ undoubtedly comes to the right conclusion (even if we might not approve of the line of argument which got him there). In this case, the defendant knew full well that the claimant was entitled to 50 shares. The defendant owned those 50 shares. He had signed a contract by which he agreed to pay the claimant partly in cash by way of a salary and partly in shares. Therefore, to withhold those shares was to withhold part of the claimant's pay. The defendant was doing this simply because he had fallen out with the claimant, and presumably because he did not want to transfer 50 shares in his company to an outsider with whom he was no longer in a working relationship. Dillon LJ presumably recognised the unfairness of this situation: 'You owed this man money and shares, and now you are trying to wriggle out of your obligations with clever legal arguments'. That is why Dillon LJ came to the conclusion that he did, and that is why he felt obliged to use the arguments and legal techniques that he did so as to come to that answer. However, he could not have known at that time that his judgment would have such an important part to play in the most significant insolvency in economic history: that of Lehman Brothers, which is considered below.

### The newer approach in *White v Shortall*

There is, however, another approach to the interpretation of the sorts of situations which arose in *Hunter v Moss*, which does not require so much violence being done to the traditional principles of trusts law. In general terms, it is perfectly possible for a settlor to create a trust with more than one beneficiary, and for the trustees to have discretion as to precisely which property is allocated to which beneficiary. For example, a trust to hold £100,000 for the settlor's only two adult children in 'equal shares' will be valid, provided that the money is in a separate bank account identifiable as such. There is no problem with providing that the trustees can divide the money between the two beneficiaries. Therefore, in the New South Wales Supreme Court in *White v Shortall*,[20] it was held that when a small number of shares (out of a larger shareholding) was to be held on trust for the claimant, it was possible to interpret those facts as demonstrating an intention that the entire shareholding was to be held on trust both for the claimant and for the defendant as beneficiaries under a single trust in the proportions identified in the contract. Just like holding the property in equal shares, holding the property in pre-determined proportions is perfectly valid. The court in *White v Shortall* was able to find just such an intention on the facts in front of it. That court also dismissed the decision in *Hunter v Moss* for all of the reasons given above. This approach was also important in the Lehman Brothers litigation. It is an improvement on the reasoning in *Hunter v Moss*. The debates raised by Lehman Brothers in this context are considered separately next.

---

[20] [2006] NSWSC 1379.

# Debate 3

## Was the failure of Lehman Brothers in 2008 sufficiently significant to justify a change in the law on certainties?

### THE LEHMAN BROTHERS INSOLVENCY

The financial crisis of 2007–09 continues to have a seismic effect on the economies of the North Atlantic even at the time of writing in 2013. It was the greatest man-made economic disaster in history. Therefore, it would be surprising if it left no mark on our society, on our politics or on our law. One area of law which has been affected by the insolvency of the US investment bank Lehman Brothers on 15 September 2008 is the requirement of certainty of subject matter in the creation of an express trust. As discussed immediately above, the traditional principle was a strict one: there cannot be a valid express trust unless the property over which that trust is to take effect is sufficiently certain. It is therefore commonly said that that trust fund must be separately identifiable, or that it must be segregated from other property.

The financial crisis in the North Atlantic countries reached its frenzied nadir in the autumn of 2008 with the insolvency of the investment bank Lehman Brothers. With the failure of Lehman Brothers came several other failures of large financial institutions. Several of them were rescued by governments, including Northern Rock, HBOS, RBS, Citigroup and AIG; others were bought by other private purchasers after they had failed, including Bear Stearns, Washington Mutual and in essence Merrill Lynch. The crisis had arisen from mortgage companies in the USA misselling mortgages to people who would not otherwise have been able to afford them,[21] by deceiving them into signing the contracts. These mortgages were known as 'sub-prime mortgages' because the borrowers' credit worth was below 'prime'. Those mortgages were sold on an industrial scale, because investment banks on Wall Street had developed what appeared to be a profitable market for bundling those mortgages into packages with other securities (a process known as 'securitisation') and selling them on to institutional investors (in a product known as a collateralised debt obligation or 'CDO'). Another market in credit derivatives grew up around speculating on the performance of CDOs (these credit derivatives were known as credit default swaps or 'CDSs'). When the borrowers of sub-prime mortgages began to default on their mortgage payments in large numbers, this caused the CDOs to fail and in turn for large payments to be required under CDSs. The financial contagion spread around the world. Citigroup alone posted losses in 2008 of more than US$60 billion. Read that number again: 60 billion dollars. In one financial year. The banking system ceased to operate, as banks could not trust one another to remain solvent. The knock-on effect in the real economies of the world was colossal. The International Monetary Fund initially put the cost of the collapse of the banking system to the real world economy at nearly US$12 trillion.

---

[21] One class of mortgage borrowers was known as 'ninjas': an acronym for 'no income, no job or assets'.

The insolvency of Lehman Brothers, a huge investment bank at the heart of the US real estate and securitisation markets, transformed a localised US banking crisis into a global panic.

For present purposes, Lehman Brothers was revealed by this crisis to have breached several of its regulatory obligations in relation to the treatment of client money and in relation to the preparation of its accounts. It emerged that Lehman Brothers had been taking, inter alia, extremely optimistic valuations of its portfolios of real estate investments and securities investments. It also emerged that Lehman Brothers had borrowed $44 for every $1 it actually owned, so that it was over-extended generally. When the market in real estate in the USA began to contract in 2006, Lehman Brothers began to slide into insolvency. In time, other banks refused to deal with it, and speculators began to bet on Lehman Brothers failing. Ultimately, the US government refused to use public money to support it. Consequently, it went into insolvency. There is an excellent literature now on the circumstances which surrounded that collapse.[22] Understanding the vital importance of the financial crisis to the world economy is, it is suggested, central to understanding the context in which the judges were dealing with that litigation and the reason why they might have felt required to come to the conclusions that they did, so as to facilitate one of the most critical and enormous insolvencies in economic history.

## Finding a trust in Lehman Brothers

When financial institutions of the size of Lehman Brothers cease to operate, there will always be litigation revolving around the eye-wateringly large sums of money which are at stake. The litigation in relation to working out the insolvency of Lehman Brothers was particularly complex, and its prosecution was intense.

In particular, when financial institutions failed, there were two issues which were critical for the finding of a trust to protect some of the creditors in the bank's insolvency. (Remember, every creditor wants to be a 'secured creditor' with assets held on trust for them, as opposed to being an 'unsecured creditor' simply waiting in hope that there will be some assets left at the end of the insolvency proceedings to pay back some of what they are owed.) First, regulated financial institutions in the UK were bound by financial regulations in the form of the Financial Services Authority's Client Assets Sourcebook ('CASS'). This rulebook implemented provisions for customer protection in the EU Markets in Financial Instruments Directive 2004 ('MiFID'). In essence, although its precise meaning was a matter for interpretation by the courts, CASS required regulated institutions to hold client assets on a statutory trust. In practice, many financial institutions simply failed to perform their regulatory obligations, and so assets were not systematically segregated into trust accounts for individual clients. Secondly, when a financial institution went

---

[22] See Alastair Hudson, *The Law of Finance*, 2nd edn (Sweet & Maxwell, 2013), Ch. 45, for a lawyer's account of the crisis. Alternatively, on the Lehman Brothers collapse, see e.g., A.R. Sorkin, *Too Big To Fail* (Penguin, 2010) and L. McDonald, *A Colossal Failure of Common Sense* (Random House, 2009).

into insolvency without having performed its regulatory obligations, the issue arose whether the client would have any assets available to it under trusts law. Were there any means by which a trust could be found so as to protect clients against 'their' assets being distributed in the general insolvency of the financial institution? This required a resolution of the debate between the traditional certainty of subject matter principle and more pragmatic approaches, as is considered next.

Lehman Brothers investment bank was poorly run in many ways. The principal focus since the financial crisis has been on the way in which Lehman Brothers mispriced the risks associated with its investments, the amount of debt it owed, its off-balance sheet Repo 105 structure in which it stripped toxic assets off its balance sheet temporarily, and so forth. However, there were many senses in which Lehman Brothers had been badly run long before then. The CASS regulations required that Lehman Brothers segregate any assets held for any individual customer off from all other assets so that those assets would be held on trust for that customer. The intention behind the regulations was that there was to be a segregated account for each customer. However, the regulations were so poorly drafted that it was unclear on what terms this trust was supposed to operate. Therefore, there was enormous flexibility in the interpretation of those regulations in individual cases.

When customers had assets held for them by Lehman Brothers, it was Lehman Brothers' practice in London simply to pool those assets together. So, instead of having thousands of segregated trusts accounts for customers and accounts for Lehman Brothers' own assets, in practice Lehman Brothers simply had one enormous account with everyone's assets mixed in together. This was in flagrant breach of the regulations. This meant that Lehman Brothers was able to treat the entire pool as though it belonged beneficially to Lehman Brothers itself, and instead only to transfer assets to customers when those customers made a demand for assets to be delivered to them. When such a demand was made, Lehman Brothers would simply dip into the pool, or acquire that type of asset in the marketplace. This was the same sort of breach of contract which had been practised in *Re Goldcorp*.

The question which arose, in trusts law terms in several cases, was whether there could be a trust even though there had not been any assets segregated to the client's account, or whether the CASS regulations could be interpreted so as to find the existence of a trust in some other way. In short, it was a choice between the traditional approach and the newer approach.

In *Re Global Trader*,[23] it was held by Park J that the failure of Global Trader to segregate assets into different accounts (so that the assets were simply held in one large pool) meant that there could not be a trust in favour of any individual client. At first instance in the Lehman Brothers litigation,[24] it was held by Briggs J that the traditional principle must mean that Lehman Brothers' clients could not have

---

[23] [2009] 2 BCLC 18.
[24] [2010] EWHC 2914 (Ch).

trusts found in their favour because none of them had assets held separately to their account.

The ramifications of failing to find a trust of some sort in the Lehman Brothers case would have been that all of the assets which should have been held for those customers would instead pass into the deep, deep hole of Lehman Brothers' insolvency, so as to be distributed among their unsecured creditors. Because there were so few assets left, there would be very little money available to meet the claims of those unsecured creditors. So the effects of the judgments of Park J and Briggs J were that none of the customers who were supposed to have assets held on trust for them by the failed bank actually had any assets held on trust for them. While this was correct in law, it disappointed those customers whose banks were simply not obeying the regulatory obligations which had been created for their protection (but poorly enforced by the regulators).

Several cases proceeded from the Lehman Brothers insolvency. We shall focus on the decision in the Supreme Court in *Re Lehman Brothers International (Europe) (in administration) v CRC Credit Fund Ltd*.[25] The question was whether or not there was a valid trust created over the assets which ought to have been held on a statutory trust under the CASS regulations. The problem in all of these cases was that Lehman Brothers had not in fact segregated all (nor even many) of its clients' assets into trust accounts. Instead, those assets were held in very large, pooled accounts which were used by Lehman Brothers as though they belonged beneficially to the bank, and which were distributed to clients when the clients issued a demand for them. However, to protect the claimants in the relevant litigation, it was necessary to find some sort of trust in their favour. In essence, the courts relied ultimately on the decision in *White v Shortall* (see above), so as to claim that they had found an intention in the CASS regulations to impose a single trust over all of the assets held in that enormous pool of assets by Lehman Brothers, and they interpreted the ambiguously drafted CASS regulations so as to permit such a finding.

### The decision in the Supreme Court

In the Supreme Court in *Re Lehman Brothers International (Europe) (in administration) v CRC Credit Fund Ltd*,[26] there were two schools of thought. Lord Walker spoke for the traditional view. In his Lordship's opinion, great harm would be caused to trusts law if it was held that there could be a trust found when no assets had been segregated off from other assets. On the facts, of course, no one had ever expressed an intention to create a single trust over all of the assets held by Lehman Brothers. Instead, the CASS regulations required that a trust was created, but those regulations were so poorly drafted that it was unclear on what basis that trust was intended to operate. This left great scope for the Supreme Court to interpret that intention. However, Lord Walker took the traditional view that even if the regulations required that a trust should be deemed to have been created, because there

---

[25] *Re Lehman Brothers International (Europe)(in administration) v CRC Credit Fund Ltd* [2012] UKSC 6.
[26] Ibid.

had not in fact been any segregation of property to be held on that trust, then a trust could not be found.

By contrast, Lord Dyson was concerned with the larger context of the Lehman Brothers insolvency, and so his judgment may be read as being a purposive interpretation of the CASS regulations which would impose a trust, which would in turn help these customers of Lehman Brothers. Lord Dyson spoke for the majority. He held that the entire pool of assets taken by Lehman Brothers could constitute a single, large trust fund. This interpretation was considered to be possible on a purposive interpretation of the poorly-drafted CASS regulations (read in tandem with the consumer protection objectives in the source legislation, MiFID 2004). Therefore, rather than needing to find a series of trust funds in favour of each customer with assets deposited with the bank (as the regulations must have intended), the single pool of property held unlawfully by the bank in breach of its regulatory obligations was taken to be a single trust fund. The terms of the trust were that each customer was a beneficiary of that trust, with the size of each customer's rights against the trust fund being in proportion to their rights against Lehman Brothers under the terms of their contracts.

One clear truth emerges from this debate. The banks were acting with shocking and knowing disregard for their regulatory obligations. And the law of trusts was being used solely for the purposes of effecting the best available means of clearing up the mess afterwards. The majority of the Supreme Court and the Court of Appeal[27] were less concerned with the coherence of trusts law. Instead, trusts law was used an instrument of a larger purpose. It is unclear whether these cases will be interpreted in the future simply as interpretations of the CASS regulations which should be restricted to their facts and not applied generally to trusts law. Alternatively, it may be that future cases will take the view that trusts law has now swung away from the traditional approach. Ironically, if trusts law does swing away from the certainty which is offered by the traditional approach then that will have been caused by the demands of a case involving a commercial insolvency, which is usually the field of practice which calls for greater certainty in the law.

Interestingly, none of these judgments presented any statistical or factual demonstration that the insolvency would be administered more efficiently by allowing one category of customer to have some beneficial right under a trust than by allowing those assets to pass into a general pot and for all of the unsecured creditors to be treated in the same manner. The judges simply assumed that the finding of a trust would benefit all parties, even though there would presumably have been unsecured creditors who thus lost access to large numbers of assets. So, it is unclear whether or not the perversion of the traditional approach is actually more effective in resolving complex insolvencies, because no evidence of that point was considered at all. By making everyone a beneficiary under a trust, it may have

---

[27] *Re Lehman Brothers International (Europe) (In Administration)* [2011] EWCA Civ 1544.

included so many claimants within the scope of that trust that there would have been many fewer assets to be distributed among them.

## THE SENSE BEHIND THE TRADITIONAL PRINCIPLE; AND ITS LIMITATIONS

The traditional principle makes great sense as part of the law on tangible property. If I am to be owner of a pig, I need to know which pig is mine. That pig must be identifiable. In P.G. Wodehouse's stories about Blandings Castle, when Lord Emsworth's prize-winning pig, 'The Empress of Blandings', is stolen from him, he has to be able to identify that pig so as to be able to recover her. Equally, if a beneficiary is to have property rights which will transcend insolvency or other challenges – as with a trust – then the trust property which receives that property must be clearly identifiable.

However, when our society moved beyond the fact of all property being tangible property into a situation in which we deal in intangible property increasingly often, it became questionable whether those same rules would be fit for purpose. The concept of copyright in English law, for example, is an ancient one; but the development of uncertificated shares (held in electronic registers), 'money' held in electronic bank accounts and everything which has flowed from the Internet, have presented great challenges to property law. Many of the largest corporations in the world – such as Google, Microsoft and Facebook – deal in intangible property at least as much as tangible property. Companies such as Apple and Nike do sell tangible goods, but their most valuable property rights are their trade marks and their patents. Importantly, their goods are manufactured by other companies in a variety of countries around the world. Apple does not own factories; Nike does not employ garment workers directly. Instead, both of those organisations enter into contracts with manufacturers in the developing world who produce their goods under licence. Google, Microsoft and Facebook deal principally in online information held in 'clouds'. While they have large computer servers, their income is derived from their contracts and their intellectual property.

The new capitalist titans do not build factories nor railroads like John Pierpoint Morgan and the capitalist titans of an earlier age. The new titans own intellectual property which earns them fantastic incomes. In the new age, intangible property has become more important than it used to be. The effect on our property law should be equally profound. The social theorist Zygmunt Bauman refers to this shift in our economic life as being the dawn of an age of 'liquidity' (as opposed to solidity) in which our social relations have become fluid, while our property has become increasingly intangible and less meaningful.[28] As the French thinker Jean Baudrillard observed,[29] our chattels are increasingly characterised by 'compulsory obsolescence', that is, our goods are expected to wear out so that we will buy new ones. The fashion industry designs our clothes to go out of fashion; the computer

[28] Z. Bauman, *Liquid Modernity* (Polity, 2001).
[29] J. Baudrillard, *The Consumer Society* (Sage, 1998).

industry designs computers which will be out-of-date or broken by the time their warranty expires, and they update their software on a weekly basis; the electronics industry designs electronic items which change software regularly and which break down completely within a couple of years. So, what does this mean for property law?

In an essay,[30] Hudson has argued that these changes in the nature of property should be recognised as constituting a distinction between property which is weighty and meaningful, and property which is 'light', 'liquid' or 'soft'. For international corporations like Nike or Apple, their property relations are light: that is, they do not have the burdens of maintaining machinery, or employing factory workers. Instead, they pay other people to do all of that for them, and Nike and Apple rely on intellectual property law (on trade marks, patents and copyrights) to protect their truly valuable property: their logos (like the ubiquitous Nike 'swoosh' and the Apple corporation's logo with an apple that has had a bite taken out of it) and their brands. For the remainder of the population (like you and me), property can be heavy. Our houses need repair; our mortgages drain a large portion of our incomes; and our chattels typically break one day after their warranty expires and so require costly replacement. Consequently, Hudson spoke of the 'unbearable lightness of property', in the sense that property rights are beneficial for the large corporations and yet burdensome for others.

And yet our property law has been slow to accommodate these changes in the very nature of the property with which we deal. A good example of that arose in the leading case of *Westdeutsche Landesbank v Islington*,[31] in which Lord Browne-Wilkinson was required to decide who owned property rights to electronic payments which had been made under a very complex financial instrument known as an interest rate swap. To begin his odyssey into the forefront of financial sophistication and the limits of property law, Lord Browne-Wilkinson held that we must treat these electronic payments as though they were 'a stolen bag of coins', and as though we wanted to recover those very coins because they were intrinsically valuable. By contrast, electronic payments are of course simply amounts of 'value' recorded in computer memories, and not gold coins with tangible existence and an intrinsic worth. This judgment was pivotal to trusts law, but it also demonstrated an odd desire to use very old-fashioned ideas involving gold coins to confront the financial instruments of a new age.

## CERTAINTY OF INTENTION

The financial crisis of 2007–09 highlighted many problems with the application of trusts law. Ironically, one of the more obscure areas of the law arises in relation to the creation of express trusts. An express trust can self-evidently be created by

---

[30] A.S. Hudson, 'The Unbearable Lightness of Property' in *New Perspectives on Property Law, Restitution and Obligations* (Cavendish, 2004), 1.
[31] [1996] AC 669.

means of a written instrument which declares itself to be a trust and which provides that identified trustees are to hold identified property on trust for identified beneficiaries. Nevertheless, such an instrument is not necessary to create a trust. A trust may be created entirely orally (except for situations involving land and some other statutory exceptions). So, trusts can be created very informally. There are situations, however, in which it is unclear whether or not an express trust has been created in these informal situations. These situations may involve ordinary people who do not have the benefit of legal advice, or they may involve large financial institutions. Examples of each situation are taken in turn.

In *Paul v Constance*,[32] the Court of Appeal inferred the existence of an intention to create a trust from the circumstances. In that case, a man had died after having paid money from a personal injury award into a bank account, having used that money with his girlfriend to pay for joint holidays and having used that account to hold their joint bingo winnings. The evidence suggested that the pair had wanted to open a joint account but that their bank manager had frowned on the idea. It was held that this suggested that the intention which the dead man had had was an intention which the law would define as being an intention to create a trust. As the sole signatory on the account, this meant the dead man had been trustee for himself and his girlfriend as beneficiaries. A claim was brought after the man's death by his estranged wife (from whom he had not been divorced) seeking ownership of the money. However, his girlfriend won out because there had been sufficient intention to create a trust. Importantly, the couple were considered to have been too unsophisticated to know what a trust was. Consequently, the court interpreted their general intentions to be an intention to create a trust.

What is important here is that an express trust can be inferred from the circumstances of a case. This is contrary to the literal meaning of the term 'express trust', because the intention to create an express trust need not be 'express' in the sense of being an explicit intention to create a trust rather than something else. Rather, the intention must be something which a court would define as being an intention to create a trust. The sorts of actions which are necessary are an intention to hold property jointly, or for one person to hold property in such a way that another person who was not expressed to be a common law owner of that property would have rights to it. However, this sort of uncertainty is not limited to the private lives of ordinary citizens. There are many commercial situations in which the parties fail to make their intentions entirely clear.

In *Brazzill v Willoughby*,[33] a trust was found in the wake of the insolvency of Icelandic bank Kaupthing and its subsidiary KSF. The UK Financial Services Authority had issued a 'supervisory order' in relation to KSF, which had required that KSF pay amounts into an account with the regulator which were equal to amounts owned to clients. It was found that this order, which had included the word 'trust', should be interpreted as having created a trust over those moneys.

---

[32] [1977] 1 WLR 527.
[33] [2010] 1 BCLC 673.

Similarly, in *Mills v Sportsdirect.com Retail Ltd*[34] it was held that KSF's decision in relation to a 'repo' transaction with one of its clients to hold payments in a separate account so that they were 'ring-fenced' and held in that client's 'box' (to quote terms used by the parties), should be interpreted as having created a trust in favour of the customer. Even though the commercial parties in these instances had not created formal trusts using written instruments drafted by lawyers as one might have expected, it was found that they had demonstrated sufficient intention to do something which the courts interpreted as constituting trusts. The effect of these trusts was to give the clients proprietary rights which survived KSF's insolvency.

## THE IMPORTANCE OF INSOLVENCY TO TRUSTS LAW

The phenomenon of insolvency illustrates why it would be unjust to award trusts randomly. In an insolvency, by definition, the insolvent person will be unable to meet their debts as they become due, and in consequence there will be more unsecured creditors with more claims against the insolvent person than there is property to meet them. Therefore, to award a trust in one person's favour is to deny access to that property to the other unsecured creditors. In a complex insolvency like the Lehman Brothers insolvency in 2008, the instinct of the judges and of the insolvency law commentators is to maximise the amount of property which is available to all of the unsecured creditors, and to be reluctant to allow some property to be hived off to particular creditors' use without a very good reason for doing so.

The litigation in relation to *Re Goldcorp*[35] is a good illustration of this phenomenon. There a company had marketed itself to the public as a means of making safe investments in gold and other precious metals. The company contracted with its customers on the basis that it would acquire gold to their order and that it would hold that gold (and other commodities) in its vaults. Therefore, the customers could supposedly have confidence that there was gold in the vaults and that their investments were safe. However, the company ran into difficulties and so lapsed into the common practice among financial institutions of acquiring only as much gold (and other metals of similar types) as was necessary to meet its obligations to its customers on any given working day. Given that most customers would leave their gold in the company's vaults, there was a commercial need to have only a fraction of the gold of different types which constituted the entirety of its clients' orders held in the company's vaults. When the company went into insolvency, its 'customers' became reclassified in everyone's minds as its 'creditors in insolvency proceedings'. At that moment it became vitally important to know which customers could identify gold that was held separately to their account, and which customers only had rights of a given value against the bulk of bullion held in the company's vaults. The certainty of subject matter rule was important to prevent some creditor-customers inappropriately getting access to gold to the detriment of

[34] [2010] 2 BCLC 143.
[35] [1995] 1 AC 74.

other creditor-customers. In this sense, insolvency law is concerned with 'equity' in the sense of 'equality' or fairness.

While trusts are ordinarily considered by equity specialists to be predicated on conscience and to be concerned with morality, insolvency lawyers see the world differently. To insolvency law specialists, trusts are simply a means of evading insolvency law treatment by holding assets on trust.[36] This characterisation is not entirely fair, of course. If the parties have been careful enough to settle property on trust, then that property is not beneficially the property of the insolvent person. Nevertheless, insolvency law permits the courts to recover property which had been settled on trust solely for the purpose of evading creditors too close to the time of insolvency.[37]

What is also important to identify is that insolvency law has a tendency to pull trusts law out of shape. The rules of trusts law are perfectly clear: there must be three certainties satisfied and there must be identified beneficiaries before a trust is valid, and the settlor's intention must be to create a trust rather than something else. However, because trusts are so often claimed by people who are creditors in an insolvency, it becomes very important in practice to try to expand the range of transactions which can be defined as being trusts so that more people can take protection under them. Consequently, the Lehman Brothers litigation has wrought damage on trusts law which may take decades to mend. After the decision of the Supreme Court, will there be a single trust in favour of multiple beneficiaries in any situation in which an insolvent person ought to have created a trust of some sort, even if that person did nothing to segregate the trust fund from other property? Will there be a trust whenever the court considers it helpful to protect unsecured creditors in an insolvency? Or will the courts slowly return to the traditional principle that there can only be a trust, whether or not there is an insolvency, if the settlor intends to create a trust and separates the trust fund from their other property? Ironically, this is one situation in which a rigid rule of trusts law requiring 'certainty' has been bent out of shape by commercial law practitioners seeking a fair outcome for their clients.

# Debate **4**

## Disagreements about certainty of objects

### THE LAW ON CERTAINTY OF OBJECTS: DISCRETIONARY TRUSTS AND FIDUCIARY POWERS

The principal, long-standing debate within the law on certainty of objects revolves around the test for certainty as to the identity of the beneficiaries who are intended to be benefited by a settlor in relation to discretionary trusts and in relation to

---

[36] R. Goode, *Principles of Corporate Insolvency* (Sweet & Maxwell, 2011).
[37] Insolvency Act 1986, s. 423.

powers held by fiduciaries.[38] The legal significance of 'powers' has been lost from the university law school curriculum, and the beacon for its importance is held aloft by the very important work of Professor Geraint Thomas in his book *Powers*.[39] The law in this area is explored in detail in the trusts law textbooks; this discussion is intended only to highlight one important aspect of the debates between the judges.

What the law *is* today is perfectly clear, even if the test itself is a little too subtle for the tastes of many law students. To decide whether or not the objects[40] of a discretionary trust or of a fiduciary power are sufficiently certain for that trust or power to be valid, the test is whether any given postulant who is under consideration to be included in the class of people who may take a benefit from that trust or power is or is not within the ambit of that class: in the event of uncertainty as to whether or not such a postulant is or is not within that class, then the trust or power is void. There are a number of questions as to what that test means, but in essence that is the test. More importantly, that statement of the test walks a fine line between the competing arguments as to what that test might mean in practice. This statement of the test *is* the law in that it is drawn from the most recent House of Lords decision on this area of law in *McPhail v Doulton*. Therefore, to the extent that this statement of the law disagrees with any of the arguments which were advanced by other judges in earlier cases, this decision of the House of Lords takes precedence over all earlier judgments and is the law.

The debate was the following one: should trusts have a test which is different from the test for powers, and in consequence is there something special about trusts which requires different, more stringent treatment than is the case for powers? In the case law, it is common to refer to a power as a 'mere power' because, in the minds of many judges, there was something less significant (in terms of the test to be ascribed to it) about a power than a trust. In this view, a trust is something complex and multi-faceted which may, for example, organise the ownership and use of property down the generations (as with a family settlement), which necessitates a rigid test. By contrast, a power may relate to a comparatively limited ability to direct the use of property, albeit that the holder of the power could not be allowed to do anything they pleased with it. So, powers may relate to powers of attorney (for example over the assets of someone who has become incapacitated) and so forth, and do not have the longevity nor complexity of a settlement, even if they are significant in other ways.

The old approach to certainty of objects, in essence, took the view that anything which was properly analysable as a trust – whether a fixed trust, a bare trust or a discretionary trust – required that a complete list of all of the beneficiaries should be capable of preparation before the trust could be considered to be valid. (In practice,

---

[38] For further discussion of the relevant principles in this area, see Hudson, above n 1, Ch. 3.

[39] G.W. Thomas, *Powers*, 2nd edn (Oxford University Press, 2011).

[40] In this context, it should be remembered, the 'objects' of a trust or power is a reference to the people (human beings or corporate bodies) which are to take a benefit from that trust or power, and not a reference to the objectives of that trust or power.

presumably, many trusts would be operated perfectly successfully under terms which would have been considered unsatisfactory by Chancery judges, provided that no one brought the arrangement before a court.) Judges such as Lord Hodson and Lord Guest in *Re Gulbenkian*[41] and *McPhail v Doulton*,[42] and Hodson LJ in *Broadway Cottages*[43] supported this approach. By contrast, the test for any sort of power could be different. (There were many different types of power in the old jurisprudence – although the modern cases on certainty of objects seem to have flattened them somewhat.) Therefore, the position used to be that there was a line drawn (by judges who held this opinion) between trusts on the one hand and powers on the other.

However, the cases after *Re Gestetner*[44] saw a dissolution of that clear line between trusts and powers. So, Lord Reid held in *Re Gulbenkian* that the question should be whether or not a person is or is not within the class, and (speaking as a Scots lawyer who had not been brought up on English trusts law) that he considered English trusts law to be overly concerned with technical rules which would have the effect of invalidating otherwise perfectly serviceable trusts in this area.

Importantly, in *Re Gulbenkian* (a case concerning a mere power) it is Lord Upjohn who gives the leading speech (in that Lord Hodson and Lord Guest agree with him). His judgment is meandering and in some places unclear. There is only one passing reference to the concept of 'is or is not' in the early part of the judgment, when otherwise his Lordship conducted a survey of all of the cases. It should be pointed out that Lord Hodson had been part of the Court of Appeal in *Broadway Cottages* which had taken the view that a complete list of objects should be required in fixed trusts. It was only in the final paragraph that Lord Upjohn returned to the idea of 'is or is not'. It is worth pointing out that Lord Reid was much clearer about his affection for the idea of 'is or is not' as a test in his judgment. The outcome was that the later decision of the House of Lords in *McPhail v Doulton* (about a discretionary trust) contains an argument (set out most clearly in the judgment of Lord Hodson) in which Lord Hodson and Lord Guest both clearly disagree with the use of the 'is or is not' test and moreover explain that they thought (when they concurred with Lord Upjohn in *Re Gulbenkian*) that Lord Upjohn was setting out a complete list test.

Therefore, Lords Hodson and Guest refused to agree with Lord Wilberforce and the other judges in the House of Lords in *McPhail v Doulton*, because Lord Wilberforce presented an interpretation of Lord Upjohn's judgment which finds that Lord Upjohn intended the test to be an 'is or is not' test. The majority of the House of Lords in *McPhail v Doulton* held that that test was an 'is or is not' test for discretionary trusts and, by interpreting Lord Upjohn in this way, for fiduciary powers as well. Whatever Lord Upjohn may actually have meant, because the

---

[41] [1968] Ch 785.
[42] [1971] AC 424.
[43] *IRC v Broadway Cottages Trust* [1955] Ch 20.
[44] [1953] Ch 672.

House of Lords in a later case interpreted him in a particular way, that later interpretation of the House of Lords in *McPhail v Doulton* becomes the definitive statement of the law at present.

In any other context outside the courtroom, we might take a different approach. Suppose you are a witness to an argument between friends in a coffee shop as to whether Beth loves Sandy or not. Suppose further that the argument revolves specifically around something which Beth said to a group of friends, including Maisie. Beth said: 'This relationship could be the most significant mistake of my life.' In the argument in the coffee shop, Jolene says: 'What Beth meant was that *ending* the relationship would be the most significant mistake of her life, and therefore she really does love Sandy.' However, Maisie says: 'I was there that night, and what Beth meant was that she considers being with Sandy will make her unhappy and so she clearly does not love Sandy. I was in the room. She was not saying she loved Sandy. She was very upset about Sandy's behaviour.' In any ordinary walk of life, we would believe Maisie's account of Beth's opinion (at least at the time Beth spoke). Maisie was there. Maisie had the chance to talk to Beth. Maisie saw the entire context in which those words were spoken. If Jolene had not been there, then Jolene could only be guessing.

However, in the legal context, we assume that the person who speaks with the highest level of legitimacy (like Lord Wilberforce as the most recent judge in the House of Lords to express a view) and authority (like Lord Wilberforce having the agreement of the majority of judges in that court) to be definitive of the point and therefore correct. Therefore, if everyone in the coffee shop chooses to agree with Jolene's analysis, then Jolene would be taken to be correct *if Jolene was in the House of Lords under the doctrine of precedent*. Lords Hodson and Guest would say: 'We were in the court with him, so we know what Lord Upjohn intended.' But the law does not work like that. Lord Wilberforce's judgment is the definitive statement of the law because it has formal legitimacy and authority, even if there were other judges in the courtroom who might have a greater claim to the correct analysis. This gives us an insight as to how the doctrine of precedent decides the outcomes of some debates, and how judges will often simply disagree about what the law should be.

## AN EXAMPLE OF WHY STRICT RULES MAY CAUSE POOR OUTCOMES

The reason why it is so important to decide whether to have a strict rule which will tend to invalidate trusts, or a slightly more relaxed rule which is more likely to validate trusts on the borderline, is that when a trust is invalidated all of the property will pass to people whom the settlor may not have intended to take all of the property and the ultimate goal[45] of the trust will be missed. Imagine a trust in which

---

[45] I use the word 'goal' here as a compromise between 'object' (which means beneficiary in this context), 'objective' (which sounds too much like 'object') and 'purpose' (because that word also has the sense of a 'purpose trust' which will ordinarily be void for breaching the beneficiary principle). Trusts law is truly a minefield, in which one must be very careful to select the correct word for each context – something which demonstrates again its nature at times as a rigid set of rules and practices.

the settlor wished to benefit his nephews, nieces and cousins with property of a value of approximately £2 million, but who was nervous about misdescribing that class or failing to include any future children in his trust instrument. Suppose, therefore, that he referred to the beneficial class of a discretionary trust as being 'my relations and other members of their families'.[46] As is typical, the trust instrument will then have identified a person to act as the residuary beneficiary in case there was any property left over: in this case, the trustees of the Lindfield Cats Home, a charity. If this particular term of the trust creating the discretionary obligation were to fail, then none of the nephews, nieces nor first cousins would receive a penny. However, the cats of Lindfield would be eating their dinners off silver plates, because all of the property would pass to the residuary beneficiary here, even though the settlor had expected that only a few pounds might fall through to the Cats Home.

This is why an overly strict rule may defeat common sense, and it may defeat the goals of settlors by allocating large amounts of money to people who were only expected to receive a small amount. In this example, if the trustees decided to operate the trust on the basis which they understood the settlor to have intended, and if the family members all agreed to consent to that, then it would be unlikely that there would be any litigation which would invalidate the trust in practice (because everyone has agreed to treat it as valid). It would only be if the trustees of the Lindfield Cats Home learned of the terms of the trust, took advice from a trusts lawyer, and then decided to commence litigation that there would be a risk of the trust being declared invalid by the courts.

A number of questions arise about the test as set out by Lord Wilberforce in *McPhail v Doulton*. First, what form must the 'postulant' take? Must the postulant be someone who is actually hammering at the trustees' door, or can the postulant be simply a hypothetical postulant whom the trustees are imagining? If the test is simply concerned with the real people who actually come forward, then it is more likely that a concept such as 'my friends' will be satisfied. However, if the trustees are to imagine hypothetical people in hypothetical situations, then it is more likely that the trustees will be able to imagine an individual who would create uncertainty. Secondly, when deciding whether or not the test is satisfied, what should the trustees actually be doing? Let us assume that the trustees are sitting in a room together behind a table. Should we assume that the trustees have placed an advert on the Internet and that they are interviewing all of the people by lining them up in the corridor outside; or should we assume that the trustees are simply asking hypothetically whether or not their task would be possible without having any real people in the corridor outside?

---

[46] The argument here would be whether the reference to 'relations' was as clear as the reference to 'relatives' in *Re Gulbenkian* [1968] Ch 785, and whether the reference to 'their families' was too vague as to the people who were intended to fall under that net: What sorts of family members? People who married into the family and their third cousins? People who lived in their house but who were not related by blood? And so forth.

Browne-Wilkinson J in *Re Barlow*[47] took the approach, in relation to the specific facts in front of him, that it would be possible to ascertain which individuals the settlor had had in mind when a trust in favour of 'friends' was created. Thus, on the facts of any particular case, it may be possible for the court to decide that it knows what a particular settlor had in mind when the trust was created, even if the words may appear ambiguous in the abstract. For example, a loner who had been an orphan, who worked alone online from his flat, and who had only two friends with whom he met once a week to discuss a shared love of Marvel comics, could be interpreted as having intended to benefit those two friends when he settled property on 'my two dear friends'.

This suggests a slightly unintellectual, but nevertheless effective, third approach to this debate: can the problem be solved common-sensically, even if the drafting of the trust is poor? In contract law, it is common for problems to be solved by taking a constructive, commercially reasonable approach to the interpretation of what the parties must have intended the term of their contract to mean. So, in trusts law, why should it not be possible to interpret the terms of the trust instrument so as to achieve the settlor's intentions? Clearly, there will be situations in which it is impossible to know what a settlor intended by the words 'hold the property on trust for *nice people*'. However, a settlor who only ever had two friends might reasonably be interpreted as having intended those people to be the 'friends' who were to benefit. Common sense is not a satisfying basis for creating law; but it may be a useful way of resolving problems between human beings, on occasion.

## HOW NEW DIRECTIONS IN THE LAW GROW OUT OF THE OLD

The alternative ways in which new laws in trusts law can grow out of the old are as a result of legal practice leading the law in a new direction. It is important to bear in mind that the law of trusts has not been created by a statute. There is no single source for the law. Instead, the law of trusts has developed after the event: that is, by the courts reacting to events initiated by practitioners and creating rules in response to those developments. The next key development in trusts law may result from the international contexts which are considered in the next chapter.

---

[47] [1979] 1 WLR 278.

# 5

# THE BENEFICIARY PRINCIPLE AND INTERNATIONAL TRUSTS LAW

## INTRODUCTION

This chapter considers trusts law from a perspective which is rarely discussed in English and Welsh law schools: that of the international use of trusts. There is a very important dimension to trusts law practice: the use of trusts in jurisdictions known as 'tax havens' or 'offshore jurisdictions' to invest or shelter assets in a tax-efficient way. Typically these offshore jurisdictions have low or effectively no taxes for foreign investors. Commonly they have specific statutory schemes in place for such overseas investors so that their trusts are treated differently from ordinary trusts: we shall consider the scheme used in the Cayman Islands by way of example. The users of these trusts structures are the international financial services providers (whether investment banks, international accountancy firms or others) who sell their tax-efficient vehicles and structures to clients from the UK, the USA and similar jurisdictions in the industrialised world. Importantly, not only do these offshore jurisdictions offer low taxes, but they also have historically refused to provide information to the tax authorities of other jurisdictions about the investments which have been made in their territories. Consequently, in the past, investors could acquire low tax, clandestine investment services.

Clearly the existence of these structures in these jurisdictions means that a large amount of tax can be avoided in the UK, the USA and so forth. During a time of economic austerity in the North Atlantic countries after the 2007–09 financial crisis, the loss of tax revenue to other jurisdictions has driven a change in policy. The scrutiny which has been turned on offshore financing by international bodies like the Organisation for Economic Cooperation and Development ('OECD') and the Financial Affairs Task Force ('FATF') had intensified already in the wake of the attacks on the World Trade Center in New York on 11 September 2001 because clandestine tax havens are the ideal mechanism for international terrorist organisations and other criminal organisations to conceal and to invest their money. Therefore, the backdrop to this chapter is the epicentre of geopolitics at the time of writing: the wherewithal to deliver terrorism, military insurgency and drug-dealing is commonly believed to be funded through offshore jurisdictions.

And at the centre of these developments, beyond all of the politics and the conflict, is the beneficiary principle. Never was there a more unlikely focus for debate: the centuries-old rule that there cannot be a valid trust without there being someone for whose benefit the trust must be performed. The debates revolving around the beneficiary principle in English law are considered first. Then we shall consider the way in which offshore trusts laws are commonly organised, and why the humble beneficiary principle is at the centre of international, political debates about recovery from the financial crisis and the funding of international terrorism.

## THE CENTRAL TRUSTS LAW PROBLEM FROM A UK PERSPECTIVE

One of the key questions, from a UK perspective, with international trusts is whether or not the specific provisions of the trusts law codes in offshore jurisdictions would be accepted as being valid under English trusts law. The central question is whether a trust which is valid in an offshore centre under its own trusts law would be considered invalid under English trusts or tax law. This is known as the 'limping trust' problem[1] because one 'leg' of the trust in England would not work, whereas the other 'leg' offshore would work. As Paul Matthews has put it, a sovereign jurisdiction may pass legislation which calls Monday Sunday and Sunday Monday, but that does not mean that UK revenue law will necessarily accept that analysis. So, offshore jurisdictions can enact whatever they please in their own law, but that does not mean that the courts of other jurisdictions which are important to their clients will necessarily take benign views of those same structures.

Let us take an example. John is a wealthy UK citizen. He is advised by his accountants to invest in a trust structure in a jurisdiction which has a statute in place which provides expressly that a trust will be valid in that jurisdiction without the need for a beneficiary: instead, there will be a so-called 'protector' who will look after John's interests in relation to the trustees. Consequently, John invests a large amount of money in that trust in that offshore jurisdiction. The trust provides that John owns no beneficial interest in the trust but that the trustees are empowered to pay the profits from the investments into a range of different objects, including a company wholly-owned by John in yet another low tax jurisdiction. In practice, of course, the trustees pay all of the profits into that company because they are accountants who are being paid a fee under a contract with John. The problem arises back in the UK. John does not want the UK tax authorities (HMRC[2]) to learn about the trust; and he is also nervous that if its terms were known about in the UK then litigation might be started by HMRC to see if John could be made liable for tax in the UK on any profits earned from that trust. Under English trusts law, HMRC might argue that the trust should be considered *by English law* as being void because no beneficiary is identified in that trust, as

---

[1] D. Waters, 'Reaching for the Sky: Taking Trusts Law to the Limit' in D. Hayton (ed.), *Extending the Boundaries of Trusts and Similar Ring-Fenced Funds* (Kluwer Law International, 2002), 243.
[2] HMRC means 'Her Majesty's Revenue and Customs', previously the 'Inland Revenue'.

required by the beneficiary principle in English law.[3] If the trust is void under English trusts law, then an English court would interpret the trust property as remaining with the settlor (i.e. John) on resulting trust and therefore John would be considered taxable under UK revenue law on the profits from the void trust as its sole beneficiary.[4]

Consequently, the trusts laws of the jurisdictions in which the investors have their domiciles[5] will still be important in practice because the financial services providers who provide offshore trusts services are ultimately in the business of servicing wealthy individuals from those jurisdictions. There is constantly an interplay between the laws of the offshore jurisdictions (which typically service the business practices of the trust service providers) and the laws of the jurisdictions in which their clients are domiciled or ordinarily resident. In practice, no one wants to risk litigation, in case an English court rules definitively that the offshore trusts services are not effective for the purposes of English trusts law. This chapter begins with an analysis of the key debate in the case law dealing with the English beneficiary principle.

## Debate 1

## What is the concept of the beneficiary in express trusts law?

### THE LAW

The beneficiary principle has developed in its modern form from the decision in *Morice v Bishop of Durham*,[6] to the effect that there must be at least one beneficiary and the identity of that beneficiary must be sufficiently certain, so that there is 'someone in whose favour the court can decree performance' in the event that the trustees are alleged to have failed in their duties. The logic of the beneficiary principle is this. First, a trust operates by the beneficiaries suing the trustees if the trustees fail to obey their obligations under the terms of the trust. Unless someone is able to bring a case before the court, the court will not be able to adjudicate on the probity of the trustees' actions. The argument, considered below, has been made that there is no reason why the person who enforces the trust in this way needs to be one of the beneficiaries: it could be someone called a 'protector' or an 'enforcer', who has no rights in the trust property but who is appointed so as to protect the position of the beneficiaries.[7] Secondly, the court must know the identity of the beneficiaries with sufficient certainty so that the court can identify in

---

[3] *Morice v Bishop of Durham* (1805) 10 Ves 522.

[4] *Vandervell v Inland Revenue Commissioners* [1967] 2 AC 291.

[5] There are complex concepts beyond the scope of this work which distinguish, for tax law and other purposes, between the domicile, the residence and the citizenship of a person. Domicile and residence can have different tax law effects in different contexts.

[6] *Morice v Bishop of Durham* (1805) 10 Ves 522.

[7] D. Hayton, 'Developing the Obligation Characteristic of the Trust' (2001) 117 *LQR* 97.

whose interests the trustees are supposed to be acting. After all, if the court does not know that, how could the trustees themselves know in whose interests they are supposed to be acting when deciding how to use their powers?

Within English trusts law, there are two approaches taken to the nature and extent of the beneficiary principle: first, that taken by Viscount Simonds in *Leahy v Attorney-General for NSW*;[8] secondly, that taken by Goff J and Oliver J in *Re Denley*[9] and in *Re Lipinski's Will Trusts*[10] respectively. Each approach is now considered in turn.

## THE NARROW MODEL

The argument that was advanced by Viscount Simonds, inter alia, in *Leahy v Attorney-General for NSW*, about the nature of beneficiaries, was that they were required to be in 'immediate possession' of their rights. So in that case his Lordship found that no valid trust was created over a sheep station of 750 acres in New South Wales in favour (after the exercise of the trustees' discretion) of the Carmelite order of nuns because the members of that worldwide order could not reasonably be understood as going into possession en masse of such a sheep station with a single farmhouse containing about a dozen rooms. Therefore, it was held that there were no beneficiaries of the right sort, and therefore no trust.

However, it could be argued that that was to misunderstand the nature of a beneficial interest; or, more accurately, it was to misunderstand the range of types of beneficial interest which are possible. For example, in a discretionary trust it is perfectly possible that many of the potential objects of the trust will never actually receive any property because the trustees may not exercise their discretion in favour of those particular objects. No one has ever suggested that discretionary trusts in general are ineffective. And yet, if we were to accept Viscount Simonds' conception of what constitutes a beneficial interest (i.e. that that person must go into immediate possession of property rights) then that would mean that discretionary trusts could not be effective because there would be objects of that trust who did not go into immediate possession of their rights: those rights could only take effect on the contingency that the trustees exercised their discretion in favour of those objects at some time after the trust was created. Therefore, the argument advanced by Viscount Simonds might be part of the reason for finding that there was no beneficial interest for the Carmelite order of nuns in that situation, but it cannot stand as a definition of the nature of the beneficial interests of all beneficiaries. We must consider alternative formulations.

The most significant alternative model of the beneficiary principle was that set out by Goff J in *Re Denley* (and approved in similar terms by Oliver J in *Re Lipinski*). In *Re Denley*, a sports ground had been left 'for the benefit of' employees of a

---

[8] [1959] AC 457.
[9] [1969] 1 Ch 373.
[10] [1976] Ch 235.

company. The trustees were granted a power to decide how the land should be used. The issue arose as to whether or not there was sufficient right here to satisfy the beneficiary principle. Goff J held that it was sufficient that the property was defined as being held 'for the benefit of' the employees of that company and, importantly, that the mischief at which the beneficiary principle is directed required merely that there was someone in whose favour the court could decree performance: that is, that it was sufficient that there were the employees of the company who could act as claimants in the event that there was any issue as to whether or not the trustees were performing their duties properly.

Interestingly, the facts of *Leahy* and *Denley* were very similar indeed when seen in the following light. Both cases involved fairly large expanses of land: one a sheep station, the other a sports field. Both cases involved a large number of people who would be theoretically entitled to use that land but who could not have used the land simultaneously. (It is true that the size of the land and the number of people were larger in the former case than in the latter, but otherwise the parallels are close.) Both cases involved the trustees having some discretion as to the precise use to which the land would have been put. And yet the different opinions of the judges as to the nature of the beneficiary principle led to different outcomes. In *Leahy*, the sheep station could have been made available for the order of nuns as a retreat, or as a convalescent home for elderly nuns or something of that sort. It would not be necessary for all of the nuns to use the land at once, just as it was not necessary for all of the employees to use the sports ground at once or at all. The overweight men of the accounting department, for example, might never find themselves on a sports field; but that would not have invalidated that trust. It is important to note that these cases were decided differently simply because the various judges believed that the law should be different.

## THE BROADER MODEL

The opinions of Goff J and Oliver J, two venerable Chancery judges who would later grace the House of Lords with their intellects, were clearly that the beneficiary principle had traditionally been exercised too strictly. Their judgments may both be read as preferring an approach in which the law of trusts is less concerned to invalidate trusts which have some potential beneficiaries and which perform socially unobjectionable activities (such as constructing a new clubhouse for a social club). As Oliver J suggested in *Re Lipinski*, it was only when the terms of the trust were extremely unclear or abstract – for example, when property was left for the benefit of a favourite pet – that trusts law should interfere and invalidate the trust.

It is useful to remember what happens when a trust is invalidated: the property passes to the residuary beneficiary named in the trust instrument (often a will in this context), or passes on resulting trust back to the settlor if there is no residuary beneficiary. The residuary beneficiary is often a charity (like an animal shelter), or a relative who was not considered worthy of a specific right under a trust.

Therefore, if the property were to pass to that person, then they would receive property not intended for them by the settlor. The question must be asked whether or not it is preferable for that property to go to the purpose or person which the settlor intended, assuming that can be identified with sufficient certainty. Goff J and Oliver J were mindful of this context (having been Chancery lawyers themselves). By diluting the strictness of decisions like *Re Grant's Will Trusts*[11] (see below) and *Leahy v Attorney-General for NSW*, it is possible to give effect to the general intentions of the settlor. In a sense, this exercise in judicial interpretation is similar to the 'cy-près' doctrine in charities law, which permits a poorly-drafted charitable trust, or a charitable intention which has become impossible to perform (for example, because the charity in question no longer exists when the trust comes to be performed), to be reinterpreted so that the settlor's general purpose may be achieved by some other, similar method.[12]

## PERPETUATION OF THE NARROW MODEL

There are, however, other judgments, like that in *Re Grant's Will Trusts*[13] delivered by Vinelott J, which command the support of venerable trusts law commentators like Professor Geraint Thomas.[14] To a certain species of trusts lawyer, the validity of a trust should depend on its careful drafting and construction. So, in *Re Grant's Will Trusts*, the testator (or his advisers) prepared a will trust which purported to create a valid trust in favour of the members of the defunct Chertsey Constituency Labour Party, and which therefore created a void 'trust' in favour of the property committee of the national Labour Party under the rules of that organisation. That committee was not a legal person and therefore could not be a beneficiary. Therefore, there was no valid beneficiary capable of taking the property and so the purported trust failed. A purposive interpretation of this arrangement could have decided that the settlor's intention was to benefit the human beings who were members of the successor group to the Chertsey Constituency Labour Party, but Vinelott J did not take that approach. Instead, his lordship's approach was a careful reading of the Labour Party's regulations and of the trust itself.

The decision of Goff J in *Re Denley* could be limited to its own facts, of course. That was the approach taken by Vinelott J. The situation in that case could have been explained as a simple discretionary trust in which the identity of all the potential beneficiaries was known (i.e. any of the employees of the company) and in which the trustees simply had to exercise their discretion as to the use of the sports ground. Therefore, on the facts of that case there was no real trusts law problem, and instead Goff J was taking the opportunity to address a broader problem which he had identified in the law. In consequence, the precise state of the law is

---

[11] [1979] 3 All ER 359, [1980] 1 WLR 360.

[12] For an excellent account, see R. Mulheron, *The Modern Cy-Près Doctrine* (UCL Press, 2006).

[13] [1979] 3 All ER 359, [1980] 1 WLR 360.

[14] G.W. Thomas and A.S. Hudson, *The Law of Trusts*, 2nd edn (Oxford University Press, 2010), 6.20.

unclear. Although, it is suggested, the weight of authority appears to be with Goff J and Oliver J, and that appears to be sentiment in many of the textbooks.

# Debate 2

## What are the issues with offshore trusts being valid under English trusts law?

### THE NATURE OF INTERNATIONAL TRUSTS LAW

International trusts law is really two things. Fist, it is the legal practice of lawyers with clients whose affairs cross borders, who use trusts to manage their property. Secondly, it is also the aggregation of the trusts laws of different jurisdictions which might apply to any given client, depending on where their property and the various beneficiaries are domiciled or resident (or have plausible claims to residence). There is no transnational law in truth which governs these international trusts. Instead, there are the trusts laws of individual jurisdictions which have different analyses of how those trusts might work, and whether or not they are legally effective.[15] Instead, practitioners are free to create their own trusts structures for their clients, and to pick from the available trusts laws of different jurisdictions in so doing. Therefore, the issues here relate to the differences between English law and the laws in offshore jurisdictions, and whether or not particular trusts models would be valid under English law.

### THE EXAMPLE OF STAR TRUSTS IN THE CAYMAN ISLANDS

In this section we shall focus on a passionate debate about the so-called 'STAR trust' created by statute in the Cayman Islands. (The term 'STAR' derives from the statute – the Special Trusts (Alternative Regime) Law 1997 – which created this 'special trust' originally in the Cayman Islands. That statute has since been consolidated into Part VII of the Trusts Law (2001 Revision).) The underlying objective of the STAR trust is to encourage investment, through financial services and trusts services providers in the Cayman Islands, by wealthy citizens of industrialised democratic countries who want to avoid taxation, or effectively by criminals who want to avoid regulatory oversight. The STAR trust may be used for more mundane purposes, but that was not the reason for introducing the legislation.

Briefly put, Cayman Islands trusts law operates as follows. There are two types of trusts: ordinary trusts and STAR trusts. The STAR trust has a simple concept at its heart: there does not need to be a beneficiary with any enforceable equitable rights, and there will be an 'enforcer' who can intercede against the trustees in the event that the trustees do not perform their duties properly. By effectively removing the beneficiaries from the picture, the tax treatment of the STAR trust is

---

[15] Aside from the Hague Trusts Convention, there is nothing which exists across borders which might be referred to as a legal code. That Convention relates to the recognition of trusts from other jurisdictions.

intended to be such that the beneficiaries are not to be treated as having any property rights in the trust fund if the settlor chooses to structure matters in that way. As will emerge below, the absence of such a beneficiary with enforceable rights may well be lawful in the Cayman Islands (as it clearly is because that sovereign nation has created a statute to that effect), but it is a different question whether that structure would be accepted as being effective under English law.

This section focuses on a part of the statutory position of the beneficiary under Cayman Islands law and on the role of the protector. In particular, this section will highlight elements of a debate between Professor Paul Matthews and Mr Antony Duckworth about the feasibility of the STAR trust. In the space available, it will not be possible to explore every crevice of that debate. At stake is the question whether or not the STAR trust could be considered to be valid under English trusts law.

### The position under the STAR trust

The position of the beneficiaries is a significant feature of STAR trusts. Under s. 100(1) of the 2001 Revision Law (which used to be s. 7(1) of the 1997 Law, which is the statute referred to in the journal literature debate discussed below):

> 'A beneficiary of a special trust does not as such have standing to enforce the trust, or an enforceable right against a trustee or an enforcer, or an enforceable right to the trust property.'

Clearly, this would not satisfy the beneficiary principle (as currently understood) in England, because the beneficiary cannot enforce the trust in their capacity as a beneficiary and the beneficiary does not have an enforceable right to the trust property. However, it is valid under Cayman Islands law.

Furthermore, under s. 100(2), only enforcers appointed for that purpose are entitled to enforce the trust. The enforcers are given the same rights as beneficiaries under an ordinary trust, although that should be interpreted to mean that they have rights of enforcement but not rights to take the trust property beneficially in that capacity. The enforcer 'has the rights of a trustee' under s. 102(b).

### The Matthews–Duckworth 'Star Wars' debate

In an article,[16] Professor Paul Matthews identified several problems with the 'special/STAR trust' arrangement. As a useful rule of thumb, Matthews warned us that if a jurisdiction creates a new trusts law regime that is not to be used by the locals and which does not apply to local land, then it is 'seriously wacky'. (For example, the Cook Islands have a scheme of international trusts which does not apply to natives of those islands.[17]) Among his principal concerns about STAR trusts, for our purposes, are the following. First, the beneficiaries are disconnected from the right to enforce the trust under s. 100(1). This may have the effect that

---

[16] P. Matthews, 'Shooting STAR: the new special trusts regime from the Cayman Islands' (1997) 11 *Trust Law International* 67.

[17] See A.S. Hudson, 'Asset protection trusts' in D. Hayton (ed.), *The International Trust*, 3rd edn (Jordans Publishing, 2011), 345.

the trustees and the enforcers may misuse the trust property against the beneficiaries' interests, given that the beneficiaries have no legal right to interfere under the statute. Secondly, the beneficiaries have no property rights in the trust fund further to s. 100(1). This means that all the beneficiaries have is the 'bare enjoyment' of the property but no means of enforcement of their entitlement to it. Thirdly, the enforcer is expressly empowered to act as though a trustee, which confuses the fiduciary structure of the trust (without the clarity of an old unit trust where one trustee would watch another). Fourthly, no STAR trust can be void due to the uncertainty of its 'objects or mode of execution', which puts it on a par with charitable trusts under English law and which expressly permits STAR trustees to use their powers to interpret those trusts so as to make them valid, thus giving them enormous power as though the settlor. Fifthly, the definition of a 'beneficiary' is so very broad – including 'a person who will or may derive a benefit or advantage, directly or indirectly, from the execution of a special trust' – as to create problems about knowing who can qualify as a beneficiary.

Duckworth had drafted the STAR legislation originally, and continues to work at a law firm in Cayman Islands advising on private client and trusts business. Therefore, he has, to employ an Americanism, skin in the game. He wrote an article in response to Matthews[18] which addressed Matthews's concerns. What emerges is that the two commentators have completely different viewpoints on the material at issue. First, Duckworth argued, the STAR trust is intended to encompass a very broad range of situations, including spendthrift trusts, in which a settlor may want to prevent the beneficiaries from taking over the property under the *Saunders v Vautier* principle because they are too young or untrustworthy, or addicted to drugs or whatever. Therefore, providing that the beneficiary has no rights is useful for the settlor in those situations. Duckworth tells us that the STAR trust is intended for the brave investor, but there is protection against breach of trust in the form of the enforcer, and the settlor simply needs to choose reliable trustees and enforcers in the same way that an English settlor needs to choose reliable trustees. Moreover, the trust instrument must deal with the precise powers, rights and obligations of the parties. (The English law response would be that English law does grant greater rights to the beneficiaries so that they can protect themselves in the event of problems.) Secondly, there are plenty of trusts in which the beneficiaries have restricted property rights in practice, such as discretionary trusts. Thirdly, the enforcer protects the beneficiaries so that the beneficiaries do not need to have equitable rights, which is a central part of the STAR concept. The beneficiary principle is therefore not necessary. Fourthly, removing the uncertainty in trusts, by means of the trustees exercising a power to decide how the property is to be appointed, is said to remove one of the principal deficiencies in English law under which trusts are susceptible to invalidity. (The English response would be

---

[18] A. Duckworth, 'STAR WARS: The Colony Strikes Back' (1998) 12 *Trust Law International* 16. In Duckworth's favour are his excellent article titles and the exquisite way in which he joins battle in writing.

that it gives the trustees unfettered power to decide to operate the trust in a way which the courts will be unable to review or validate.) Fifthly, the definition of beneficiary was intended to be 'compendious', hence its breadth.

Matthews responded in another article;[19] Duckworth in yet another article;[20] until Matthews called a halt.[21] Matthews stressed the difference between the property rights which all of the beneficiaries acting together have in the trust property, even in discretionary trusts (where the class is closed and the property must be exhausted), as distinct from the STAR arrangement. The final question became whether the STAR trust would be considered to be valid under English law. Matthews began by arguing on the basis of the inalienability principle. Duckworth shifted the debate to the beneficiary principle and argued that many English law trusts such as discretionary trusts have complex equitable proprietary interests, and charitable trusts have no property rights for the people who benefit from their activities at all. Matthews rightly expressed the English law position on the beneficiary principle at present: if there is a STAR trust without beneficiaries with any rights in the property (whether rights to control the trustees or property rights in the trust fund) then there is no beneficiary, and therefore there is no valid trust. There was simply no common ground between these commentators: one setting out the problems from an English law perspective, and the other advocating a business model which he had created in his own jurisdiction.

Professor David Hayton, as he then was, addressed the problem of the beneficiary principle head on.[22] In essence, Hayton revisited the detail of the judgment in *Re Denley* and its use of the principle which was identified in *Morice v Bishop of Durham*, to the effect that the mischief at which the beneficiary principle is directed is ensuring that there is someone in whose favour the court can decree performance. As Hayton explained the reasoning in *Denley*, there do not need to be beneficiaries with immediate possession of rights in the trust property; rather, it is enough if there is someone who can control the trustees by taking them to court, so that there is then someone in whose favour the court can decree performance. By extension, Hayton argues that the enforcer (or protector) concept provides someone in whose favour the court can decree performance of the trust: that does not need to be the beneficiary. Thus, argues Hayton, the trust's irreducible core content can include beneficiaries without rights against the trustees.

This argument is advanced so as to allow English trusts law to assist Cayman Island and other offshore trusts models to flourish. It suggests that English trusts law could develop to assist financial services activity in other jurisdictions. Quite why the English jurisdiction and the UK public exchequer *should* take this step is unclear, as is considered at the end of this chapter. There is nothing in it for

---

[19] P. Matthews, 'STAR: big bang or red dwarf?' (1998) 12 *Trust Law International* 98.

[20] A. Duckworth, 'STAR WARS: Smiting the Bull' (1999) 13 *Trust Law International* 158.

[21] P. Matthews, 'Paul Matthews writes ...' (1999) 13 *Trust Law International* 168.

[22] Hayton, above n 7. See also the essays in D. Hayton, *Extending the Boundaries of Trusts and Similar Ring-fenced Funds* (Kluwer Law International, 2002) (including a reprint of the *LQR* article).

English law, nor for the UK public exchequer except a large fall in the amount of tax that will be received from people who take advantage of those newly reinforced trusts structures.

## Protectors

### Whether protectors are fiduciaries or beneficiaries

Protectors do not exist formally in English trusts law and yet they are used frequently. Moreover, the term 'protector' (as well as other purported synonyms such as 'enforcer') has no single definition but rather is used in many different ways. Those two sentences may seem to present an impossible pair of paradoxes, but they are a fair representation of the position. It is commonly the case that someone is appointed under the terms of a trust to look after the interests of the beneficiaries by controlling some of the trustees' functions, or to ensure that the settlor's intentions are put into effect by trustees operating under a discretionary trust, or using fiduciary powers of appointment or advancement. This may be done by giving the protector a right to veto the actions, decisions or exercises of discretion by the trustees; or by giving the protector the right to appoint trust property for specified purposes; or by giving the protector the right to appoint or remove trustees; or by giving the protector the right to negotiate and to settle trustees' fees and other commissions. The protector may be a specialist with a power to oversee the trustees' dealings with particular property, for example a tree surgeon overseeing the treatment of trees held on trust, or a horse whisperer overseeing racehorses held on trust. This needs to be done, for UK tax purposes, in such a way that the trustees do not appear to have their freedom to manage the trust's affairs controlled by the protector.[23]

It is important to recognise that in the English trusts lexicon there is no single definition of what is meant by the term 'protector'. The question arises as to the proper analysis of the protector's role under English trusts law. Under many other systems of trusts law – particularly in offshore jurisdictions – specific legislation has been drafted to specify the role and purpose of such protectors. In England and Wales, however, no such legislation nor any such case law principles exist. Thus the following analysis is predicated entirely on a commonsense attempt to categorise the sorts of roles which are granted to protectors.

The first possibility is that protectors are in fact trustees themselves. The careful structuring of the tax avoidance specialist will seek to have the protector occupy no trustee-like role; however, if the protector is able to veto the decisions of trustees and so forth then the issue must arise whether or not the protector is acting as some sort of trustee. If the trustees decide to invest in x and the protector intervenes to prevent an investment in x, how are we to understand the power of this protector? This person has the right to gainsay the decisions of trustees and therefore she must be acting with a power equivalent to that of trustees. Could this

---

[23] See R. Venables, *Non-resident Trusts* (Key Haven Publications, 2005).

protector act capriciously in so doing? The answer must be 'no'. The protector is empowered to act in relation to another person's right in property, namely that of the beneficiaries. This must constitute a fiduciary role to the extent that it involves control of the decisions of the trustees themselves. It would be possible to have other roles allocated to the protector – such as making the tea at trustees' meetings – which would not be fiduciary in nature. However, in general terms, given that the protector's actions will have direct effects on the rights of the beneficiaries to the trust fund, it must be the case that the protector is occupying a fiduciary capacity in deciding whether or not to gainsay the decisions of the trustees. Taking control of the decisions of the trustees in this manner means that the protector is able to take control of the 'rudder' guiding the trustees' actions and decisions. If this person was not named 'protector' in the trust instrument already then any person who took control of the trust in this fashion would be considered to be a trustee de son tort and so be construed to be a trustee. Either way, the protector is acting 'in loco trustee' and so must be considered to be a species of trustee with control over certain aspects of the trust property.

The second possibility relates to the preceding paragraph, whereby the protector exists so that there need not be any beneficiary with vested proprietary rights which might attract liability to tax. The trustees' aim (in their alternative role beyond the trust as a financial services provider) is to seek investors who will contribute to the trust fund in the expectation that the presence of a protector will replace the need for the beneficiaries to have any vested proprietary rights in that trust fund; if the investors retain no proprietary rights then it is hoped that there will be no tax payable on any profits their investments realise, and furthermore the protector's presence will also enable them to supervise the activities of the trustees on behalf of the beneficiaries. The difficulty, as explained in the previous paragraph, is that English law does not permit a trust without a beneficiary. Thus, even if an offshore jurisdiction were to enact legislation permitting a trust to exist without investors needing to have equitable proprietary rights, there would be the problem that such a trust would not be recognised as being valid in England and Wales and therefore the investor would be treated as continuing to hold an equitable interest in her investment on resulting trust principles. For this English law analysis not to work, the protector would be required to have the equitable interest in the property vested in it. That would be something which the investor may not wish to countenance, particularly given that the purpose of the transaction would be to transfer the profits to the investors so that the protector would not really be intended to hold the equitable interest. The consequence of pretending that the protector owned the equitable interest, when in reality it would be treated as though it remained the property of the investor, would be that the trust would be treated as being a sham and the equitable interest treated by English law as belonging to the investors.

### How the protector could operate in practice
Having considered the circumstances in which a protector would be a fiduciary or, worse, a beneficiary, this section considers how, in general terms, the protector

could function in practice. There are three models: the private industry model, the private beneficiary model and the public model.

First, the private industry model. A protector could be appointed by the trusts service provider who sells the trust structure to investors. It would need to be asked who that person might be. Akin to an old-fashioned unit trust model, it could be a person separate from the service provider whose sole role is to hold the fund for safekeeping. Such a person, if holding the property, would be a trustee properly so-called and so not a separate person. Therefore, it is supposed that the protector would have to have a different role from that. It would then need to be asked who pays for the protector. If the service provider were to pay the protector's expenses and fees then the protector would be nothing more than a creature of the service provider. If the protector were acting for a number of trusts operated by the service provider, then there would be a very close link between the two people which would call into question their independence. In a small island community, in any event, one would have to query the credibility of a system in which the protectors would not become so close to the service providers as to call into question their independence. There are then issues regarding who would oversee the functioning of the system to ensure that the protector was keeping a sufficiently close watch over the service provider, what punishments the service provider would face for failing to acquire the services of a protector, and so forth. All-in-all, this structure seems to lack credibility, unless the protector is a person independent of the trustees and the trusts service provider.

Secondly, the private beneficiary model in which, presumably, the beneficiaries themselves would pay for the protector. To pay for a professional protector would add to the costs of investing and would be unattractive to the investor. A cheap protector, though, would probably offer no genuine protection at all. Further, how could the beneficiaries select the protector if the beneficiaries are not known to one another (and so could not agree on a single protector) and if the identity of the only professionals available was proprietary knowledge held by the service provider?

Thirdly, the public model, in which the protector is an official appointed by the government of the state in which the services are provided. We are asked to bear in mind, it should be recalled, that the continued rude health of offshore trusts services is vital to the island economies involved, and therefore we must proceed cautiously with ideas of well-funded public protectors aping the scale of the UK's Financial Conduct Authority. If the trusts services sector is indeed so important to the island economies, then there is immediately a difficulty with appointing a public official whose diligence might constitute a threat to the free functioning of those activities. Assuming a diligent public servant insulated from the island's economic future (and from the fear of forcing service providers to move their operations elsewhere), how broad would this person's remit and function be? Financial services regulation in the European Union (EU), for example, contains detailed codes on matters such as financial promotion, market abuse and conduct of business. Each area (and many more) has detailed rulebooks which are maintained and implemented by different departments of the regulatory body. Significantly, while the Financial Conduct Authority in the UK is concerned to protect the integrity of the financial markets and to protect the public interest, any 'protection' of investors in private trusts services will be directed only at the limited needs of the investors as beneficiaries. This, after all, is the purpose of replacing the beneficiary principle with a protector: to consider the narrow interests of the investor-beneficiary – to maintain secrecy, to minimise the liability to tax, and to satisfy the courts in England and elsewhere that there is just enough of a structure here to permit them to relax their laws.

This would be a shameful premise on which to alter English law so as to remove the beneficiary principle and to permit protectors to displace the need for a beneficiary. A protector is an anaemic sop to the policy underlying the beneficiary principle, but it will offer no valuable regulatory function whatsoever. More interesting in this regard is the introduction of the EC Savings Directive and other, similar international initiatives which compel provision of information by service providers in many contexts. This development is interesting not only because it threatens the secrecy of some funds but also because it demonstrates what real regulation is about. Real regulation is predicated on public policy which is concerned primarily with the public good and with shining a light into the dark corners of financial activity. The term 'transparency' is important in EU financial regulation because it underpins the common policy of the Member States to prevent fraud and criminal activity from thriving in the shadows by making all of the relevant information visible to investors and to regulators alike. By contrast, offshore trusts services rely on opacity to function. They cannot be relied upon to introduce 'protective' structures which will meet the case.

## DIFFERENCES IN THE USE OF TRUSTS IN OTHER JURISDICTIONS

The preceding discussion has outlined some of the key differences in municipal trusts laws outside England among the offshore jurisdictions. The principal use of trusts which was outlined above was regulatory avoidance. There are, however, different cultural considerations which arise when trusts are introduced to legal systems which had not previously included trusts as part of their jurisprudence. The two examples given here are Malta and Sicily.

I was asked to address a conference on the trust at the invitation of the University of Catania, Sicily. Sadly, one of the connections which many people make when they hear about Sicily is with the Mafia. That is, of course, to overlook the beauty of the island; the dramatic, volcanic presence of Mount Etna seemingly wherever you are; and the vibrancy of the street life. The conference itself took place in a beautiful villa in Catania. Before the conference began, on a bright, sunny morning, dozens of elegant cars disgorged dozens of elegant Sicilians outside the entrance. Somewhat disconcertingly, we had had to pass through gates guarded by gun-toting Caribinieri before we were allowed to pull up next to the classically delightful villa. The conference venue itself was accessed down several flights of stairs, which opened out unexpectedly into a large, ultra-modern, underground meeting venue, with a stage at one end (complete with microphones organised on a long, cloth-covered table), a suite of booths for translators to deliver simultaneous translations of the speakers' words into Italian via the headphones concealed in the arm rests of every seat, and exquisitely comfortable seating for about a hundred people. The slick modernity of the underground conference venue was such a surprise, after the traditional, chocolate box beauty of the villa at ground level, that it was like entering a Bond villain's lair.[24]

The purpose of the conference was to consider the use of trusts in Sicily. As is usual on these occasions, the English trusts lawyer wants to speak in detail about recent case law on specific uses of the trust, while the overseas audience wants to consider at a more abstract level what the uses of trusts could be in their jurisdiction which are not already catered for (by company law and contract law), and what the risks might be. What was particular to Sicily, however, was the concern that the trust threatened to make it easier for participants in organised crime to conceal their ill-gotten gains.

Next to me on the speakers' dais was a young judge. His role in the Sicilian legal system was both to investigate Mafia-related crime and to bring its participants to trial.[25] This young man had a constant armed guard, as did many of the people in the audience. So, whereas my English discussion of equity and trusts can begin with Aristotle and ideas of conscience, for a criminal law judge in Sicily, the principal use of a trust would be to conceal criminals' assets. (Indeed my talk was almost entirely centred on exploring this cultural difference.) The challenge for this judge, in a legal system which used trusts, would be to track down criminal assets hidden in trust funds. Because ordinary trusts do not require registration, there is no public record of the beneficial ownership of their property, nor of the trustees, nor of the property which they hold. Therefore, for an investigator it is difficult to identify criminal property, when compared to the public registration which is required for companies. Consequently, trusts can be used to achieve secrecy for wrongdoing settlors who are, for example, criminals. Paradoxically, the conscience-based trust may be the organised criminal's best friend.

By contrast, the remarkable jurisdiction of Malta is approaching the trust quite differently. The history of Malta is predicated on its physical presence as a solid rock in the middle of the Mediterranean. The heroic resistance of its people during the Great Siege of 1565 and the role played by Malta during the Second World War are only parts of the story of this island. The next chapter in its history began when it joined the EU and, like Cyprus, was assumed by many people (eager to make an untaxed profit from financial speculation) to be a sort of offshore jurisdiction within the EU, thus having many of the clandestine advantages of an offshore

---

[24] Seriously. It was only missing a map of the world, scientists with clipboards and a sinister voice counting down the time to lift-off. It was just like a James Bond film from the 1970s. There was, after all, even a nearby volcano.

[25] The excellent Italian film *La Scorta* (1993; dir. Ricky Tognazzi) is a vivid depiction of the life of a 'Mafia judge', and the dangers which they and their families face.

jurisdiction with the protections afforded by EU law. However, the Malta Financial Services Authority has always made it clear that it will prevent any harm being caused to the island by its financial system and by these sorts of opportunists.

When Malta decided in the twenty-first century to introduce trusts law by statute into its legal system, two things were evident. First, the trusts laws of Malta would require the registration of trusts, thus making it more difficult to use Maltese trusts to conceal property or beneficial ownership of property. Secondly, Maltese trusts law would focus only on the express trust, leaving the 'remedies' (as they would put it) associated with constructive trusts and so forth out of their jurisprudence. The utilitarian purpose of the express trust would be to facilitate investment by 'funds' in the island's economy and to grant the people of Malta the advantages of the trust structure. While the law of trusts in Malta has been interpreted in accordance with English law principles,[26] it is otherwise predicated entirely on its own statute.

Two points emerge from these discussions. First, the trust has a pragmatic use in many non-Anglophone jurisdictions which did not have the trust as part of their legal systems. There is no interest there in the historical pedigree of English trusts law, nor in its centuries of precedent. On the downside, what this does mean is that their trusts laws will not have the principles built into them which have proved necessary over the centuries in England and Wales to resolve situations in which trustees commit fraud, in which it is unclear at which point in time the objects of a discretionary trust acquire vested interests, and so forth. Without the English general principles, it is more difficult to generate principled answers to these questions. Secondly, the trust may pose the problem of being used, de facto, for illegal purposes because it is so adept at concealing ownership, at concealing property, and at concealing the terms on which the trustees are required to act. Consequently, a system of registration and regulation akin to company law in most jurisdictions becomes necessary to combat this sort of behaviour. That many jurisdictions do not have a system of registration demonstrates that they are open to this sort of abuse: omission seeming very similar to commission.

## Debate 3

### How should international trusts law be understood politically and morally?

#### IS INTERNATIONAL TRUSTS LAW IMMORAL?

The question which arises in relation to the sorts of trusts structures used in offshore jurisdictions for tax avoidance purposes, which have been considered in this chapter, is whether or not they are simply immoral. The answer must be: yes.

---

[26] The first case in Maltese trusts law adopted statements in Hudson, *Equity & Trusts* as being correct statements of the law in Malta.

The purposes of the clients who use offshore trusts services are solely to avoid regulatory oversight or their tax responsibilities. Those clients are necessarily very wealthy individuals (so as to be able to afford the fees involved in acquiring this sort of sophisticated legal and financial advice). The reason they invest in jurisdictions like the Cook Islands, the British Virgin Islands or the Isle of Man is that they do not want to contribute their share to the cost of maintaining the society in which they live in the UK, or the USA or wherever by paying taxes there. Instead, they use the roads, are defended by the police and armed forces, and so forth, all of which are funded by their taxpaying fellow citizens. Paying taxes is perhaps the most moral thing that a person can do in a civilised society – through our taxes we fund our common life.[27]

Offshore jurisdictions have always traded on their secrecy, even though most of them are reliant on countries like the UK and the USA for military and other kinds of support. This use of secrecy has meant that criminal and terrorist organisations have been able to use these services beyond the oversight of authorities in the jurisdictions which they want to attack or in which they want to conduct other criminal activities. The financial services industries have become the most significant businesses in terms of their size on these islands, although it is questionable to what extent ordinary islanders derive a benefit from the high finance which is notionally conducted nearby. That these jurisdictions host this sort of activity is demonstrative of a lack of morality.

There are jurisdictions in Europe which conduct the same sorts of activities. In Switzerland – inside Europe but outside the EU – the banking industry has long relied on the secrecy of its activities (and the possibility to have anonymous, numbered bank accounts) as a unique selling point. In recent years, the Swiss have been forced to agree to exchange information with the EU. Scandals about the quantity of stolen gold and other property that was deposited with Swiss banks by the Nazis during the 1939–45 war continue, quite rightly, to embarrass the Swiss nation, and in particular its bankers. Liechtenstein is a tiny, snow-covered territory in Europe which exists, so far as one can tell, solely to ensure that hospitals are not built in EU countries, by sucking capital away from the tax authorities in those countries and into its low-tax financial services industry. The Channel Islands, which are UK protectorates, serve the same function, as does the Isle of Man.

Luxembourg has become infamous because, in spite of being inside the EU, it allows large numbers of multinational corporations to register in its territory and to use 'transfer pricing' techniques to move their income there for tax purposes. As a result, companies like Amazon and Starbucks effectively pay no tax in the UK. Starbucks has a subsidiary in Luxembourg which buys coffee from suppliers around the world and then sells that coffee to other Starbucks subsidiaries in

---

[27] By contrast 'philanthropists' are often wealthy people who pay little tax but who insist on public celebration when they do contribute anything to the common wealth. Charities in practice are repositories for tax avoidance in many circumstances, as successive reworkings of the regulation of charities have acknowledged. Taxes are to be preferred to charities.

various European countries. Coincidentally, the charge which the Luxembourg subsidiary levies for that coffee is exactly the same as the other subsidiaries' annual profits in the UK, thus leaving no taxable profits in the UK. Alternatively, these sorts of internal movements of money within corporate groups are achieved by way of charges being levied between subsidiary companies to use the business's intellectual property which is also registered in low-tax Luxembourg. In Ireland, the investment zone around Dublin, with its low tax structure, has attracted a large number of technology companies like Dell.

When a country sets up a low-tax zone to encourage investment, it is impossible for that country to protest at the amount of tax it can raise there; but in relation to the use of complex trusts schemes offshore, the questions are different. The use of tax avoidance structures of this sort is demonstrative of a decision by the individual client to avoid being part of a civilised society. It is a decision to distance oneself from the obligations which are accepted by other members of society towards the human beings around them.

The common riposte is that tax avoidance is lawful, and that it is tax evasion which is illegal. It is true that tax evasion is illegal. However, tax avoidance may be conducted disingenuously, and in consequence it cannot be known whether or not a purported tax avoidance structure is lawful until it is examined by a court. There are examples in investment banking, especially in the 1990s, of creating entirely disingenuous derivatives structures which were organised entirely on the basis that they appeared at first blush to fall outside the concepts which were contained (on an entirely literal reading) in the statutes at the time, and which were never revealed to the tax authorities so that their efficacy could not be analysed. Much of the beauty of offshore trusts structures has been their secrecy: if no one knows where the money is then no one can tax it or recover it. While all tax laws deliberately create excluded categories of activity which are deliberately encouraged by being exempted from tax, the sorts of tax avoidance structures which are being considered here trade on finding unintentional gaps in the tax laws which may be exploited.

What is remarkable is how little effort tax authorities have devoted hitherto in combating these jurisdictions. Territories like the Cook Islands would struggle without the protection New Zealand offers them; the Isle of Man similarly in relation to the UK. Even in times of economic austerity, those tax authorities and their governments have been slow to take action.

## SHAKY PRACTICE: A TRAVESTY OF A MOCKERY OF A SHAM

A particularly important issue in the treatment of tax avoidance structures in English trusts law is the pretence that an arrangement has the feature $x$ when the true state of affairs is $y$. In defining what is meant by a 'sham', Diplock LJ held that a sham constitutes:[28]

---

[28] *Snook v London and West Riding Investments Ltd* [1967] 2 QB 786, 802.

'acts done or documents executed by the parties to the "sham" which are intended by them to give to third parties or to the court the appearance of creating between the parties legal rights and obligations different from the actual legal rights and obligations (if any) which the parties intended to create ...'

Therefore, a sham is a scheme of action or a pattern of documentation which seeks to create the impression that the state of affairs is one thing when in fact it is something else. An example would be the purported creation of a trust to make it appear that the settlor had divested herself of property, whereas in fact the property is still be held for her use and enjoyment such that it could be said that she still owns it outright.[29] It is a requirement of finding a transaction to be a sham that the parties to that sham intended to deceive other people as to the nature of their true rights.[30] For example, when Mr Wyatt claimed that his interest in his home had been settled on trust for his wife and daughters, but when he had nevertheless used the house as security for loans for his business and when he had failed to tell his wife about the trust so that it was not mentioned when the couple divorced, it was held that the trust was in essence a sham.[31]

It commonly happens that trust structures are created to give the appearance of one state of affairs when the truth is actually something different. Much of commercial life is artificial. For example, the company is treated as being a legal person with the ability to make contracts, to own property and so forth, even though it has no tangible existence but rather acts through its human agents. No one questions the validity of this model of the company with legal personality and with limited liability for its shareholders. However, these things can be taken too far. It happens that professionals sometimes operate their offshore trusts structures ineffectively. For example, imagine a financial services firm in London selling tax avoidance advice to a British client in London, to the effect that a trust resident in a particular offshore jurisdiction would be efficient for her. The firm should ensure that employees in the offshore jurisdiction actually manage the trust in that jurisdiction, that the assets of the trust are resident in the offshore jurisdiction and so forth. However, because the managers and the client are in London, it sometimes happens that the professionals and the client meet in London to conduct the trustees' meetings. To keep up appearances, they would (as I have seen myself) fax the minutes of that meeting to the office in the offshore jurisdiction, so that the appearance of meetings being held in the offshore jurisdiction could be maintained. What sometimes happened, however, was that the fax was placed straight on the file, complete with the London fax number of the professionals printed at the top of it, thus demonstrating that the meeting was actually held in London. The tax structure, under UK revenue law, will generally be dependent on the trust actually being managed from the offshore jurisdiction and its controlling mind (as

---

[29] *Minwalla v Minwalla* [2004] 7 ITELR 457.
[30] *Scott v Federal Commissioner of Taxation (No 2)* (1966) ALJR 265, 279, *per* Windeyer J.
[31] *Midland Bank v Wyatt* [1995] 1 FLR 697.

well as the majority of its trustees) being resident in the offshore jurisdiction. The sham of management in the offshore jurisdiction, with the reality of management being conducted in London, may well unpick the validity of this structure for tax purposes.

## THE CHANGING CONTEXT OF THE LAW IN OFFSHORE JURISDICTIONS

The four criteria which the OECD used to identify 'tax haven' status were as follows:

1. the levying of no or only nominal taxes;
2. a lack of the transparency which would ensure open and consistent implementation of tax laws and the preparation of appropriate accounting information;
3. the absence of laws concerning sharing information with the relevant agencies of other governments or supra-national bodies, including bank secrecy; and
4. the lack of any need for any substantial activities to be carried on in the jurisdiction. (This fourth criterion was dropped in 2001.)

Having identified a list of such jurisdictions, the OECD set out to cajole them into changing their laws.[32]

An important part of this development was the effect of two OECD reports. The first identified a list of 38 'unco-operative tax havens' in 1998. The concern is with the quality of the administrative practices in those jurisdictions in sharing information with other governmental and supra-national agencies. The second report, which has been updated annually since 2000 under the title *Towards Global Tax Co-operation*,[33] surveys the tax and trusts laws, and also assesses the administrative practices of a growing number of jurisdictions, not just those which were considered to be transparent in relation to the assets and activities within their jurisdictions. Thirty-five jurisdictions which were originally identified on the OECD list in 1998 as being 'unco-operative tax havens' have since given undertakings to implement transparency standards and to engage in the exchange of information with other jurisdictions for tax purposes. Consequently, there are no jurisdictions on that list today, although the amount of information which is actually being provided is unclear and the OECD retains clear concerns about corruption in many jurisdictions in the world.[34]

The work involved in greater tax co-operation is an ongoing project. Consequently, while many of these jurisdictions have not recently changed their substantive law, their administrative practices and public policy pronouncements on international co-operation have changed. It is a classic demonstration of the difference between the form which the law takes and the substantial effect of its implementation. In this new world, being identified as a tax haven is not a good

---

[32] These changes are discussed in Hudson, above n 17, at 442 *et seq.*
[33] *Towards Global Tax Co-operation 2010* (OECD Publishing, 2010).
[34] Ibid, accessed on 29 June 2011.

thing: nevertheless, the Internet positively hums with enthusiastic websites offering advice on finding 'tax havens' and offering professional services in them. The upshot of the OECD initiative was a change of the culture in those tax havens and an ostensible readiness to become more co-operative. Whether real change has been effected remains to be seen.

## THE DEVELOPMENT OF FINANCIAL REGULATION

It is worth spending a moment on the development of international financial regulatory standards in offshore jurisdictions. While the principal focus of the legal treatment of asset protection in the literature has focused on questions of shielding assets from insolvency and on questions of tax efficiency, there is a growing perception that asset protection structures are used for regulatory avoidance and to facilitate international criminal activities. Indeed, it is a fear that these structures could be used for those purposes, particularly in the wake of the 9/11 terrorist attack on New York, allied to long-standing concerns about regulatory avoidance more generally, which has led to pressure being applied to offshore jurisdictions to become more open about the asset protection and other activities which are conducted through their territories. In the wake of the global financial crisis which began in 2007 there is also a renewed focus on fighting tax avoidance structures as a means of increasing governmental revenue in developed jurisdictions. The types of regulation which have increased in intensity in recent years are money-laundering regulation, financial stability regulation, and insider dealing and market abuse regulation, as well as the private law context of conduct of business regulation. International standards on distinct areas of financial regulation, ranging from the maintenance of bank capital to minimum standards of information provision in the issue of securities, have begun to inform many of the jurisdictions which were formerly identified as being 'unco-operative tax havens'.

The response of the offshore jurisdictions to the larger project of regulating financial markets and dealing with corruption and bribery has been piecemeal. On the one hand, tightening regulation and increasing the level of transparency in jurisdictions as diverse as large and developed Switzerland at one end of the scale and the small island nations at the other, carries the risk that investment will fall and that business will leave, seeking other jurisdictions with less regulatory oversight. On the other hand, a perception of legitimacy is necessary to attract legitimate investment and to allow those offshore jurisdictions to avoid pariah status in the context of increased concerns about global security.

The financial service providers who deal in the offshore jurisdictions are local professionals, but they are more commonly subsidiaries of global investment banks and similar financial institutions, and affiliates of accountancy and law firms. Therefore, the local regulation of these service providers is, at one level, only a part of the regulatory tapestry.

## IN CONCLUSION

Perhaps the final word should be left to that great champion of a moral form of equity, Lord Denning. His Lordship was asked in *Re Weston's Settlement* to award a variation of a trust in favour of a child beneficiary on the sole basis that it would avoid UK tax by 'exporting' that trust outside the UK. Lord Denning held as follows:[35]

> 'Many a child has been ruined by being given too much. The avoidance of tax may be lawful, but it is not yet a virtue. The Court of Chancery should not encourage or support it – it should not give its approval to it – if by so doing it would imperil the true welfare of the children, already born or yet to be born.'

Lord Denning's complex, esoteric creativity as a judge is very much out of fashion. As an undergraduate law student in the late 1980s, I found that much of the law I was studying was a reaction to Denning's creativity in the 1970s as the courts took the opportunity to unpick many of his developments. However, what Lord Denning did have, on occasion, was a clear eye for the morally correct approach to the law. In *Re Weston* he appears to have hit the nail on the head. The ultimate irony in trusts law is that a doctrine which began life as a means of ensuring just outcomes on Aristotle's model, has since become used in practice so as to elude tax and to fund international crime.

---

[35] [1969] 1 Ch 234, at 245.

# 6

# TRUSTEESHIP

## INTRODUCTION

The role of the trustee is central to an express trust. While trusts law generally considers that ultimate ownership rests with the beneficiaries, all of the hard work in the management of the trust is carried out by the trustees. This chapter examines some of the key debates in the legal treatment of trustees and their duties. There are three key issues identified here. First, whether or not there is an 'irreducible core' content to trusteeship, as has been suggested, and whether the law on excluding trustees' liabilities undermines the very concept of there being such an irreducible core. Indeed, the remaining debates in relation to the concept of trustees that are considered in this chapter all seem to call into question whether there is such a core content. The second issue asks whether or not there is really such a thing as one single kind of trustee, especially given the number of types of trustee which are subject to statutory regulation of different kinds. The third debate considers the investment of trusts, and asks how the Trustee Act 2000 has impacted on the standards imposed on trustees but not on very important types of trusts like pension funds and unit trusts.

## Debate 1

### What does it mean to be a trustee?

The central problem with trusteeship is knowing what trusteeship involves. What are the obligations imposed on a trustee? What standards must the trustee observe? The term 'trusteeship' connotes the state of being a trustee; but, significantly, the precise obligations which are bound up with being a trustee will mean different things from context to context. The point about fiduciary duties in general terms is that they differ from context to context: they arise 'sub modo'. The same is true of trustees, as is explained below given the different contexts in which trustees operate and the different legislative codes which bind some of them (such as unit trusts and pension funds). There are also differences within what we might term 'ordinary trusts'. For example, a trust which compels a person to invest trust property differs from a trust which compels a person to maintain a house for the occupancy of the beneficiaries. The former trust involves expertise in investment markets (whether the trustees are expert, or whether the trustees delegate their powers to investment professionals), whereas the latter involves basic property management (whether the trustees clear the gutters themselves, or whether the trustees delegate their powers to others). The former context also involves regulation by the Financial Conduct Authority beyond the reach of trusts law; whereas the latter context may involve the Trusts of Land and Appointment of Trustees Act 1996, informing the rights of the beneficiaries and the obligations of the trustees.

## THE IRREDUCIBLE, CORE CONTENT OF TRUSTEESHIP

Professor David Hayton first proposed the idea that trusts law should recognise an 'irreducible core content' of trusteeship in an essay published in 1996.[1] His point was that we should draw a line beyond which any arrangement created between parties should not be considered to be a trust. Why is this necessary? There are many circumstances in which people want to create a trust so that they can have the benefit of trustees managing their property, but without some inconvenient tax treatments of specific types of trusts or without some inconvenient aspects of mainstream trusts law which are excluded in the trust instrument (such as the beneficiary principle). The question then is whether those people have created a trust or something else, like a contract, an agency or a bailment arrangement. Many settlors may therefore wish to have the benefits of a trust in some senses (for example, to acquire protection against insolvency) while not having the features of a trust in other senses (for example, avoiding having a vested equitable interest in the property for tax purposes).

The approach which Millett LJ took to the concept of the 'irreducible core content of trusteeship' in *Armitage v Nurse* was the following:[2]

> '[T]here is an irreducible core of obligations owed by the trustees to the beneficiaries and enforceable by them which is fundamental to the concept of a trust. If the beneficiaries have no rights enforceable against the trustees there are no trusts. But I do not accept the further submission that their core obligations include the duties of skill and care, prudence and diligence. The duty of trustees to perform the trusts honestly and in good faith for the benefit of the beneficiaries is the minimum necessary to give substance to the trusts, but in my opinion it is sufficient.'

So, there we have it: the irreducible core content of a trust is an obligation to be honest. There must be some duties imposed on the trustees, but they need not be as demanding as being skilful, careful, prudent or diligent. So apparently, you can be a trustee as long as you are honest, but you can also be untalented, cack-handed and careless without necessarily calling your performance into question.

---

[1] D. Hayton, 'The irreducible core content of trusteeship' in A. Oakley (ed.), *Trends in Contemporary Trusts Law* (Oxford University Press, 1996), 47.
[2] [1998] Ch 241.

This standard is not particularly demanding – if all that is required is that the trustees must not be dishonest then that does not mark trustees out as being very different from parties to an ordinary contract, let alone other forms of fiduciary. There must be an argument that this approach to fiduciary duties for trustees is simply wrong in principle. Trustees are expected to occupy a radically different relationship to their beneficiaries – which includes bearing liability to them for any loss caused by breach of trust, an obligation to take no unauthorised profits and so forth – from the sorts of relationships which arise in ordinary contract law.

Professor Hayton saw the core of the trust concept as being a 'duty of confidence imposed on a trustee in respect of particular property and positively enforceable'[3] by a beneficiary. This includes a power to make the trustees account to the beneficiaries. What is lacking, however, is any statement as to whether a trust requires a beneficiary with a proprietary right in the trust property, or a trustee who owes obligations of good conscience and so forth. Instead, the limitation is on the role of the trustee.

The important sub-text among the commentators is that there should be two changes made to traditional trusts law. First, that trustees should be entitled to have their liability for breach of trust limited by the terms of the trust instrument, so that the trustees are liable to compensate the beneficiaries for any loss they suffer only if the trustees were actually dishonest. This issue is considered next. Secondly, that a trust should be allowed to exist under English law without the need for a beneficiary with a vested interest (so that tax-free investments may be made through trusts in the way that is discussed in Chapter 5).

## EXCLUSION OF LIABILITY

A particularly significant question in trusts law practice is whether or not trustees may limit their liabilities for breach of trust, or exclude them entirely. The position under English law at present is that trustees may have their liabilities for breach of trust limited in the trust instrument for any malfeasance, from innocent carelessness up to gross negligence.[4] Therefore, even a professional trustee (that is, someone who charges for the service of acting as trustee, whether a solicitor, an accountant or a banker) can avoid liability for breach of trust on the basis that they were careless, negligent or grossly negligent. Trustees may not exclude their liability if they have been dishonest.[5] The question which arises is whether a person who is able to act negligently in breach of trust without having to compensate the beneficiaries (and while still charging their fee) can really be considered to be a trustee who is acting in good conscience at all.

So, if a trustee is entitled to exclude some of the liabilities, can that person really be considered to be a trustee? In essence, is there some minimum level of liability

---

[3] Hayton, above n 1.
[4] *Armitage v Nurse* [1998] Ch 241.
[5] Ibid.

which must be borne by all trustees so that they can still properly be considered to be trustees as opposed to something else? The existence of the law on exclusion of liability means that express trusts law comes to resemble contract law in one important respect: the liabilities of the parties are limited by an instrument (whether trust or contract), and are thus not determined entirely by the general law.

The debate runs as follows. On the one hand, a person who agrees to act as a trustee may require the reassurance that their liabilities will be limited before they agree to act. In particular in relation to professionals (such as solicitors and accountants, or even non-professionals like bankers), the service which is rendered as part of the trustee's role will be paid for under a contract as well as regulated by a trust instrument. In such a situation, before they agree to act, professionals acting as trustees will require their contractual and fiduciary liabilities to be limited both by the contract they will create with their client (i.e. the settlor) and by the trust instrument which sets out their fiduciary obligations. Consequently, acquiring the best trustees in many circumstances will require that those trustees have the protection of exclusion of liability provisions.

On the other hand, if there is something special about the fiduciary obligations of a trustee, then they should be protected by trusts law. Maintaining the distinctiveness of trustees' obligations requires that those obligations cannot be excluded by the trust instrument and reduced, in effect, to mere contractual obligations. In differentiating between a trust and a contract, the two main features of the trust are that the beneficiaries acquire proprietary rights in the trust property and that the trustees owe fiduciary and proprietary obligations to the beneficiaries in relation to the trust property (as opposed to purely personal obligations in damages and so forth under contract law). Therefore, to maintain the integrity of the trust concept requires that there is something distinct about it. So, let us consider what some of those things might be.

As outlined above, in *Armitage v Nurse*, Millett LJ considered that the irreducible core of the trust concept required that trustees must be honest. This seems a very thin distinction between the trust and anything else. Without becoming metaphysical, it is difficult to imagine a situation in which the law actively permits or supports dishonesty. In general, the law sets its cap against dishonesty, as with liability for theft, dishonest assistance, civil fraud, criminal fraud, misrepresentation and so forth. Thus, nothing is achieved by drawing the line at what makes something a trust as opposed to a contract by identifying the prevention of 'dishonesty' as being the principal point of distinction.

In the Privy Council decision in *Spread Trustee Company Ltd v Hutcheson*,[6] two dissenting judgments by Lady Hale and Lord Kerr doubted the validity of the *Armitage* principle. As Lord Kerr put it:[7]

---

6 [2012] 1 All ER 251. See generally P. Matthews, 'The efficacy of trustee exemption clauses in English law' [1989] Conv 42, which is referred to extensively by the Privy Council.

7 [2012] 1 All ER 251, at [180].

'If, as I suggested at the beginning of this judgment, the placing of reliance on a responsible person to manage property so as to promote the interests of the beneficiaries of a trust is central to the concept of trusteeship, denying trustees the opportunity to avoid liability for their gross negligence seems to be entirely in keeping with that essential aim.'

In other words: if trustees are retained to look after other people's property then it makes sense to prevent those trustees from excluding liability for their own negligence. It can hardly be said to set too high a standard for a trustee to avoid grossly negligent performances of their duties. Lord Kerr reminded us that the claimant in *Armitage v Nurse* was a 17-year-old girl who was reliant on the trustees' looking after her rights in the property before those trustees were negligent. Allowing trustees to limit or exclude their liabilities in these circumstances cannot possibly encourage them to strain every sinew in the service of that beneficiary. It is a sign of a slack professional culture that professional trustees put the avoidance of liability before caring for their beneficiaries.

On the one hand, it could be said that the duties of a trustee require more than that the trustee is simply honest. Instead, we should recognise that the fiduciary duties of the trustee require good conscience, the avoidance of conflicts of interest, the avoidance of taking unauthorised profits from the fiduciary office and so forth.[8] On other hand, it could be said that if the standards of trusteeship are set too high then that will dissuade people from acting as trustees. In particular, this may deter professional people from acting as trustees. Therefore, the approach which the law should take is to permit professional people to limit their liabilities by means of an exclusion of liability clause in the trust instrument. The approach which the law takes generally to exclusion of liability language is that it may exclude liability for anything except dishonesty. However, the ramification of permitting the exclusion of liability is that only trustees with sufficient expertise (or with sufficiently good legal advice) will exclude their liabilities in practice, whereas ordinary members of the public who act as trustees will not know that they should exclude their liabilities, and informal trusts like that in *Paul v Constance*[9] will arise verbally without any possibility for the limitation of liability clauses to be drafted.

In consequence, it is more likely that professional trustees will avoid liability for their own carelessness or negligence when that causes loss to the trust, than ordinary members of the public who have agreed to act as trustees. This is a key paradox in trusts law. Professional trustees will ordinarily be paid for their work. Usually they will have marketed themselves as being highly competent professionals, while insisting on exclusion of liability language being included in the trust instrument. They may even carry on the business of trustees as their sole professional activity,

---

[8] For a full discussion of the obligations of trustees, see Alastair Hudson, *Equity & Trusts* (Routledge, 2014) Ch. 8.

[9] [1977] 1 WLR 527.

like the trust management subsidiaries of banks. By contrast, non-professional trustees are unlikely to have held themselves out as having expertise in trust management, and they are more likely to be acting as trustees as a favour to someone else on an unpaid basis. And yet those non-professional trustees will face personal liability for the entire loss suffered by the trust in the event that they commit a breach of trust – a contingency which is all-the-more likely because they are not professionals. Therefore, permitting the exclusion of liability by professional trustees merely encourages them to be careless in their work because they face no potential liability unless they are consciously dishonest.

This is not the case in other areas of law. In finance law, for example, professionals are not permitted to exclude their liability for any breaches of conduct of business regulation when dealing with their customers. What is interesting is that the judges and practitioners in the trusts law field appear to be decades behind the forefront of commercial regulation. The ideology which began to take hold in the UK from the late 1970s onwards was that free markets should be allowed to flourish and that agencies like the law should not interfere in their free operation. As a part of that ideology, it was felt that contract law should not impose any restrictions on the ability of commercial people to contract free of any interference not included in their contracts by themselves voluntarily. Financial regulation takes the opposite approach in the twenty-first century: it is accepted that banks and financial institutions may not act entirely as they please. Instead, those institutions are required to act in the best interests of their clients and to ensure the best available prices for their clients, and are precluded from excluding their liabilities. The modern approach to commercial regulation does not permit commercial people to act as they see fit, although that change in ideology has not percolated down into contract law.

## Debate 2

### Are all trustees the same?

There are significant differences between different types of trustees. This section considers some of the key differences between those different types of trustee.[10] There is nothing unusual in the idea that there is a core minimum to a trustee's obligations when there is no standard form of trusteeship in any event. In this debate we consider the distinction between trustees used in unit trusts, pension funds and so forth, and ask what makes them different.

Some trustees are subject to formal regulation by statutory regulators, whereas other trustees are not. Ordinary trustees are not subject to regulation, unless there is something special about their situation. This is a key point of differentiation between some trustees and others. It is this differentiation which is the key to

---

[10] A.S. Hudson, 'The Regulation of Trustees' in M. Dixon and G. Griffiths (eds), *Contemporary Perspectives on Property, Equity and Trusts Law* (Oxford University Press, 2007), 163.

understanding how the obligations of trustees should be understood in modern trusts practice: as obligations created and limited by trust instruments, as obligations supervised by regulators, as obligations defined by statute or as obligations conceived of entirely in the case law.

The first point, then, is to understand how differentiated trust practice has become: that pension trust schemes differ markedly from trusts of land, from unit trusts and so on. The coverage offered by traditional trusts law is no longer absolute, that is, the decisions of the courts of Chancery are no longer the whole of the law of trusts. So, for example, trustees in unit trusts and occupational pension fund schemes are regulated by the Financial Conduct Authority and the Pensions Regulator respectively. The presence of these regulators constitutes a very different form of oversight from the traditional trusts law model which is based on beneficiaries bringing trustees' malfeasance before the courts, as expressed in the words of Lord Grant MR in *Morice v Bishop of Durham* to the effect that 'there must be someone in whose favour the court can decree performance'.[11] Successive incursions by public policy, in the form of statutory regulators (as in unit trusts and pension funds) and statutory codes on particular uses of trusts (such as the Trusts of Land and Appointment of Trustees Act 1996 and the Trustee Act 2000), are contributing to these marked differences between various forms of trust. Consequently, it is tempting to see trusts law as breaking apart in the way that Lord Browne-Wilkinson predicted that it might in *Target Holdings v Redferns* when he suggested that:[12]

'In the modern world the trust has become a valuable device in commercial and financial dealings. The fundamental principles of equity apply as much to such trusts as they do to the traditional trusts in relation to which those principles were originally formulated. But in my judgment it is important, if the trust is not to be rendered commercially useless, to distinguish between the basic principles of trust law and those specialist rules developed in relation to traditional trusts which are applicable only to such trusts and the rationale of which has no application to trusts of quite a different kind.'

His Lordship assumed that there would need to be a distinction between family settlements which would be subject to their own 'special rules', and other trusts which are used in the commercial context.

In this vein, Professor Hayton has suggested[13] that trustees of pension funds should be considered to be different from trustees of other trusts. This argument appears to be unobjectionable on its face: there is something different in the quality of acting as trustee of a large pension fund when compared to a trustee of, say, a will trust of an individual of limited means. This barely scratches the surface of

---

[11] (1805) 10 Ves 522.

[12] [1996] AC 421.

[13] D. Hayton, 'Pension Trusts and Traditional Trusts: Drastically Different Species of Trusts' [2005] *Conv* 229.

differentiation in trusts law, however. In truth, there have long been great differences between various forms of trust and the various uses to which trusts are put in practice. At the simplest level there were distinctions between strict settlements and other settlements at the very least from the enactment of the Settled Land Act in 1925, as with trusts of land in 1996 with the Trusts of Land and Appointment of Trustees Act, pension fund trusts with the Pensions Act 1995, unit trusts most recently with the Financial Services and Markets Act 2000, and so on as considered below.

Consequently, there is something different about being the trustee of a pension fund when compared to other forms of trustee. If what is meant by this observation is that those trustees must be subject to principles of fiduciary law which are modified to account for their particular context, then the argument seems sensible; whereas, if what is suggested is that pension fund trustees should be subjected to none of the ordinary principles of fiduciary law which apply to trustees generally, then the argument is problematic.

## Debate **3**

### How does the law on the investment of trusts operate?

#### THE ISSUES CONSIDERED IN THIS DEBATE

One of the more important, practical questions governing trusts is the manner in which trusts law deals with the investment of trusts. Following on from the earlier debates in this chapter, there are several different species of trust with different investment objectives and different regulatory schemes governing them. The treatment of trusts investment in most university courses is limited to the investment of ordinary trusts, ignoring many different types of trust which are subject to their own principles: those different types of trust are considered first. Then there are several questions as to the manner in which financial theory should interact with the law on the investment of ordinary trusts.

#### TRUSTEES UNDER FINANCIAL REGULATION

In the financial context, there are several types of fiduciary which are subject to statutory regulation beyond the ordinary law of trusts. So, whereas an ordinary trustee under a traditional trust may limit her liability for any infraction except dishonesty (see above), trustees of regulated trusts are typically not permitted to exclude their liabilities in general terms. Consequently, a trustee of a pension trust under s. 33 of the Pensions Act 1995 bears 'liability for breach of an obligation under any rule of law to take care or exercise skill in the performance of any investment functions', and it is further provided that this liability 'cannot be excluded or restricted by any instrument or agreement'. There is also a statutory restriction placed on the ability of the manager of a unit trust to seek to restrict its own liability in the following terms:

'Any provision of the trust deed of an authorised unit trust scheme is void in so far as it would have the effect of exempting the manager or trustee from liability for any failure to exercise due care and diligence in the discharge of his functions in respect of the scheme.'[14]

So, any provision of the trust deed of an authorised unit trust scheme will be void if it has the effect of exempting the manager or trustee from liability for any failure in due care and diligence.

## THE EXAMPLE OF UNIT TRUSTS

Following on from the above, unit trusts are mutual investment funds which are marketed by financial institutions which operate as their 'scheme manager' and different entities which operate as their 'trustee' – that is, there are two types of fiduciary in a unit trust. The purpose of a unit trust, which is defined as being a trust in UK law further to s. 237 of the Financial Services and Markets Act 2000, is to collect investment capital from the public and to invest it on their behalf according to the terms of the trust instrument. Unit trusts are regulated by the Financial Conduct Authority (FCA) further to the 2000 Act, and under the Collective Investment Schemes (COLL) rulebook which forms part of the *FCA Handbook* (which is the regulatory rulebook governing the conduct of investment business in the UK). Therefore, 'trustees' in relation to unit trusts are governed not only by trusts law but also by the conduct of business and financial promotion rules in the *FCA Handbook*. Those 'trustees' have the terms of their fiduciary duties informed by the FCA rules and not simply by trusts law. The *FCA Handbook* imposes a number of positive obligations on those 'trustees', including obligations to act in the best interests of the client, to ensure 'best execution' (i.e. the best available price and performance) and to ensure that the products sold are suitable for the client (including an obligation to give risk warnings in certain situations). Self-evidently, the context of the fiduciaries in relation to a unit trust is very different from that of the trustees of an ordinary trust. The fiduciaries in a unit trust may not exclude their liabilities, unlike a trustee under an ordinary trust.

Similarly, in relation to pension trusts there is a complex regulatory scheme overseen by the Pensions Regulator in the UK, further to the Pensions Act 1995 and successor legislation. Pensions are trusts, but the obligations which are incumbent on their trustees are very different again from ordinary trusts. Occupational pension schemes occupy such an important role in our social life that they require regulation. Again, trustees in pension funds are not permitted to limit their liabilities in the trust instrument, just as fiduciaries in unit trusts are not permitted to do that. In short, every regulated form of trust is not permitted to allow the limitation of trustees' liabilities: it is only traditional trusts law which continues to permit exclusion of liability.

---

[14] Financial Services and Markets Act 2000, s. 253.

## THE STANDARD OF 'PRUDENCE'

The traditional standard of behaviour under the old case law for trustees when investing the trust fund was 'prudence'.[15] The modern sense of the word usually has connotations of caution, carefulness and an aversion to risk-taking. Gordon Brown used to talk of prudence when Chancellor of the Exchequer, and for him it had connotations of caution, paying down debt and yet allowing the economy to grow. In his case, of course, that began as a boom then developed into less and less paying off of the national debt, and ended in a financial crash in 2007–08. However, the language of prudence was meant to suggest someone who was careful and thrifty with finances. For trustees, the lodestar is to avoid loss for the trust fund or else the trustees would bear personal liability for that loss if there had been any breach of trust bearing some causal connection to that loss.

However, that is not the only meaning for the very old concept of 'prudence'. In the *Oxford English Dictionary*, the concept of prudence is not just about 'caution' but it is also about 'wisdom', and also about 'earning a profit'. These are three quite different senses. Caution suggests avoiding risk, which in turn (in modern finance theory) means earning a lower profit. The risk associated with investments is related to the return which they will generate: a high risk earns a high return. So, if you lend money to a risky client, you charge them a high interest rate; whereas a dependable client is only charged a low interest rate. For the bank, the risky client earns it a higher profit (provided that that client actually pays what they owe) so as to compensate the bank for taking the risk of that loan. The idea of 'wisdom' in this sense of prudence suggests a careful understanding of an investment and a selection of investments which will generate a good profit while being structured so that they will perform: for example, a good finance lawyer will organise appropriate means of taking security and of drafting the loan contract so as to minimise the practical risks to the bank in making a loan. A wise investor will take appropriate risks in the right circumstances, and will be able to select unwise investments (at whatever price) which should be avoided. Thus, prudence comes to be linked to earning a profit as a result of using wisdom, knowledge and expertise to take sensible risks.

Nevertheless, the idea of 'prudence' haunts trust investment. Michael O'Higgins, of the Pensions Regulator, has encouraged pension fund managers (in effect, the trustees) to take greater risks in their investments on the basis that at present the trustees of pension funds interpret the concept of 'prudence' in the old case law to mean 'caution', 'taking great care', and 'avoiding hazard'.[16] However, the economy, at the time of writing in 2013, is suffering in the wake of the financial crisis because there is insufficient investment capital being applied to existing businesses and to new businesses, with the result that there is little or no economic growth after the contraction of the economy after the credit crunch which began

---

[15] *Speight v Gaunt* (1883) 9 App Cas 1.
[16] In a speech to the Professional Pension Show, accessible via www.thepensionsregulator.gov.uk/press/.

in 2007. Therefore, encouraging trustees to invest more proactively – especially in relation to pension funds, which remain some of the most significant investors in the UK economy – is central to fuelling economic growth by making more capital available. There is also a problem with pension trustees making too little profit for their beneficiaries, who require their pensions to be paid now and in the future. Therefore, the meaning of the word 'prudence' is at issue, because the economy requires that trustees earn greater profits in a context in which they are also being prudent.

The UK Coalition Government, as part of a concerted effort to kick-start that part of the economy and to recover the image of the City of London after a slew of banking scandals, commissioned Professor John Kay (the journalist and academic) to analyse what is needed to reinvigorate the London stock market (in which pension funds and other trust funds remain the largest investors).[17] His conclusion was that there is too little trust in the stock market, and that to recover trust (ignoring the collapse in confidence in banks which had been shown to have engaged in many criminal and otherwise unlawful practices) the Law Commission should consider the law relating to fiduciary duties in that context. At the time of writing, the Law Commission has not produced any meaningful proposals.

One way forward for the Law Commission would be to draw a parallel in trusts law with the FCA Principles for Businesses rulebook, which requires that professional trustees act with integrity, and the FCA Conduct of Business sourcebook, which requires that regulated trustees act in the best interests of their clients, procure best execution for their clients and provide only suitable investments for their clients. It has been argued by Hudson that these regulatory standards ought to be interpreted as creating fiduciary obligations in private law.[18] The trusts law standard of good conscience is similar in its methodology of establishing a high-level principle to the regulatory standard of 'integrity', except that financial regulation has no jurisprudence to guide its development and interpretation. Consequently, the law on trust investment could develop by drawing together the regulatory principles governing trustees acting in the course of their business and the ordinary law of trusts governing trust investment.

## THE EFFECT OF THE TRUSTEE ACT 2000

The Trustee Act 2000 effected a significant change in trusts law relating to investment.[19] Whereas the case law has always contained a standard of 'prudence', as considered above, the Trustee Act 2000 created a new standard of reasonableness which applies to all trusts which do not have their own statutory code, or which do not have their own trust investment provisions in their trust instrument. The ideology which underpinned the 2000 Act was that the trustees should be treated

---

[17] 'Kay Review of UK Equity Markets and Long-Term Decision-Making', Final Report, July 2012.
[18] Alastair Hudson, *The Law of Finance*, 2nd edn (Sweet & Maxwell, 2013), Ch. 5.
[19] For a discussion of the law on the investment of trusts, see Hudson, above n 8, Ch. 10.

as not having any limitations on their power to invest and as though they were the absolute owners of the trust property, again provided that there was nothing to the contrary in the trust instrument. The previous legislation had been more restrictive on the powers of trustees, and the standard of prudence required that the trustees were cautious when making investments. Cautious, safe investments, in modern finance theory, earn low profits precisely because they are safe: investors are compensated for the level of risk that is taken. Therefore, trustees were only able to earn low profits on trust investment. Hence the impetus to create the new Trustee Act 2000 to permit more progressive trust investment.

The Trustee Act 2000 marked a change away from 'prudence', with its overtones (apparently) of caution, towards 'reasonableness': this meant that trustees could make any reasonable investment, without needing to prioritise caution. Section 4 of the Act requires that trustees take into account the standard investment criteria, that is, that the trustees must diversify the trust's investments and that the trustees must invest in suitable investments. Section 5 imposes a duty on the trustees to take proper advice in making their investment decisions. These provisions are based on the fashionable investment practice at the end of the twentieth century century of 'portfolio investment'. In essence, portfolio investment involves spreading the risks by investing in a large number of different types of investment in different markets. By switching the principal concept to that of reasonableness, this means that trustees investing a trust fund which the settlor wanted to be invested aggressively may take risks in investments such as derivatives and complex securities, instead of limiting their decisions to safe investments, as might be suitable for a trust established by a settlor who wanted the trustees to exercise caution. The portfolio investment approach is discussed below.

## WHETHER 'PORTFOLIO THEORY' IS THE BEST APPROACH

The modern law of trusts – which began in this context in the late 1980s – is still caught up in the language used by Hoffmann J and American jurists in the early 1990s with a twist in finance theory which had seen the financial market collapse in 1987 when many investors and companies lost money because they were exposed to specific markets. The mood in financial markets changed from investing in narrow fields and moved instead into investment across 'portfolios'. As financial markets became more volatile, it became clear that it was possible to be wiped out if all your investments were in one single market sector or in one geographical location. Therefore, professional investors began to erect groups or packages of many different investments in different market sectors in different geographical locations – known as a 'portfolio' – so that a downturn in one market would not affect the entire portfolio but would be balanced out (it was hoped) by profits in other parts of the portfolio.

In consequence, because the case law in this area moves much more slowly than finance theory moves, trusts law is still locked into the judgment of Hoffmann J in

*Nestlé v NatWest*[20] and its affection for portfolios. Now, the concept of portfolios is still used by many investment managers in relation to very large funds, but even then the investment managers tend to select a specific range of investments which they will make. Unit trusts are required by regulations to identify the types of investment which they will make, and therefore they tend to identify particular market sectors in which they will focus their activities. But there are many, much more successful investors – like Warren Buffett of Berkshire Hathaway – who eschew the entire concept of portfolio investment on the basis that the use of a portfolio necessarily assumes there will be some losses, but that those losses will balanced out by profits elsewhere in the portfolio. Buffett asks why one would assume there will be losses. Better, in Buffett's view, to select a few investments which will all make money, than to make a large number of investments and accepting some of them will fail. Buffett typically makes a few, large investments in companies on the basis of their sound management and, ideally, an ability to control the price of the goods or services sold. This suggests a very different approach to investment theory.

Moreover, even in relation to firms which make portfolio investment, the mathematics which underpin the portfolios have changed markedly, often involving derivatives strategies and not simply an estimate of earnings-per-share growth. The use of the Black-Scholes options pricing model in derivatives theory has revolutionised the ways in which financial instruments are used within portfolios. It has also become clear (to everyone who would not have believed it before) that the financial crisis destroyed the credibility of derivatives as a means of controlling or removing risk. Ironically, in 1998, two of the Nobel laureates behind the Black-Scholes and related mathematical models ran a hedge fund, Long-Term Capital Management, which collapsed spectacularly in 1998 as a result of the Russian government's announcing it would not be paying out on all of its obligations. Their sophisticated models had not prevented their firm from going into bankruptcy.

The preceding discussion shows that the movements in finance theory are difficult to map, but they have moved beyond simple 'portfolio' theory into something far more mathematically complex and, we now know, dangerous. Moreover, the case law standards which control trusts law are out of step with those finance theory developments. This is why it is suggested that it would be more effective for the protection of beneficiaries to bring the high-level principles in trusts law closer to the principles of financial regulation – especially conduct of business regulation, with its focus on the best interests of the client and so forth – so that what is 'reasonable' for a trustee is interpreted closely with the way in which a professional trustee acting on behalf of clients in a trust situation is required to act under statute in regulations which are enforced by the Financial Conduct Authority.

---

[20] *Nestle v National Westminster Bank* [1993] 1 WLR 1260.

## WHEN WILL TRUSTEES EVER BE LIABLE FOR BREACH OF TRUST FOR INVESTMENT?

There is a question whether or not a professional trustee will ever be held liable for breach of trust. If a professional trustee cannot be held liable for breach of trust in practice, it should cause us to ask whether or not the law of trusts is appropriately organised, because there should be circumstances in which trustee could be held liable for the logic of trusts law to work. The logic of trusts law, as outlined in Chapter 4, is that there must be someone in whose favour the court can decree performance: that is, there must be a beneficiary, so that the courts can control the trustee when the beneficiary brings the trustee to court.

To begin at the beginning, if professional trustees are entitled to rely on the exclusion or limitation of their liabilities for carelessness or gross negligence (for actions for which there could be no exclusion of liability under financial regulation, as discussed above) then that greatly limits the actions which may be brought against trustees. In effect, liability can be fixed on trustees only for dishonesty. Approaching the question from another direction, after *Nestle v NatWest*, trustees will not be liable as professionals for breaches of trust which cause loss to the trust, if they were acting in the same way as would be suggested by the consensus of other market practitioners. Therefore, negligent or borderline dishonest behaviour may be excused if it is the market norm. Thus, trustees will be liable only for actions which no other market actor would have taken, and for actions which are also dishonest. Moreover, there must be a breach of trust, of course, which involves an express term of the trust which is breached, or else some standard of the general law which has not been excluded by the trust instrument. Furthermore, that breach of trust must have been the cause of the loss, and not some movement in market prices. So, even if the trustee is dishonest, following a maverick investment strategy, and purportedly acts in breach of the express terms of the trust, if the loss was caused by the movements in a market (e.g. an unexpected market fall) and not directly by the breach of trust, then the trustee may well still not be liable for breach of trust.

Therefore, professional trustees will be liable for breach of trust only if they are dishonest (because the trust instrument will have excluded all other liabilities, the Trustee Act, and the case law standards), if they act in a way that no other professional does, if they breach a clear term of the trust, and if the loss is caused by their action in a market which otherwise rises. It is very hard to imagine circumstances in which this liability would arise, unless a professional trustee was actually stealing money from the trust.

Consequently, if the only liability for breach of trust which attaches to trustees is limited to acts of theft or embezzlement, then the law of trusts has been reduced almost to vanishing point. There is nothing special about the fiduciary duties of trustees in such a situation. There is no irreducible core of trusteeship at that point. Practical matters have effectively removed trustee liability in investment matters, unless those trustees are actually liars or thieves.

# 7

# RESULTING TRUSTS

## INTRODUCTION

The resulting trust is one of the more enigmatic equitable doctrines: not least because every commentator has a (different) view on how it should operate and be understood. The most recent, leading judicial statement of the manner in which resulting trusts operate was that of Lord Browne-Wilkinson in *Westdeutsche Landesbank v Islington*, as considered below.[1] Unfortunately, it opened as many debates as it resolved. Significantly, it rejected the principal argument posited by Peter Birks in property law, to the effect that unjust enrichments should be addressed by a greatly enlarged 'restitutionary resulting trust'. Lord Browne-Wilkinson confirmed that the ambit of the resulting trusts doctrine was limited to only two categories, but in so doing he disturbed some earlier understandings of this doctrine. Therefore, this chapter considers, first, the nature of the resulting trust after the decision of the House of Lords in *Westdeutsche Landesbank v Islington*; secondly, whether resulting trusts operate automatically; thirdly, how resulting trusts operate in relation to illegal activities; and, fourthly, whether the *Quistclose* trust can be understood as a type of resulting trust.

## Debate 1

### What is the nature of the resulting trust after *Westdeutsche Landesbank v Islington*?

#### THE WESTDEUTSCHE LANDESBANK MODEL OF THE RESULTING TRUST

The leading speech of Lord Browne-Wilkinson in *Westdeutsche Landesbank v Islington LBC* set out the two situations in which his Lordship considered that a resulting trust would arise. This section sets out those categories; later sections will consider how desirable the categories are. In essence, Lord Browne-Wilkinson's judgment should be understood as the currently definitive statement of what the law 'is', even though there are many debates as to what the law 'ought' to be.

---

[1] [1996] AC 669.

## Lord Browne-Wilkinson's categorisation of resulting trusts

The first category of resulting trusts relates to situations in which a person makes a contribution to the purchase price of property, and the second category relates to situations in which the settlor has failed to explain the allocation of equitable interests in property. Purchase price resulting trusts arise so as to recognise that a person who has contributed to the purchase price of property acquires an equitable interest in that property in proportion to the size of her contribution. That equitable interest is held on resulting trust for the contributor. This first category affirms the long-standing principle in *Dyer v Dyer*,[2] that where a person contributes to the acquisition of property, that person receives a corresponding proportion of the total equitable interest in that property on resulting trust.

The second category of resulting trust arises automatically where there is a gap in the equitable ownership of property. The underlying rationale for the law of trusts declaring such an automatic resulting trust is the principle of English property law that there cannot be property which does not have an owner. This second category of resulting trust is problematic. What triggers the automaticity of the resulting trust? Is it the common intention of the parties, or moral questions such as conscience, or a need to fill the gap in the equitable title in the property? As Lord Browne-Wilkinson put it, an automatic resulting trust arises 'where A transfers property to B on express trusts, but the trusts declared do not exhaust the whole beneficial interest'.[3]

## Lord Browne-Wilkinson's explanation of the resulting trust

Lord Browne-Wilkinson took the view that resulting trusts arise on the basis of the common intention of the parties. As his Lordship put it:

> 'Both types of resulting trust are traditionally regarded as examples of trusts giving effect to the common intention of the parties. A resulting trust is not imposed by law against the intentions of the trustee (as is a constructive trust) but gives effect to his presumed intention.'[4]

Therefore, Lord Browne-Wilkinson took the view that all resulting trusts arise on the basis of the 'common intention' of the parties. This is easy to understand in relation to the purchase price resulting trust because in that instance it is necessary that all of the relevant parties agree that the claimant is intended to acquire an equitable interest in the property as a result of contributing money to its purchase. For example, the claimant must not have been intended merely to make a loan to the defendant, such that the claimant was intended only to have the loan repaid and to acquire a proprietary right in the property as well. Even if the claimant contends that she expected to acquire such a right in the property, that would not be appropriate if the other parties understood that the claimant was only making them a loan.

[2] (1788) 2 Cox Eq Cas 92.
[3] [1996] 2 All ER 961, 990.
[4] Ibid.

## The criticism of the 'common intention' idea

The presence of *common* intention is more difficult to explain in relation to the other type of resulting trust, where one party had intended to transfer property but had failed to do so for some reason. In such a situation, it would appear that the appropriate intention is the intention of the putative transferor and not necessarily the intention of anyone else. If I am to make a gift to you, then it is only my intention as the outright owner of the property in question which is important; you can want the property as much as you like, but that cannot force me to transfer it to you if I do not want to do so (without some other factor, like a contract or a prior declaration of trust, being present). There may well be cases in which two parties agree that property will be transferred as part of some larger transaction but the transfer fails for some reason and so there is found to be a resulting trust: in such a situation, it may be that the *common* intention of the parties is significant in that it may bind (or permit) the owner of the property to act as she wishes to do. Otherwise, it is less clear that the common intention of the parties is significant.[5]

Chambers has criticised the 'common intention' model of the resulting trust:[6]

'[I]t is clear that a common intention is not a requirement for a resulting trust, which can arise even though one of the parties is unaware of the transfer.[7] Lord Browne-Wilkinson's speech in *Tinsley v Milligan*[8] indicates that he is mixing the requirements for resulting trusts with those for constructive trusts in the context of family home ownership. That case involved a resulting trust based on the common intention of the parties. Both parties had contributed to the purchase of a house and their intentions were relevant as providers. However, his lordship did not distinguish between the resulting trust based on their contributions and the constructive trust based on a "common intention acted upon by the parties to their detriment".'[9]

So, by way of example, in *Vandervell v IRC*[10] it can only have been the intention of Mr Vandervell which was remotely important when Mr Vandervell decided to transfer a parcel of valuable shares from his own trust to the Royal College of Surgeons so that the College could receive a dividend on those shares. The issue was the ownership of an option to buy back those shares after the dividend had been paid. It was held that the option should pass on resulting trust to Mr Vandervell's trust, because that part of the equitable interest had been missed out in the transfer arrangement. It is the titleholder in property who decides how that property is to be treated; whereas the intention of the recipient is unimportant.[11] However, in a case like *Westdeutsche Landesbank v Islington*,[12] where there was a

---

[5] R. Chambers, *Resulting Trusts* (Clarendon Press, 1997), Ch. 1.
[6] Ibid, 37.
[7] *Ryall v Ryall* (1739) 1 Atk 59.
[8] [1994] 1 AC 340.
[9] Ibid, 371.
[10] [1967] 2 AC 291.
[11] This is so particularly if the recipient is a volunteer. In the event that the recipient has given consideration, the law of contract and the principle of specific performance are applicable.
[12] [1996] AC 669.

void commercial contract between two parties acting at arm's length, it might seem appropriate to talk of a common intention.

## THE THREE PRINCIPAL MODELS OF THE RESULTING TRUST IN THE LITERATURE

Despite this variety of opinion, there are in truth only three key views on the nature of the resulting trust in the literature. Each is outlined in turn here.

The first view is that championed by Professor Birks and Dr Chambers, to the effect that the resulting trust achieves restitution of unjust enrichment by ensuring that equitable title in property results back to its original owner on the happening of some unjust factor.[13] It is an important part of this theory that the resulting trust comes into existence because the transferor did not intend the transferee to take the property beneficially. Rather, where there has been some unjust factor, such as mistake or failure of consideration, which has caused the property to be passed to the defendant, equity operates to reverse that unjust enrichment by subtracting the property which has been passed to the defendant by means of the imposition of a resulting trust on the defendant. The vision of the resulting trust asserted by the Restitution School was that of a response which would be imposed in *any* situation in which a defendant was unjustly enriched by virtue of property being passed to him from the claimant. It was considered that the resulting trust would apply in relation to proprietary claims, whereas the common law action for money had and received would effect restitution of unjust enrichments in relation to personal claims.[14] This form of restitutionary resulting trust had a simple shape: by permitting the property to 'jump back' on resulting trust, the title in that property was being restored to its original owner to reverse the unjust factor which had caused it to be passed to the defendant initially, by subtraction of the property itself. This vision of the greatly enlarged resulting trust was rejected by the House of Lords in *Westdeutsche Landesbank v Islington* – in favour of the two forms of resulting trust set out above – and appears to have disappeared into the ether as a result.

The second view is that the resulting trust is a doctrine of limited application which arises in two circumstances:

1. where the claimant has contributed to the purchase price of property; or
2. where the claimant has failed to dispose adequately of all of the equitable interest in property.[15]

This was the view of the majority of the House of Lords in *Westdeutsche Landesbank v Islington*. In truth, the two forms of resulting trust appear to have little in common with one another. That is, there does not seem to be anything distinctive

---

[13] See generally P. Birks, 'Restitution and resulting trusts' in Goldstein (ed.), *Equity: Contemporary Legal Developments* (Jerusalem, 1992), 335.

[14] *Westdeutsche Landesbank v Islington LBC* [1996] AC 669.

[15] Lord Browne-Wilkinson in *Westdeutsche Landesbank v Islington LBC*; W. Swadling, 'A new role for resulting trusts?' (1996) 16 *LS* 110.

in terms of common features between those two models of resulting trust. This division between two types of resulting trust is similar to that of Megarry J in *Vandervell No 2*[16] but is predicated on a rejection of the idea that property always passes back on resulting trust to its previous owner in the event that a transfer of such property fails.

The third view follows on from this second view, and provides that the resulting trust is indeed a limited doctrine which is restricted to a limited range of categories and no further.[17] The nub of this third view is that the resulting trust is really a form of default rule in the law of property. In effect, that means that where there is uncertainty as to the property-holder of property where some proposed transaction or trust has failed, it is to the rules on resulting trust that one has to look, and those rules tell us to declare that title remains in the hands of the last beneficial owner. This principle emerges from those old English property law cases in which it was held that it was impossible for there to be a gap in the beneficial ownership, and similarly that it was impossible for title simply to be abandoned by a titleholder without its being transferred to another person or held on trust.[18] This idea is considered in greater detail below in the subsection headed 'AN EXAMPLE SUGGESTING AN ANSWER' in relation to the second debate.

## Debate 2

### Does property move in a resulting trust?

#### THE PROBLEM

Does property actually need to move in a resulting trust? Birks suggested that the term '*resulting*' trust is derived from the Latin *resalire*, meaning to 'jump back' – that is, the equitable interest in property 'jumps back' to its original beneficial owner.[19] This is a convenient explanation of that form of resulting trust which arises when a transfer has failed. It suggests movement. However, this is a less convenient explanation of the purchase price resulting trust.

As outlined above, not all resulting trusts can be considered to be '*resulting trusts*' at all because in some circumstances no title leaves the settlor. If that is so, is it correct to say that any property actually moves back to the previous equitable owner of that property on resulting trust? In short the problem is this: there is nothing to suggest that resulting trusts necessarily *return* property to the settlor in all cases because it can be shown that in some cases the courts are in truth merely recognising that the property rights in issue have *remained* with the settlor throughout.

---

[16] [1974] Ch 269.

[17] C. Rickett and R. Grantham, 'Resulting trusts – a rather limited doctrine' in P. Birks and F. Rose (eds), *Restitution and Equity* (Mansfield, 2000), 39.

[18] *Dyer v Dyer* (1788) 2 Cox Eq Cas 92.

[19] P. Birks, *Introduction to the Law of Restitution* (Clarendon Press, 1989), 62.

## AN EXAMPLE SUGGESTING AN ANSWER

By way of example, in *Essery v Cowlard*,[20] property was to have been held on the terms of a marriage settlement but the marriage settlement did not come into existence because the marriage never took place, and consequently the equitable interest in the property was held on a resulting trust in favour of the putative settlors of that marriage settlement. In that context there was no marriage settlement onto which the settlors' property rights could have passed, and therefore it is not meaningful to say that title left the settlors only to be returned to them by means of resulting trust. It would be more satisfying to say that the order of the court recognised the continuing existence of the settlors' property rights and thus recognised that the settlors *remained* equitable owners of the property on the basis that the intended marriage settlement did not come into existence.

An alternative view might be that if the trustee was vested with the legal title in that property, there was sufficient dealing with the property and the trustee should be deemed to hold the property on resulting trust for the settlors. This view, it is suggested, raises difficulties. It is not clear when the resulting trust would come into existence, nor what the trustee's responsibilities would be if it did. It is clear on these facts that the marriage settlement did not come into existence, and therefore that the trustee was never vested with either the powers or the obligations of trusteeship. The neater approach, it is suggested, is to recognise that no rights ever left the settlor in that case.

On this model, the resulting trust is perhaps better understood as an *explanation* as to why the property rights remain with the putative settlors of the failed trust, as opposed to becoming vested in some other person. In essence, the resulting trust is a convenient device for failed transfers of property because it explains why property should remain in the hands of the original owner: when a transfer of property has failed, and we need to know who owns the property as a result, it is better to recognise that the property rights have simply never left the hands of their original owner. That original owner sought to transfer those property rights elsewhere, she failed to do so, and consequently she should be taken to have remained the owner of those property rights.

There is another context in which it is useful to use a resulting trust device: the dead horse problem. If you were a farmer in the eighteenth century who owned a horse, and if your horse died while you were riding it to market, then you might well prefer to abandon your horse and find another means of getting to market. The horse would simply lie in the road and pose a problem to all other road users. Clearly, it would be preferable for the farmer to continue to be the owner of the horse, and thus to be responsible for moving the carcass off the roadway and dealing with any subsequent problems. Consequently, it is a general rule of English property law (except for some cases in the area of theft) that it is impossible simply to abandon property. Instead, if the owner of property wants to be rid of it, she

---

[20] (1884) 26 Ch D 191.

must agree with someone else that that other person will become the owner of the property. Resulting trusts are part of the same logic: if no new owner can be found for that property then the property is considered to remain the property of its original owner. The explanation that Birks employs is that the property passes away and then bounces back, but the more useful model might simply be to recognise that the property remains in the same place throughout, unless and until a new owner can be found for it.

## THE GILLINGHAM BUS DISASTER MODEL

There is another model of the resulting trust which, in effect, throws doubt on Birks's model. It has been advocated by Professor Geraint Thomas and was first presented in the judgment of Harman J in *Re Gillingham Bus Disaster Fund*.[21] In that case, to put the matter briefly, moneys had been raised for the victims of a bus crash, but more money was raised than was needed for those victims: the question arose, inter alia, as to whether the surplus moneys should be held on resulting trust or passed *bona vacantia* to the Crown. Harman J described an automatic resulting trust as operating in the following terms:[22]

> 'The general principle must be that where money is held upon trust and the trusts declared do not exhaust the fund it will revert to the donor or settlor under what is called a resulting trust. The reasoning behind this is that the settlor or donor did not part with his money absolutely out and out but only sub modo[23] to the intent that his wishes as declared by the declaration of trust should be carried into effect. When, therefore, this has been done any surplus still belongs to him. This doctrine does not, in my judgment, rest on any evidence of the state of mind of the settlor, for in the vast majority of cases no doubt he does not expect to see his money back: he had created a trust which so far as he can see will absorb the whole of it. The resulting trust arises where that expectation is for some unforeseen reason cheated of fruition, and is an inference of law based on after-knowledge of the event.'

What emerges significantly from this judgment is the idea that a resulting trust does not necessarily involve any property moving at all from the settlor. Instead, the property may be said to remain with the settlor throughout on the basis of a resulting trust. This is a judicial conceptualisation of the ideas which were set out above. What Harman J had in mind specifically was that the resulting trust in this context arises 'sub modo': that is, on the basis of its own terms and in reflection of its own circumstances.

Many of the alternative models of the resulting trust are determined to find that there is one model of resulting trust which fits all circumstances. However, this is contrary to the underlying project of the courts of equity: equity prefers to dress

---

[21] [1958] Ch 300.

[22] Ibid, 310.

[23] The expression 'sub modo' means 'in accordance with its own terms', or 'in accordance with its own circumstances'.

the details of the trust or the remedy to meet the circumstances, by reference to general principles. Interestingly, Harman J did not see the resulting trust as being the result of the mindset of the settlor. Instead, the resulting trust arises by operation of law when the trust cannot be performed or completed.

# Debate 3
## When is it right to ignore illegal acts in awarding resulting trusts?

One of the most vital debates within resulting trusts has related to illegal acts and the availability of trusts as a response. The cases arose in relation to people who sought to put their property beyond the reach of their creditors, contrary to insolvency law: that is an illegal act under English law. When a person transfers property to a third party and then later wants to recover that property, it is usual for that person to argue that the property should be treated as having been held on resulting trust for them throughout the transaction. However, when they go into insolvency (and thus commit an illegal act), the resulting trust may be refused on the basis that 'he who comes to equity must come with clean hands'.[24] Nevertheless, the approach that has been taken in recent cases is this: if the resulting trust is based on something other than the illegal act, then the resulting trust may take effect even if there is some illegal act in the background. The leading cases will illustrate the point.

In *Gascoigne v Gascoigne*, it was held that the claimant was not entitled to a resulting trust in favour of himself because he had committed an illegal act. Therefore, the assets continued to be owned by the person who had legal title over them. This is the foundation of the principle that an illegal act will preclude a person from being entitled to any equitable interest, including a resulting trust.

The problem arises when a person wants a resulting trust in their favour but when they have also committed an illegal act. Suppose that Michael fears that he is about to go into insolvency. Consequently, he transfers all of his property to his wife, Susan, in the hope that if the worst happens then he will be able to argue that his house, his car and all his belongings are actually owned by his wife. This is an illegal act under insolvency law. However, Susan divorces Michael at the same time as his insolvency is going ahead: after all, money troubles are one of the key reasons for relationship breakdown. Michael will want to argue that the property is actually held on resulting trust for him because he had not intended to make an outright gift of it to his wife, merely to have her pretend to own it for insolvency purposes. His wife would have argued (before the Equality Act 2010) that there must be a presumption that her husband intended to make a gift of the property to her, and furthermore that Michael's illegal act must mean that he is precluded by the rule in *Gascoigne v Gascoigne* from taking the benefit of a resulting trust.

---

[24] *Gascoigne v Gascoigne* [1918] 1 KB 223.

Nevertheless, the insolvency creditors will want to argue that the property should be treated as having passed back to Michael on resulting trust, because if the property is owned beneficially by Michael then it forms part of his estate and so can be passed out among his insolvency creditors.

So, in *Tinker v Tinker*,[25] Mr Tinker divorced his wife and sought to retain assets for himself on resulting trust principles on the basis that they had been put in his wife's name only so as to put them beyond the reach of his creditors. However, Mr Tinker had told his insolvency creditors that he did not have any interest in those same assets because they were held by his wife. Lord Denning held, in essence, that Mr Tinker could not have it both ways: either the assets were held on resulting trust for Mr Tinker, with the result that they could be used to defray his debts to his creditors; or they belonged beneficially to his wife so that his wife was entitled to take them. It was held, on balance, that the assets belonged beneficially to Mrs Tinker.

## TINSLEY v MILLIGAN

A good example of this phenomenon of identifying the link between an illegal act and a resulting trust arose in *Tinsley v Milligan*,[26] where a lesbian couple, Kathleen and Stella, had acquired property to use as a guest-house. They were joint owners of it in equity. However, Kathleen agreed that she would not appear on the legal title of the property so that she could acquire housing benefit illegally. When the couple separated, Kathleen argued against Stella that Kathleen was entitled to ownership rights on resulting trust principles, because she had contributed to the purchase price of the property. Stella counter-argued that Kathleen should be prevented from asserting such a resulting trust because she had committed an illegal act. (This extraordinary argument overlooked the fact that Stella had conspired with Kathleen in this plan.)

When is it wrong to rely on equitable remedies, particularly if one's rights depend on that doctrine? Had Kathleen paid for her crime when the criminal justice system punished her, or should she also be punished by losing her private law rights? Could Stella in good conscience take the entire ownership of the property when she had known of Kathleen's behaviour, and given that Kathleen had contributed to the purchase price of that property?

The Court of Appeal[27] advanced an interesting argument that there is a 'public conscience' which would be offended if a criminal like Kathleen was able to assert title to property which had been bound up with her criminal act. In essence, if equity is built on morality then it would be wrong to allow a criminal like Kathleen to use a resulting trust to acquire a part of her property back. Lord Goff, in the minority in the House of Lords, took a similar view: in essence, Kathleen had acted illegally and therefore could not have the benefit of an equitable doctrine like the

---

[25] [1970] P 136.
[26] [1994] 1 AC 340.
[27] [1992] Ch 310.

resulting trust. However, is this argument watertight? Kathleen was not a drug dealer who had bought her house with the proceeds of her crimes.[28] Instead, she bought a house with legitimate money and then committed a criminal offence. This was the approach which Lord Browne-Wilkinson and the majority of the House of Lords took. Significantly, his Lordship looked at the source of Kathleen's rights. Kathleen's right in the property came from the fact that she paid for those rights with legitimately earned money. Her criminal act was separate from the acquisition of those rights. Therefore, it was held by the majority that Kathleen was entitled to rights in the property on resulting trust principles. Thus, the bluff ethical arguments of the Court of Appeal were relegated behind a more sophisticated inquiry into the source of the parties' respective rights.

### TRIBE v TRIBE

Perhaps the most interesting example of the ethical issues in this area arose in *Tribe v Tribe*.[29] Tribe Senior feared that his business was about to go into insolvency because it owed large amounts of money under a dilapidations clause on its lease over business premises. In consequence, Tribe Senior decided to transfer all of his shares in the family company to his son, Tribe Junior.[30] Junior purportedly acquired those shares under a contract under which he was required only to pay an under-value for those shares. That amount was never paid. Nevertheless the shares were transferred to Junior by Senior. (This opened the possibility that this sale at an under-value could have been undone by insolvency creditors under s. 423 of the Insolvency Act 1986.) In the event, Senior managed to avoid the insolvency of the company by agreeing with the landlord that the lease would be surrendered, with the result that the dilapidations amounts did not need to be paid. At this point, Senior sought to recover the shares from Junior. Junior refused to retransfer the shares on the basis that a transfer from a father to a son should be presumed under English law to constitute a gift from father to son (under the ancient presumption of advancement). Senior argued that his intention had only been to put the property beyond the reach of any insolvency creditors (and not to make a gift of them to Junior), with the effect that those shares should be held on resulting trust by Junior for the benefit of Senior. Junior argued that Senior could not rely on a resulting trust because he had committed an illegal act in seeking to put property beyond the reach of his creditors.

The Court of Appeal (in particular Millett LJ) held that there had not actually been an illegal act committed because the company had not actually gone into

---

[28] The Proceeds of Crime Act 2002, for example, recovers criminal property from convicted criminals – criminal property is property which has been acquired as part of a criminal lifestyle. In that case, there is a need to establish a connection between the criminality and the purported ownership of the property. Kathleen would not have lost her property rights on a Proceeds of Crime Act analysis either.

[29] [1995] 3 WLR 913.

[30] If you are a fan of 1980s pop and of pop group Frankie Goes to Hollywood, you will agree that this is a situation in which 'two Tribes go to war'. And a point is all that they can score.

insolvency. Consequently, Senior was entitled to his resulting trust because there had not been an illegality. In moral terms, however, Senior had done everything necessary to perform the illegal act. He had, in effect, the 'mens rea' of the illegal act, in that he intended to defraud any creditors, and he had performed all of the 'actus reus' of that illegal act that was necessary for him to perform. But, through good luck or clever negotiation, the final element of the actus reus had not been committed because the company had not actually gone into insolvency.

Nevertheless, morally, Senior had done everything to constitute an illegal act. In *Equity & Trusts*,[31] Hudson compares the mental state of someone like Tribe Senior, who intends to carry through his illegal action, with an assassin who lines up a target in his sights and fires the bullet, only to have the target killed at the last second by a passing bus. The assassin would also have intended to commit a criminal offence, but his performance of that act was only prevented by another intervening act at the last moment. Tribe Senior intended to commit the illegal act of putting property beyond the reach of his creditors, and he carried out all the actions involved in that, but was saved from so doing by the landlord agreeing to a surrender of the lease. Morally, Tribe Senior and the frustrated assassin appear to be in similar positions. Tribe Senior had sinned in his heart. He had intended to commit the illegal act. Therefore, ethically he was in the same position as if the company had actually gone into insolvency. So, why should equity excuse him when he had acted unconscionably? The only answer on those facts must be that Tribe Junior was the only other person who could have acquired those shares and he was a conspirator in this arrangement. Tribe Junior had no better claim, morally speaking, to the shares than Tribe Senior. Therefore, the outcome was the least bad result among the available options.

## Debate 4

### What is a *Quistclose* trust and why is it so difficult to tell?

#### ENTERING INTO AN ANCIENT DEBATE

In the movie *Troll Hunter*, the main characters hear rumours of vicious trolls in the Scandanavian wilderness, and then later they hear the roars of unseen monsters echoing in that same wilderness when they go in search of the legendary trolls. The film is shot as a documentary with hand-held cameras. (*Beware*: spoiler.) Late in the film, when the largest mountain trolls become visible on the snow-covered tundra, the human beings are terrified and bewildered. They witness extraordinary violence of a sort which they had only thought possible in legend.

This is a little, I would suggest, like the experience of undergraduate law students stumbling upon trusts lawyers debating the nature of *Quistclose* trusts. These ancient, mis-shapen creatures (with their craggy faces, their yellow teeth and

---

[31] A.S. Hudson, *Equity & Trusts*, 538.

their inexplicable ear-hair) roar at one another in an ancient, primal tongue which only they seem able to understand. Long-standing enmities and beliefs are given flesh as they fight and roar. Neither will give way. There is no give and no take possible between them.

Trolls behave in much the same way.

And yet *Quistclose* trusts are, in essence, quite simple. When a borrower of money goes into insolvency, the loan moneys (assuming they are still identifiable as such) are taken to be held on trust for the lender if the loan contract had specified that those moneys were only to be used for a specified purpose. With a sense of unease, trusts law trolls the world over will reluctantly accept that much. The fearful student may wish to withdraw at this stage. A brave student may nevertheless wish to know how each of the trolls would explain *the nature* of that *Quistclose* trust. It is at that moment that the roaring really begins.

## THE THREE DIFFERENT MODELS CONSIDERED BELOW

The first question is whether one is talking about the *Quistclose* trust as actually described by Lord Wilberforce in the House of Lords in *Barclays Bank v Quistclose*;[32] or whether one is talking about defining the *Quistclose* trust as belonging to one of the species of existing trusts (express, resulting or constructive); or whether one is talking about the *Twinsectra* model of this kind of trust which was set out by Lord Millett; or whether one has some preferred model of one's own. (Each of these possibilities is considered in turn below.) In essence, what most of the commentators are doing is attempting to explain in the abstract the conceptual nature of *all* trusts of this sort. What they generally do not accept is that the nature of equitable rights and obligations in this sort of arrangement will depend upon the precise contractual terms on which and the circumstances in which *each individual* underlying loan came into existence. A failure to acknowledge these differences at the starting-point is commonly the root of the troll-like bellowing that ensues, with few of the protagonists really listening to one another.

To digress for a moment, most academic disagreements can be found in this sort of problem. When academics disagree starkly, that is generally because the issue at hand raises questions which go to the heart of their very different worldviews. Some people like freedom, other people like order. Unlike Jack Spratt and his wife (where, in the nursery rhyme, he could eat no fat and she could eat no lean), it is unusual for academics with completely differing tastes to be able to reconcile with one another. (There are some delicious exceptions to this rule, but many academics are a curmudgeonly bunch.) If one sees this sort of problem as a question of the nature of a resulting trust then that will suppose one sort of answer; alternatively, if one sees this sort of problem as a sub-set of contract law with a proprietary result then that will suppose a different sort of answer. How one frames the question will lead ineffably to one's answer. If the commentators could understand one

---

[32] [1970] AC 567.

another's starting-points, then the debates might come to more satisfactory conclusions.

## The model in *Barclays Bank v Quistclose*

In the appeal in *Barclays Bank v Quistclose* itself, Lord Wilberforce delivered a judgment which seems, to modern eyes, to be ancient in its own way. In that case, Quistclose had loaned money to Rolls Razor solely for the purpose of paying a dividend to its preferred shareholders. However, Rolls Razor went into insolvency, and so its bankers, Barclays, purported to use those loan moneys, which were held in one of Rolls Razor's bank accounts, to pay off the overdraft which Rolls Razor had from Barclays. It was held that the equitable interest in the loan moneys should belong to Quistclose because of the term in the loan contract specifying the sole use of that money, and therefore none of those moneys could be used by Barclays to pay down the overdraft. The real question, however, is the precise legal basis on which those loan moneys 'belonged' to Quistclose.

Significantly, Lord Wilberforce held that the doctrines of common law and equity would combine in loan contracts of this sort. Thus, if the terms of the contract suggested that the loan money was to be used for a specified purpose and if that purpose was performed, then it would be common law doctrines which would govern the transaction through the law of contract. However, if the borrower went into insolvency then 'the remedies of equity' would intervene to protect the lender. The remedies of equity in this context operated by means of a 'primary trust' (permitting the use of the loan moneys for the specified purpose) and then by means of a 'secondary trust' to protect the lender. These categories of primary and secondary trust are unique to this area of the law, and Lord Wilberforce did not explain what he meant by them. Most commentators assume that the secondary trust is intended to be a resulting trust which carries the equitable interest in the loan moneys back to the lender. But what all the commentators seem to miss is that Lord Wilberforce intended there to be a combination of common law and equitable doctrines to govern this species of loan transaction, and moreover that the terms of the loan contract should really guide us as to the rights which the lender is intended to have in detail.[33]

The language used in Lord Wilberforce's judgment is open and vague as to conceptual detail. It is almost lyrical in its determination that two completely different fields of law – common law and equity – will work together so as to produce a coherent result to a practical problem. What bedevils much debate about *Quistclose* trusts is that most commentators are concerned to decide what sort of trust is at question in all *Quistclose* arrangements – that is, for example, the question on which Lord Millett focused in *Twinsectra v Yardley* (see below). By focusing on the nature of the trust which Lord Wilberforce intended, the

---

[33] E.g., W. Swadling, 'Orthodoxy' in W. Swadling (ed.), *The Quistclose Trust* (Hart Publishing, 2004), 9, which does not even mention those parts of Lord Wilberforce's judgment which set out his Lordship's actual opinion.

commentators miss the important fact that Lord Wilberforce himself was seemingly unconcerned about the precise nature of the trust, and equally unconcerned about the model of trust which he had created. If he had been concerned about it then he would most probably have defined exactly which form of trust he meant. He would have hung a label on the trust. But he did not do that. Instead, he talked in terms of over-lapping common law and equitable remedies combining so as to achieve the appropriate result on a case-by-case basis. The appeal in *Barclays Bank v Quistclose* itself had been framed in terms of a resulting trust, and the House of Lords made that order, but Lord Wilberforce did not actually use the expression 'resulting trust' in his judgment. Instead, the commentators hone in on his distinction between 'primary' and 'secondary' trusts as containing the answer to which category of trust his Lordship must have meant.

The key passage in Lord Wilberforce's judgment was the following, in relation to a loan contract in which the moneys had been advanced on the condition that they could be used only for the payment of a dividend to preferred shareholders:[34]

> 'There is surely no difficulty in recognising the co-existence in one transaction of legal and equitable rights and remedies: when the money is advanced, the lender acquires an equitable right to see that it is applied for the primary designated purpose:[35] when the purpose has been carried out (i.e., the debt paid) the lender has his remedy against the borrower in debt: if the primary purpose cannot be carried out, the question arises if a secondary purpose (i.e., repayment to the lender) has been agreed, expressly or by implication: if it has, the remedies of equity may be invoked to give effect to it, if it has not (and the money is intended to fall within the general fund of the debtor's assets) then there is the appropriate remedy for recovery of a loan. ... I can appreciate no reason why the flexible interplay of law and equity cannot let in these practical arrangements, and other variations if desired: it would be to the discredit of both systems if they could not. In the present case the intention to create a secondary trust for the benefit of the lender, to arise if the primary trust, to pay the dividend, could not be carried out, is clear and I can find no reason why the law should not give effect to it.'

Therefore, the *Quistclose* trust arises from the interplay of the ordinary principles of the contract of loan at common law and the equitable principles which prevent ownership of the loan money being passed to a third party if that loan money is misused. The manner in which the *Quistclose* trust arises, then, is by means of a 'secondary trust' coming into existence for the benefit of the lender if the 'primary trust ... could not be carried out'. The question on which the commentators have fixed is the meaning of the primary and the secondary trust (not jargon used elsewhere in trusts law), and not the inter-play of common law and equitable doctrine as part of a loan contract. In a loan contract, the repayment obligations of the borrower are governed by contract law (that is, common law). Given the context

---

[34] Ibid, 581.
[35] *In re Rogers*, 8 Morr 243, *per* both Lindley LJ and Kay LJ.

of the loan term which specifies that the money can be used only for a particular purpose, Lord Wilberforce then relies on the 'remedies of equity' (not a specific type of trust) to protect the lender's rights.

Consequently, Lord Wilberforce was, on the face of his judgment (as opposed to the sub-text which the commentators always seek), interested in the way in which the common law and equity in tandem would provide an answer to the question, on any given set of facts, and as to what sorts of rights the claimant-lender might have to recover the loan moneys. His Lordship was actually concerned with whether or not the contract itself could be interpreted as intending the creation of any right for the lender in the loan moneys once they were paid to the borrower; his lordship was also concerned with the rights which contract law would create for the parties, and only then was his Lordship concerned with the role which the 'remedies of equity' (not specifically a resulting trust) might play in protecting the lender against the borrower's failure or inability to make repayment. This is not a straightforward process of a trust being imposed and the question being as to the classification of that trust. Instead, the primary and secondary trusts (those previously unknown and gnomic concepts) are the remedies which equity uses once the borrower has taken the money in practice and is prevented by its insolvency from making repayment.

## The *Twinsectra* model

It is this last conceptualisation of the *Quistclose* trust which we should pursue into the model advanced by Lord Millett in *Twinsectra v Yardley*.[36] Lord Millett upheld the theory of the *Quistclose* trust being a resulting trust, but explained its nature differently from Lord Wilberforce in *Barclays Bank v Quistclose*. We shall focus on two passages in particular from his Lordship's speech. First, paragraph 81 of the judgment, which reads as follows:

> 'On this analysis, the *Quistclose* trust is a simple commercial arrangement akin … to a retention of title clause (though with a different object) which enables the borrower to have recourse to the lender's money for a particular purpose without entrenching on the lender's property rights more than necessary to enable the purpose to be achieved. The money remains the property of the lender unless and until it is applied in accordance with his directions, and insofar as it is not so applied it must be returned to him. I am disposed, perhaps pre-disposed, to think that this is the only analysis which is consistent both with orthodox trust law and with commercial reality.'

The second sentence is problematic: 'The money remains the property of the lender unless and until it is applied in accordance with his directions, and insofar as it is not so applied it must be returned to him.' There is a clear contradiction in terms here: if the money *remains* the property of the lender then how can it possibly be *returned* to him? If I retain property then I cannot possibly ask you to return

---

[36] [2002] 2 AC 164.

it to me later, because I have kept it. Imagine that you ask to borrow my umbrella because it is raining and I refuse to lend it to you; if I were then to come to you the next day and demand that you return my umbrella, you would say 'Well, you kept your umbrella so how can you possibly have it returned to you?' It is the same problem with Lord Millett's formulation here: if the lender retains the money, it cannot logically be returned to him. What we might take Lord Millett to mean is that *ownership* of the money in equity remains with the lender even if *possession* of the money is passed to the borrower, such that the borrower has to return *possession* of the money to the lender. Similarly, Lord Millett's reference to 'the property' is unclear, because we cannot know if it means retention of absolute title (which would negate the possibility of there being a trust), or whether it is supposed to mean only retention of an equitable interest under a trust.

Paragraph 100 from Lord Millett's speech also presents problems:

> 'As Sherlock Holmes reminded Dr Watson, when you have eliminated the impossible, whatever remains, however improbable, must be the truth. I would reject all the alternative analyses, which I find unconvincing for the reasons I have endeavoured to explain, and hold the Quistclose trust to be an entirely orthodox example of the kind of default trust known as a resulting trust. The lender pays the money to the borrower by way of loan, but he does not part with the entire beneficial interest in the money, and in so far as he does not it is held on a resulting trust for the lender from the outset. Contrary to the opinion of the Court of Appeal, it is the borrower who has a very limited use of the money, being obliged to apply it for the stated purpose or return it. He has no beneficial interest in the money, which remains throughout in the lender subject only to the borrower's power or duty to apply the money in accordance with the lender's instructions. When the purpose fails, the money is returnable to the lender, not under some new trust in his favour which only comes into being on the failure of the purpose, but because the resulting trust in his favour is no longer subject to any power on the part of the borrower to make use of the money. Whether the borrower is obliged to apply the money for the stated purpose or merely at liberty to do so, and whether the lender can countermand the borrower's mandate while it is still capable of being carried out, must depend on the circumstances of the particular case.'

Again, as with paragraph 81 above, there is a problem in that we are told that the money 'remains throughout in the lender' and yet that 'the money is returnable to the lender'. Furthermore, the *Quistclose* trust is held explicitly to be a resulting trust, even though ownership of the money is said to *remain* with the lender. Therefore, this is not a resulting trust as Professor Birks has explained it, because that sort of resulting trust requires that equitable ownership of the property has passed away and that it then 'jumps back' to the lender. That cannot happen if the lender *retains* equitable ownership of the loan money throughout the loan contract. Instead, this model of resulting trust resembles the model advanced by Harman J in the *Gillingham Bus Disaster Fund* case, as was set out above, where the unallocated portion of the property is said to remain throughout with the original owner of that property (i.e. the lender in this context).

On this basis, we must reject Professor Birks's analysis of a resulting trust and instead accept that Lord Millett has established that resulting trusts are merely a 'default trust' in which a court of equity simply recognises that when there is a question as to the ownership of property, then we should recognise that the last owner of that property is still its owner.

We are told that the borrower has merely a power to use the money for the described purpose. The money is said 'to be returnable to the lender' (oddly, even though the lender has nevertheless retained equitable ownership of it) because the power disappears (apparently) once it is not performed. In the final sentence of paragraph 100, Lord Millett acknowledges that the precise nature of the parties' obligations will depend upon the precise terms of the contract between them. Therefore, we have a very stylised form of resulting trust in the speech of Lord Millett. This model is necessary for Lord Millett's analysis, and yet his Lordship delivered a dissenting speech in the House of Lords, and as such it is difficult to know what the force of this model is in English trusts law. What is important to note is that subsequent cases have supported it, and thus have lent it some gravitas. It is nevertheless suggested that the better analysis would be to infer the existence of an express trust (just as in *Re Kayford*[37]) from the circumstance.

### The practical use of a *Quistclose* trust in banking transactions

Significantly, in practice many other things are essential in the process of creating loan contracts, even though they are rarely discussed in the commentaries or in the judgments. A well-drafted contract will specify in detail the precise rights of the lender and the manner in which the loan moneys must be held before they are used for the specified purpose. Therefore, in most circumstances, the nature of any given *Quistclose* arrangement will be dictated by the terms of the contract which creates it. In those cases it is unlikely that there will be any need to take the case to court if the contract is well drafted.

The principal usefulness of the *Quistclose* trust is probably that it enables the claimant to begin equitable tracing (which, it is commonly accepted, is dependent on there being some pre-existing equitable interest which a contract of loan in itself will usually not create but which a *Quistclose* trust certainly can). Equitable tracing may be essential to identify and recover moneys which have been paid into a bank account and mixed with other money. The contract must specify the purpose for which the money is being lent and the ramifications of non-use with sufficient clarity. Remarkably, for a *Quistclose* point to arise that is worth taking to court, the contract must be specific as to those elements of the transaction but silent as to the question of the precise property rights of the lender. This would be very sloppy drafting indeed.

A well-drafted loan contract should make these matters plain. Indeed, a well-organised banking arrangement (in which the lender does not trust the borrower

---

[37] [1975] 1 WLR 279.

sufficiently) should provide that the moneys are kept in a separate bank account until the moment at which they are to be applied in the discharge of their contractually-stipulated purpose. Such a contract would obviate the entire *Quistclose* debate because that contract would specify the rights of the parties at each stage and would ensure that the bank retained control of the money until the last second. Therefore, by definition, the debates about *Quistclose* trusts are concerned only with badly drafted loan contracts: consequently, it is unsurprising that those cases are difficult to analyse precisely because they are exceptionally badly organised commercial arrangements from the start.

### That we cannot know the nature of a *Quistclose* trust by its label

The philosopher Ludwig Wittgenstein advanced the opinion in his *Tractatus Logio-Philosophicus* that we know what things are because we know what they are called. So, for example, we know what a table is because we know that it is called a 'table' and that that categorisation describes all of the essential features of a table. When we come to the questions surrounding *Quistclose* trusts we can see that Wittgenstein would have faced a different problem. We know what these concepts are called (i.e. '*Quistclose* trusts') but we do not necessarily know what that label means. They are said to operate in so many different ways that the label does none of the work of a definition. Wittgenstein recanted his view later in life, but never wrote another complete book setting out his new approach.[38] It is common in life for us to know things without knowing what they are called.

In a wonderful moment in his diaries, the English humourist Alan Bennett describes how he took his mother (then, sadly, in the early stages of dementia) out for a drive in the countryside. Mrs Bennett looked down at the sheep on the hillside and remarked that she knew what the sheep were, but that she could not remember what they were called. As Alan Bennett wryly remarked: 'Thus Wittgenstein was routed by my mother'.[39]

---

[38] The posthumously published book, *Philosophical Investigations*, collects together his later writings, although they do not resemble a complete book of the sort suggested by the *Tractatus*.

[39] A. Bennett, *Writing Home* (Faber, 2006).

# 8

## CONSTRUCTIVE TRUSTS

## INTRODUCTION

The constructive trust is central to equity's mission to deal with unconscionable behaviour, to prevent formal legal rules from permitting an unjust outcome, and to prevent clever tricks and devices from allowing claimants to be treated unconscionably. There will always be situations in which some judges will wish to set a formal rule of law aside because its outcome on the facts of that case would be unpalatable. There are other judges who will shrug their shoulders and wonder at the injustice of the rule they are obliged to follow. The constructive trust is both a countervailing rule for judges of this second type, and a helpmeet for judges of the former type.

Constructive trusts come into existence 'by operation of law' – that is, without the need for a settlor or any other party to show an intention to create an express trust. The circumstances in which this operation of law will take effect were set out by Lord Browne-Wilkinson in the House of Lords in *Westdeutsche Landesbank v Islington LBC*,[1] in the simple proposition that a person will be subject to a constructive trust when they have knowledge of some factor in relation to property which ought to have affected their conscience (see further below).

Before essaying a programme of categorisation, however, it is worth recalling the words of Edmund-Davies LJ in *Carl Zeiss Stiftung v Herbert Smith & Co.*, that:

> 'English law provides no clear and all-embracing definition of a constructive trust. Its boundaries have been left perhaps deliberately vague so as not to restrict the court by technicalities in deciding what the justice of a particular case might demand.'[2]

This statement indicates that the constructive trust is not a certain or rigid doctrine. Indeed, it is wilfully undefined so that its central principles – built around ensuring justice on a case-by-case basis, akin to the Aristotlean model – can be moulded to fit particular circumstances. In *Paragon Finance plc v D.B. Thackerar*

---

[1] [1996] AC 669.
[2] [1969] 2 Ch 276, 300.

& Co.,[3] Millett LJ, a significant voice among the equity specialists, attempted a general definition of the doctrine of constructive trust:

'A constructive trust arises by operation of law whenever the circumstances are such that it would be unconscionable for the owner of property (usually but not necessarily the legal estate) to assert his own beneficial interest in the property and deny the beneficial interest of another.'[4]

There is a general principle to which all constructive trusts may be said to correspond. That principle correlates with the core role of equity as a jurisdiction which acts *in personam* against the conscience of the individual defendant.[5]

The most important recent statement of the core principles governing constructive trusts was made by Lord Browne-Wilkinson in *Westdeutsche Landesbank Girozentrale v Islington LBC*,[6] in the following terms:

'(i) Equity operates on the conscience of the owner of the legal interest. In the case of a trust, the conscience of the legal owner requires him to carry out the purposes for which the property was vested in him (express or implied trust) or which the law imposes on him by reason of his unconscionable conduct (constructive trust).
(ii) Since the equitable jurisdiction to enforce trusts depends upon the conscience of the holder of the legal interest being affected, he cannot be a trustee of the property if and so long as he is ignorant of the facts alleged to affect his conscience, ie until he is aware that he is intended to hold the property for the benefit of others in the case of an express or implied trust, or, in the case of a constructive trust, of the factors which are alleged to affect his conscience.'

Thus we have the central principles that knowledge of a factor which should have affected the defendant's conscience in relation to property will give rise to a constructive trust. That is the central, deontological principle which governs the law on constructive trusts (as that term was explained in Chapter 1). Given that this is the most recent statement of the basis on which constructive trusts operate by the House of Lords, that is a statement of what the law *is*.

## THE STRUCTURE OF THIS CHAPTER

The principles governing constructive trusts are an enormous topic in themselves. This chapter does not pretend to be a textbook coverage of them. The field of 'constructive trusts' could be taken to cover all trusts implied by law which are not resulting trusts, and by some accounts even the law on proprietary estoppel. It is defined by the House of Lords to cover all trusts arising by operation of law *sui generis* where the defendant has knowingly acted unconscionably. That is a field

---

[3] [1999] 1 All ER 400.
[4] Cf. *Westdeutsche Landesbank v Islington LBC* [1996] AC 669.
[5] J. McGhee, *Snells' Equity*, 30th edn (Sweet & Maxwell, 2000), 41.
[6] [1996] AC 669.

which covers trusts arising by operation of law to prevent unconscionability, proprietary claims in the wake of tracing actions (Chapter 11), claims for dishonest assistance and unconscionable receipt (Chapter 10), and trusts over the home (Chapter 9).[7] Among the sub-species of constructive trusts which have been observed are constructive trusts imposed when: contracts to acquire property have been formed,[8] bribes have been taken by fiduciaries and invested profitably,[9] unauthorised profits have been taken by fiduciaries in circumstances where there is a conflict of interest,[10] a person has used statute as an engine of fraud,[11] pre-contractual negotiations have caused one person to assume liabilities in reliance on the actions of another[12] and so forth. Importantly, many of these types of constructive trust are debated in the case law (with situations like the pre-contractual negotiations cases being overturned,[13] for example). That should not surprise us: an area of our private law which is so focused on achieving 'conscionable' outcomes – or, rather, preventing 'unconscionable' outcomes – ought properly to generate debate (among judges, academics, practitioners and non-lawyers) as to the moral choices that are being made. All areas of moral debate in society generate discussion, and so it is entirely healthy that the principles relating to constructive trusts should also generate debate and disagreement. That debate and disagreement will properly lead to cases being overruled, principles being demolished and re-established, and the boundaries of the law shifting over time. That is the business of constructive trusts.

So, this chapter will not seek to be a textbook on constructive trusts. Rather, it will focus on three particular areas of debate within constructive trusts law. The principal focus will be on the debate about bribes, and whether constructive trusts or the common law on debt is the proper response to a bribe being taken. This debate is very current (at the time of writing), it has divided opinion neatly into two camps (with equity traditionalists on one side and common lawyers concerned with insolvency law on the other), and it goes to the heart of what it means to impose a constructive trust. As a result, it stands as an example of the entire debate.

Secondly, we shall consider the complaints made by the Oxford Restitution School about constructive trusts. In essence, the members of that school of thought (as was discussed in Chapter 3) consider that constructive trusts do not arise on a sufficiently clear basis (unlike their taxonomy with its focus on events like mistake, undue influence and so forth), that they are too subjective in their

---

[7] For further discussion of these topics, see A.S. Hudson, *Equity & Trusts*, (Routledge, 2014), Chs 12–20.

[8] These arise on a 'sub modo' basis, i.e. on their own terms in their own circumstances: *Jerome v Kelly* [2004] 2 All ER 835, [2004] UKHL 25.

[9] *Attorney-General for Hong Kong v Reid* [1994] 1 AC 324.

[10] *Boardman v Phipps* [1967] 2 AC 46.

[11] *Rochefoucauld v Boustead* [1897] 1 Ch 196, as explained in *Paragon Finance plc v DB Thakerar & Co.* [1999] 1 All ER 400.

[12] *Banner Homes Group plc v Luff Development Ltd* [2000] Ch 372.

[13] *Cobbe v Yeoman's Row Management Ltd* [2008] 1 WLR 1752.

creation and that they prevent the development of ordered legal principles. This second debate links back explicitly to Chapter 3.

Thirdly, we shall consider the debate as to whether or not constructive trusts may be thought of as a coherent doctrine. There are so many sub-species of constructive trusts – as outlined above – that it would be possible to argue that they are sub-doctrines with no link to one another and therefore that the entire area of law should be dismissed as an incoherent mess. On the other hand, it might be argued that constructive trusts are all based ultimately on the concept of good conscience that was discussed in Chapter 1, and therefore that while they appear to be different in practice, they have the same root. After all, we do not say that the biology of flowers is incoherent just because the flowers of different plants look different. When we look beneath the surface, or when we look beyond the different shape and colour of the flower, we are able to identify common, literal roots to those plants, we can identify the clear features of different species of plant which function similarly and we can therefore understand the deeper pattern that links all of those plants together within the total ecology.

## Debate  1

### Should the receipt of bribes give rise to a constructive trust?

#### WHAT IS THE QUESTION?

The title for this debate is deliberately slightly vague. A better title might have been: 'Should the receipt of bribes *by fiduciaries* give rise to a constructive trust?' However, that raises a question in itself as to whether any person who receives a bribe should be considered to be a fiduciary: after all, if a person is worth bribing then it is likely that that person occupies a position of sufficient sensitivity that they are worth bribing, and therefore it is likely that they should be considered to be a fiduciary as a result. So, a British army sergeant was held to be a fiduciary when he assisted smugglers to pass through army checkpoints,[14] a security guard was considered to be a fiduciary when he assisted armed robbers to steal from his employer[15] and so forth. Neither of those categories of people would ordinarily be considered to be a fiduciary, because their rank or role is too junior within their organisations, but at the moment they perform a role which is worthy of a bribe then the courts have defined them as being fiduciaries when acting in that particular role. Therefore, there is an argument as to whether or not these principles apply to the private law analysis of all bribes in any event. The question could also, arguably, be altered so as to read: 'Should the *earning of profits from the* receipt of bribes give rise to a constructive trust?' However, that question would ignore the

---

[14] *Reading v Attorney-General* [1951] 1 All ER 618.
[15] *Brinks Ltd v Abu-Saleh (No. 3)* [1996] CLC 133.

fact that the bribe itself is also a profit from the transaction, and is itself an item of property the ownership of which should be questioned.

It is important to bear in mind that bribery is a very important topic among public policymakers around the world. In some jurisdictions, bribery and corruption are so endemic that they are very easy to spot. Indeed, academics such as Professor Amanda Perry-Kessaris have examined patterns of bribery and made the observation that in countries which are very corrupt, bribery is actually quite transparent and may be factored into your business model as a cost of doing business, like a lawful tax.[16] It is in jurisdictions or situations in which corruption is hidden that it is difficult to anticipate the cost of doing business, because it is difficult to know in advance who will need to be bribed and how much that bribe will need to be. In jurisdictions with low corruption, one can rely on the unlikelihood of needing to pay a bribe to predict one's costs. Nevertheless, in the UK, corruption has been found in the creation of large-scale contracts by large manufacturers and others, and consequently the Bribery Act 2010 introduced a range of criminal offences related to bribery. The principal offence in s. 1 is that of promising or giving a financial or other advantage to another person so as to induce or reward that other person for improperly performing a function or activity.

There are many international bodies and initiatives which seek to control bribery.[17] As a result, there is a growing part of corporate practice (not limited to lawyers) which requires that businesses, governments and others create complex practices to prevent bribery and corruption in their activities. Consequently, we can see an international acceptance that, to quote Lord Templeman in *Attorney-General for Hong Kong v Reid*,[18] '[b]ribery is an evil practice which threatens the foundations of any civilised society'.

Bribery is therefore a very serious issue. While it may not appear to occupy the same, first-line moral ground as murder, for the purposes of this debate we can acknowledge that it is serious and that it is immoral. For a person to make a bribe or to receive a bribe is unconscionable in the objective sense we established for that term in Chapter 1. From that beginning, we need to consider whether or not bribes should give rise to a constructive trust.

## THE LAW IN SUMMARY

At the time of writing, the legal position, which has swung like a pendulum between two points of view, may be understood as follows. A decision of the Court of Appeal in *Lister v Stubbs* in 1890[19] held that when a bribe is received, that bribe

---

[16] A. Perry-Kessaris, 'Use, Abuse and Avoidance: Foreign Investors and the Legal System in Bangalore' (2004) 12 *Asia Pacific Law Review* 161.

[17] For example, the OECD Convention on Combating Bribery of Foreign Public Officials in International Business Transactions in 1999, the United Nations Convention Against Corruption, the US Foreign Corrupt Practices Act, through to the World Economic Forum's clunky 'Partnership Against Corruption Initiative'.

[18] [1994] 1 AC 324.

[19] (1890) 45 Ch D 1.

should be treated as a debt which is an amount of money equal to the bribe, which is owed at common law by the recipient of the bribe to their employer or to whomever they have wronged by taking that bribe.

A decision of the Privy Council in *Attorney-General for Hong Kong v Reid* in 1993,[20] in a powerful judgment by Lord Templeman, held (on an appeal from the New Zealand Court of Appeal which was not bound by the English Court of Appeal) that when a bribe is received by a fiduciary, that bribe is held on constructive trust from the moment of its receipt by the fiduciary, with the result that any profit which is taken from that bribe or any property which is acquired with that bribe is also held on constructive trust for that beneficiary. Moreover, held Lord Templeman, if any property acquired with that bribe decreases in value, then the fiduciary must not only hold that property on constructive trust but they must also account in cash for the decrease in that value so that the full amount of the bribe is accounted for by the fiduciary. *Lister v Stubbs* was rejected, by a careful consideration of all of the case law which had preceded that decision.

Latterly, a decision of the English Court of Appeal in *Sinclair Investments (UK) Ltd v Versailles Trade Finance Group plc*[21] has created a distinction between situations in which a fiduciary takes an unauthorised profit by misusing trust property (which will lead to a constructive trust over that profit and any further property acquired thereby) and cases in which a fiduciary receives a bribe without using any trust property to do so (which will not lead to a constructive trust but which will rather lead to a debt claim at common law as in *Lister v Stubbs*). The decision in *Reid* was rejected for the reasons given below.

A more recent decision of the English Court of Appeal in *FHR European Ventures LLP v Mankarious*[22] was able to distinguish *Sinclair v Versailles* on the facts in front of it, and to find that there was a constructive trust in a situation in which a fiduciary (an agent) had taken a secret commission from a vendor of land, which meant that the agent agreed on behalf of its principal to acquire the land at a higher price than would otherwise have been required to be paid. The Chancellor (Sir Terence Etherton) also expressed the view in his judgment that the Supreme Court should rule as to whether or not the Court of Appeal in *Sinclair* had been correct to overrule *Reid*. No such judgment has been delivered at the time of writing.

The following discussion considers the debate between these two opposing points of view. First, this is done by analysing the judgments on the *Reid* side of the argument and on the *Sinclair* side of the argument. Then the debate in the academic literature is considered. In discussing the two competing lines of authority, the arguments in favour of each approach are stated in the most rhetorical way possible, so as to give life to the force with which each camp holds to its convictions.

---

[20] *Attorney-General for Hong Kong v Reid* [1994] 1 AC 324.
[21] [2011] EWCA Civ 347.
[22] [2013] 3 WLR 466.

## THE JUDGMENT OF LORD TEMPLEMAN IN *REID*

The Privy Council in *Reid* comprised not only Lord Templeman (who delivered the only judgment) but also Lord Goff, who agreed with Lord Templeman. Therefore, there was a large amount of experience and expertise in equity in the court. Indeed, the judgment of Lord Templeman was in line with the sort of focus on 'justice' and morality which was typical of Lord Goff. In *Tinsley v Milligan*,[23] for example, Lord Goff delivered a dissenting judgment in which he refused to allow a resulting trust to be awarded to someone who had bought a share in a house with legitimately earned money, because that person had concealed her ownership from the social security authorities so as to acquire housing benefit illegally. Similarly, in his Lordship's contribution to the law on change of position, Lord Goff expressed himself as being concerned with the balancing of the justice between the parties to litigation.[24] Lord Goff was, of course, one of the fathers of restitution in English law which sowed the seeds for the Oxford School. Therefore, the moral base to the decision in *Reid* is not unusual.

In *Reid* their Lordships were confronting a criminal who had not only committed a crime, but who had received corrupt payments to obstruct the prosecution of criminals. It is difficult to imagine a worse crime committed by a public official, and certainly not one involving a Director of Public Prosecutions. Therefore, it is entirely appropriate that Lord Templeman judges that defendant (in the most literal sense of the word) by describing bribery as being an evil practice. Clearly, the focus of these judges is on preventing that defendant from taking profits from these bribes in the form of the valuable pieces of land which he had been able to acquire in New Zealand with that money, and which he had put into the name of his wife and his solicitor, presumably in an attempt to put them beyond the law. It would be an odd legal system which did not have as its first objective the prevention of immoral behaviour of this sort.

Then Lord Templeman did what any good lawyer would do: he went through the competing authorities and identified why he supported some and not others. It is important to note that he did not simply exercise his discretion and find 'he did right, and you did wrong'. Instead, he worked his way through the authorities. So, Lord Templeman found support in *Keech v Sandford*,[25] *Fawcett v Whitehouse*[26] and *Sugden v Crosland*,[27] all of which pre-dated *Lister v Stubbs* and all of which held that a fiduciary was obliged to act for his principal, was not permitted to have any conflict of interest and was therefore required to hold any profit which he took for himself as part of the trust fund. Several other cases were cited in Lord Templeman's chronological approach to the case law which come to the same conclusion, and this culminated in the House of Lords decision in *Boardman v*

---

[23] [1994] 1 AC 340.
[24] *Lipkin Gorman v Karpnale* [1991] 2 AC 548.
[25] (1726) Cas *temp* King 61, [1558-1774] All ER Rep 230.
[26] (1829) 1 Russ & M 132, 39 ER 51.
[27] (1856) 3 Sm & G 192, 65 ER 620.

*Phipps*[28] which held that any profit taken in a situation in which there is a conflict of interest (not necessarily involving misuse of the trust property itself) must be held on constructive trust. That case in itself had relied on a line of authority in the House of Lords from *Keech v Sandford* through *Bray v Ford*[29] and *Regal (Hastings) Ltd v Gulliver*,[30] all of which had identified the cornerstone of this area of law as being the avoidance of any conflict of interest by a fiduciary as giving rise to a constructive trust. So, there are four House of Lords authorities asserting this as a general principle which gives rise to a constructive trust; the cases on bribes which went the other way (like *Lister v Stubbs*) were therefore the anomalous exceptions. There are also decisions like that of Lord Jessel MR in *Re Caerphilly Colliery Co., Pearson's Case*[31] ('the most distinguished equity judge of his generation'), which held, in Lord Templeman's summary, that the recipient of a bribe holds both the bribe and the property representing the bribe on constructive trust.

Lord Templeman also addressed cases which went against him. There is nothing less surprising in English law than that there will be cases either way. So, in relation to *Tyrrell v Bank of London*,[32] the court is criticised for giving no reasons nor any authority for its observations. Admittedly, the account of *Metropolitan Bank v Heiron*[33] is presented with greater rhetoric than is entirely helpful: we are told it was decided 'perilously close to the long vacation without citation of the relevant authorities'. That judgment considered that a bribe created an equitable debt but not a proprietary right. However, Brett LJ did find that a proprietary right could be declared by the court: the precise genesis of that property right puzzles Lord Templeman, unless it is in the form of a constructive trust.

So, the judgment of Lord Templeman is founded on a review of the authorities. That review of the authorities is partial in that his Lordship clearly preferred one approach to the other approach, but it is nevertheless a review of the authorities. There is also the important moral base for the judgment. Not only did Lord Templeman identify the 'evil' involved in bribery, but he also identified that '[e]quity however which acts in personam[34] insists that it is unconscionable for a fiduciary to obtain and retain a benefit in breach of duty'.[35]

Therefore, unconscionability is at the heart of this judgment, as one might expect from the traditional equitable language. Lord Templeman did have an explanation which justified the finding of a proprietary right which is also based on ancient equitable principle: because equity looks upon as done that which ought to have been done, when the defendant received the bribe he should have handed it over to his principal, and therefore equity will treat him as having

---

[28] [1967] 2 AC 46.
[29] [1896] AC 44.
[30] [1942] 1 All ER 378.
[31] (1877) 5 Ch D 336.
[32] (1862) 10 HL Cas 26, 11 ER 934.
[33] (1880) 5 Ex D 319.
[34] Meaning that it considers the situation of the individual defendant, in this context.
[35] [1993] 1 All ER 1, 4.

handed the bribe over, such that an equitable property right must be deemed to have passed in that bribe and consequently over any property subsequently acquired with that bribe.

Consequently, Lord Templeman based his judgment both on a moral base and on a property law justification for finding the constructive trust which was supported by his review of the authorities. In that sense, Lord Templeman's judgment was a classic of the equitable canon, in that it married a deontological use of moral principles with a consequentialist analysis of the existing authorities.

At its root is a very simple proposition: if a person deliberately does wrong (in particular where that wrong is a criminal offence) then that person should not be entitled to keep any profits which result from that wrong. This, incidentally, is also the basis of the Proceeds of Crime Act 2002 which achieves a different kind of restitution of criminal property by creating an asset recovery mechanism to appropriate from a criminal any property which has been earned by criminal conduct. That is the heart of money laundering law. The decision in *Reid* is therefore in line with the modern approach in criminal law to the treatment of profits taken from crime. By contrast, the decision in *Lister v Stubbs* was located within a welter of competing authority with which it did not deal adequately, and in which the world appears to operate in a moral and social vacuum.

## THE DECISION IN *SINCLAIR v VERSAILLES*

The case of *Sinclair Investments (UK) Ltd v Versailles Trading Ltd*[36] (which had, incidentally, already given rise to several cases in the preceding years which had all adhered to traditional equitable principles) led the Court of Appeal to return to *Lister v Stubbs*. Let us take a practical example to explain the argument. Suppose that Bernice is trustee and that she holds several racehorses on trust for Charles. Alfie pays a bribe to Bernice to induce her to breach her obligations to Charles. In essence, the decision in *Lister v Stubbs* had proceeded on the idea that it would be very peculiar to award a proprietary right in favour of Charles because Alfie had paid money to Bernice. If Charles had never owned that money previously, and if that money had never formed part of a trust fund which Bernice had held on trust for Charles, then why should Charles be said to own it? So, when Alfie pays his own money to Bernice, any claim which Charles might wish to bring cannot sensibly be said to be based in property law. Instead, that claim must be based on some other, personal basis between Charles and Bernice. It is accepted that it is wrong for Bernice to take a payment in breach of her duties (especially a bribe inducing her to breach her obligations to Charles) if she is acting as a fiduciary in relation to Charles (such as holding property on trust for him or acting as his agent), and that Bernice should account to Charles for the amount of that payment. The key point here is that there is no reason why Charles should be said to *own* the bribe itself: it was never his money.

---

[36] [2011] 3 WLR 1153.

Things would be different, however, if Bernice had actually used Charles's property in some way to acquire the bribe. For example, if Alfie had paid a bribe to Bernice to procure the sale of a racehorse from the trust fund to Alfie at an under-value, perhaps by Bernice claiming that the horse was no longer capable of racing. If Bernice had sold one of Charles's racehorses at an under-value so as to earn the bribe, then that would clearly create a link between Charles's property and the payment made to Bernice. The Court of Appeal in *Sinclair v Versailles* accept that that would create a constructive trust because Charles's property had been misused. However, if it was merely Bernice's office as fiduciary which led to the payment then Charles has not had his property interfered with, and therefore the Court of Appeal in *Sinclair v Versailles* held that that would not create a constructive trust.

The justification for this approach in *Sinclair v Versailles* which is typically advanced by the academic scholars, is that in cases of insolvency it is wrong to grant property rights to people without some clear basis for those property rights. This argument is considered below. It must be said that this justification, however, is intent on rewriting the law on constructive trusts to deal with cases of insolvency even though there might not be an insolvency at issue in all cases. It would be preferable to leave the law of trusts alone and to create an exception to deal specifically with cases of insolvency if that is considered to be the real problem.

The facts in *Sinclair v Versailles* related to a fraudulent trading scheme in which Cushnie pretended to be operating an investment firm by manufacturing false records of transactions. On that basis he was able to acquire investment capital from investors, supposedly to make investments on their behalf. Instead, Cushnie simply paid back the investors a percentage of their capital investment as 'profits' and lived on the rest of the capital, using it to buy a very expensive house in Kensington in London amongst other things. This sort of scheme is known as a 'Ponzi scheme' – the convicted fraudster Bernie Madoff operated a similar scheme in New York for decades before the financial crash in 2008. It relies on the fraudster continuing to find new investors to keep money flowing into the scheme: this is done on the promise of seemingly very high profits which are taken from distributing the new capital among the investors. When Cushnie and his firm went into insolvency, the only significant asset remaining was the Kensington house. Arguments were raised, inter alia, that the house should be held on constructive trust, because it had been acquired with false payments equivalent to secret commissions and bribes. That is why the Court of Appeal wanted to resist a constructive trust: if a constructive trust had been found then that house would have been held for one group of claimants as beneficiaries but not made available to any of the other unsecured creditors of Cushnie's scam. Consequently, Cushnie's insolvency prompted the court to reject the *Reid* analysis so that it could come to the outcome it preferred. That required a return to the *Lister v Stubbs* approach.

Oddly, Lord Neuberger justified this approach by saying that there was no justification for arguing that the fiduciary was obliged to take the bribe for the beneficiary, even though Lord Templeman and several of the authorities had demonstrated exactly such a principle on the authorities, as well as the argument which underpinned it – you can explain why you think an argument is unsatisfactory, but you cannot say that that argument does not exist. Even more oddly, Lord Neuberger bolsters his findings by observing that there are more articles in favour of *Lister* than *Reid*. It should be noted, first, that that is true only *after* the decision in *Reid* (whereas *Lister* was roundly dismissed beforehand); secondly, that the academics who write articles, more often do so to disagree with judgments out of cussedness and because it is easier to disagree; and, thirdly, that nearly all of the equity treatises and textbooks agreed with the decision in *Reid*, whereas the articles are commonly written by the Oxford Restitution School and their fellow travellers.

## THE ARGUMENT FOR *LISTER v STUBBS* IN THE RECENT LITERATURE

The arguments in favour of *Lister v Stubbs* which are presented separately by Professor Graham Virgo[37] and Professor Roy Goode,[38] are dominated by the law of insolvency. Both ask the question: Why should there be a proprietary right when a fiduciary receives a bribe? The reason why they both ask that question is that they fear for the creditors of the recipient of the bribe. If the recipient of the bribe is required to hold that bribe on constructive trust for the beneficiary of its fiduciary duties, that bribe will not be available to be passed among its creditors when it goes into insolvency.

Of course, one might also ask the question: What if the recipient of the bribe does *not* go into insolvency? If the recipient of the bribe does not go into insolvency then it will have to account for an amount of cash equal to the bribe, but it will be able to keep any profits which it has made on investing that bribe and any valuable property bought with that bribe. Therefore, the principal Virgo and Goode argument only applies if there has been an insolvency.

The other argument which Professor Goode raises is that there is no basis for a proprietary right in any event, other than some hand-wringing about morality. That, however, is completely to overlook that the conscience-based trust is predicated on a moral base, and that the immorality of the defendant is all that is required to trigger a proprietary obligation which the recipient of the bribe owes to the beneficiary of their relationship. The rationale for the proprietary base is that it is wrong for the recipient to keep either the bribe or any property which flows from the bribe. This is an entirely appropriate situation in which a constructive trust should be imposed to prevent the recipient from taking an unconscionable benefit from its breach of fiduciary duties.

If the insolvency situation is thought to be such a significant exception to that general principle in policy terms, there should simply be a legislative carve-out for

---

[37] G. Virgo, 'Profits obtained in breach of fiduciary duty: personal or proprietary claim?' (2011) 70 *CLJ* 502.
[38] R. Goode, 'Proprietary liability for secret profits – a reply' (2011) 127 *LQR* 493. The reply is to the article by Hayton J, below. See also R. Goode, 'Proprietary Restitutionary Claims' in W. Cornish et al. (eds), *Restitution: Past, Present and Future* (Hart Publishing, 1998), 63.

insolvent recipients of property in situations such as bribes, just as there is a carve-out under s. 423 of the Insolvency Act 1986 which prevents sales at an under-value and so forth transferring property beyond the reach of insolvency creditors. However, there is no need to allow insolvency law to prevent the imposition of a perfectly principled constructive trust in other circumstances.

## THE ARGUMENTS OF THE EQUITY TRADITIONALISTS IN THE RECENT LITERATURE

The equity traditionalists have resisted the *Sinclair* decision. Hayton J[39] (formerly Professor Hayton, author of *Underhill and Hayton on Trusts and Trustees*) and Sir Peter Millett[40] (formerly Lord Millett) have both written articles in support of the approach in *Attorney-General for Hong Kong v Reid*.

Hayton focused on whether or not the Court of Appeal had been bound to follow the earlier Court of Appeal decision in *Lister v Stubbs* as opposed to the Privy Council decision in *Reid*. From the perspective of trusts law, Hayton identified the old principle that the beneficiaries are entitled to argue that the trustee was bound to invest on behalf of the trust, and therefore that when the trustee took a bribe and invested it then the trustee should be deemed to have made that investment on behalf of the trust, with the result that the bribe and the profits should be added to the trust property.[41] As Kekewich J put it, the court 'treats the trustee as having received such a bribe not on his own behalf but on behalf of and as agent for the trust'.[42] This creates a link between the bribe and the trust property, which Hayton wants to do so as to justify the imposition of a constructive trust.

Hayton criticised the distinction that is made in *Sinclair v Versailles*, 'between profit made from exploitation of *property* and profit made from exploitation of *office*, a proprietary remedy being available in the former instance but not the latter'.[43] In many circumstances, the use of the office and of trust 'property' may overlap: as where an army officer uses his uniform to enable contraband or drugs to cross a checkpoint, given that the uniform is army property and the officer's rank attaches to the office. By way of a final word, Hayton points out that the Federal Court of Australia in *Grimaldi v Chameleon Mining NL (No. 2)*[44] rejected the analysis in *Sinclair v Versailles* in favour of the decision in *Reid*, albeit that the Australian constructive trust is a discretionary remedy unlike the English institutional trust. Importantly, the Federal Court of Australia found that *Lister* had placed an 'anomalous' limitation on the extent of the English constructive trust.

---

[39] D. Hayton, 'The extent of equitable remedies: Privy Council versus Court of Appeal' (2012) 33 *Company Lawyer* 161.

[40] P. Millett, 'Bribes and secret commissions again' (2012) 71 *CLJ* 583.

[41] This point was made originally by P. Millett, 'Bribes and secret commissions' [1993] *Restitution Law Review* 7, 20.

[42] [1896] 1 Ch 71, 77.

[43] Hayton, above n 39, 163.

[44] [2012] FCAFC 6.

Millett takes a very different, and more direct, tack. Millett argues that the Court of Appeal in *Sinclair* was 'incorrect' and that:[45]

'The duty of the trustee is to serve the interest of the principal to the exclusion of his own interest. A fiduciary who keeps a profit for himself abuses the trust and confidence placed in him by the principal. He is bound to hand it over to his principal the moment he receives it. Equity's response to a breach of this duty is to enforce the duty by means of the constructive trust.'

What is interesting is that Hayton and Millett are both reluctant equity specialists, in that they refuse to allow themselves to take Aristotle's approach, i.e. to use equity to achieve a just outcome.[46] Instead, they are careful to find a proprietary base on which their constructive trusts may be erected. Lord Templeman was bolder than that. Lord Templeman was prepared to identify bribery as an evil practice, to focus on the unconscionability of someone taking a profit from such an evil practice and to impose a constructive trust as a result. It is breath-taking in its simplicity. And, unlike much of our modern law-making, it deals simply with right and wrong.

## IN CONCLUSION

There are three approaches to bribes. First, that constructive trusts should be seen as a means of avoiding insolvency, and therefore as being a bad thing. This is the approach taken by commercial lawyers like Professor Goode, who see the risk of insolvency as being the most significant factor in cases of this sort. Secondly, that the law of trusts is a technical discipline which can establish a principled basis for a trust to be imposed over a 'false fiduciary' who misuses either their office or trust property. Thirdly, that the law of trusts rests on a moral basis which in itself can justify the imposition of a constructive trust to prevent unconscionable benefit being taken from a breach of trust, or a conflict between fiduciary duties and a fiduciary's personal interests.

That there are simply three different points of view about this issue would seem normal in any other walk of life. In relation to legal questions it can seem surprising to students. However, we have identified that there are debates here in which different people simply see the same legal question from entirely different perspectives. Those people are unlikely to change their minds, or to be convinced by one another's arguments. Indeed, in disagreeing with one another they are positively Edwardian in their politeness. However, what this demonstrates is that the perspective from which one approaches a question will often dictate the answer. If you approach the question of constructive trusts from the need to protect unsecured creditors in an insolvency, then you will follow Goode and Virgo and

---

[45] Millett, above n 40. This quotation, which summarises the pith of Millett's excellent article, is taken from the Abstract.

[46] More accurately, of course, Aristotle's approach involved circumventing statute when the legislator had failed to anticipate a specific factual scenario and had thus made an 'error', as was discussed in Ch. 1.

prevent constructive trusts from being imposed. If you approach the same question from the need to prevent immoral benefits being taken from abusing a fiduciary office then you are likely to impose a constructive trust over that profit. It is all a question of perspective.

## Debate  2

### Objections to the notion of a constructive trust

This short debate considers whether the constructive trust is useful at all. One school of thought considers that it is not a helpful concept in the first place. The next debate considers a subtly different question: whether the manner in which the constructive trust is said to arise is the most propitious.

The Oxford Restitution School generally considers the constructive trust to be the enemy of the sort of private law which they would like to see in English law. Their vision for the future was outlined in Chapter 3 of this book. In particular, Peter Birks was clear about his difficulties with the constructive trust:[47]

> 'Can the words "constructive trust" be dispensed with? They are certainly not very useful. They do not tell you anything about the quantum of the interest (fee simple, life estate or something tailored *ad hoc*) which the court will recognise. They do not tell you anything about the event which raises the interest, except negatively that it is not an express, implied or presumed declaration of trust. Worse than being uninformative, they also confuse. First, because they are not unequivocal in their reference to rights *in rem* rather than to rights *in personam* or to the concurrent availability of both in the same set of facts. Secondly, because they are surrounded by an unintelligible and infinitely damaging dispute as to whether they should be regarded as referring to rights at all or only to remedies or a remedy.'

The argument which Birks makes is that the conscience which is at issue here is simply whatever the judge in any given case thinks subjectively that it is. Moreover, the term 'constructive trust' is criticised for being too little defined; and yet we do not criticise the term 'tort' for being too ill-defined, instead we look at the case law in which the term 'tort' is used and we decide what it means from there, by observing that the different torts fall into different categories with different features (many of which are hotly contested between the judges and the commentators). The doctrines of constructive trust are very clear about what property is held on constructive trust (i.e. whatever property was treated unconscionably by the defendant or its traceable proceeds) and they are equally clear about the level of compensation which must be paid under a personal claim for dishonest assistance or knowing receipt. The division between those two types of case also expresses the division between *in personam* and *in rem* rights. There is no damaging dispute here: assistants and recipients further to a breach of trust will be

---

47 P. Birks, *An Introduction to Restitution* (Clarendon Press, 1989), 89.

liable for personal remedies, whereas all other constructive trusts are proprietary. In that sense, Birks's specific complaints do not hold water.

The following response to Birks's argument is typical of the equity specialist. It comes from the Australian lawyers Young, Croft and Smith in their excellent book, *On Equity*:[48]

> 'From time to time it is stated that unconscionable conduct is merely conduct that the particular judge before whom the case is heard considers to be unfair. Birks, for instance, described "unconscionability" as a term that "simply conceals private and intuitive evaluation".[49] This is incorrect, and has been considered incorrect for centuries. Lord Eldon, for instance, in *Gordon v Gordon*,[50] warned that it was "the duty of the Judge to make a covenant with himself not to suffer his feelings to influence his judgment".'

Again, the Oxford School's caricature of equity is that equitable doctrines and remedies arise entirely chaotically, whereas any study of trusts law demonstrates that Chancery judges in fact deliver judgment in reliance on precedent (or else they distinguish earlier precedents using exactly the same techniques as common law judgments). These arguments were considered in Chapter 3: you are referred back to that discussion if you want to revisit that general territory. By contrast to these caricatures of equity, as is considered below, much trusts law scholarship focuses on how even the most discretionary of remedies (for example, proprietary estoppel) is subjected to precedent. Thus, even the most deontological of doctrines succumbs to consequentialism in practice. This was the lesson we took from observing Lord Templeman's judgment in *Reid*: even though it is often dismissed as being emotional and based on moral considerations alone, it is actually constructed on the basis of deontological principle and a thorough, consequentialist review of the authorities.

# Debate 3

## Are constructive trusts incoherent as a doctrine?

There is one central debate at the heart of the law on constructive trusts: given that there are so many sub-species of constructive trust, should they be considered as being entirely distinct doctrines which operate randomly and incoherently, or should they be considered as being collected under a single, high-level principle of good conscience? This section considers that issue.

### IS THE DOCTRINE OF CONSTRUCTIVE TRUST A COHERENT ONE?

It has been suggested that the doctrine of constructive trusts may serve only to confuse because it is not clear on what basis constructive trusts arise, because they

---

[48] P. Young, C. Croft and M. Smith, *On Equity* (Law Book Co., 2009), 111.
[49] P. Birks, 'Equity, Conscience, and Unjust Enrichment' (1999) 23 *Melbourne University Law Review* 1, 22.
[50] (1821) 3 Swans 400, 468; 36 ER 910, 919.

are sometimes personal and sometimes proprietary, and because they do not constitute a coherent doctrine.[51] The contrary point of view is that constructive trusts offer an important means for judges to ensure that justice is done on the facts before them as they see it – having listened to the witnesses and examined the evidence – so as to prevent a benefit being taken from unconscionable conduct. So, do constructive trusts constitute a coherent doctrine or not?

First, the argument that constructive trusts do not arise on a coherent basis. If one looks at all of the various types of constructive trust considered in this chapter, and also looks at the doctrines of dishonest assistance and knowing receipt (which arise on the basis of constructive trusteeship) in Chapter 10, and also at the common intention constructive trusts in Chapter 9, then it is plain that these constructive trusts are not identical. Some arise on the basis of dishonesty, others on the basis of knowledge, others on the basis of a common intention between the parties as to their shared ownership rights. Those triggers are not identical. Similarly, the constructive trust in *Boardman v Phipps*[52] arises so as to prevent conflicts of interest; the constructive trust in *Attorney-General for Hong Kong v Reid* arises on the basis of equity looking upon as done that which ought to have been done so as to take possession of a bribe; the common intention constructive trust in *Lloyds Bank v Rosset*[53] and *Jones v Kernott*[54] arises so as to effect mutual understandings, or in relation to conduct in the form of contributions to the purchase price of property; the constructive trust in *Jerome v Kelly* arises as a trust sub modo in relation to a contract to transfer property; the constructive trusteeship in *Royal Brunei Airlines v Tan*[55] arises in response to dishonesty. All of these cases were at the House of Lords or Privy Council level, and do not include the many decisions of more junior courts which take other approaches still; and yet it is apparent that they do not arise on exactly the same basis. These various courts do not even refer to each other – rather, they seem to be deciding points which are specific to their own particular form of constructive trust. The key words they use in reaching their judgments – conscience, dishonesty, conflict of interest, that which ought to be done and so forth – are different. Therefore, we could say that constructive trusts lack coherence.

The alternative point of view is that constructive trusts are ultimately predicated on a single, deontological principle. To make this argument would require us to return to the House of Lords decision in *Westdeutsche Landesbank v Islington*.[56] As was discussed at the beginning of this chapter, Lord Browne-Wilkinson reminded us that equity has always operated on the basis of conscience; since the *Earl of Oxford's Case* in 1615 this has been the case, as considered in Chapter 1. Constructive trusts are therefore said to arise on the basis

---

[51] Birks, above n 47, 89.
[52] [1967] 2 AC 46.
[53] [1991] 1 AC 107.
[54] [2011] UKSC 53.
[55] [1995] 2 AC 378.
[56] [1996] AC 669.

of the defendant's knowing of some factor which affects her conscience in relation to property. That is a perfectly viable, underpinning principle on which to base a legal concept like the constructive trust. The other House of Lords and Privy Council cases considered above may be understood as operating on a basis similar to that principle, even if they do not use the exact same language. While they do not use exactly the same terminology all of the time, all of their principles operate on a set of concepts which are very similar to saying that the defendant has acted unconscionably. That is so whether the test applied is one of allowing a conflict of interest, or acting dishonestly, or seeking to deny someone rights in a home for which she has paid in part, or seeking to renege on a contractual obligation to transfer property: each of these tests could be understood as responding at root to a requirement that the defendant act in good conscience, just as *Westdeutsche Landesbank v Islington* and the *Earl of Oxford's Case* required.

Either you are convinced that this area is sufficiently explicable on the basis of a deep, underpinning notion of conscience, or you consider it to be based on no valid organising concept and instead as comprising a scattering of unconnected doctrines. Your approach to that question is probably expressive of your view of this area of law as a whole.

## CATEGORISING CONSTRUCTIVE TRUSTS

### A taxonomy of constructive trusts

Elias presented an attempt at a taxonomy of constructive trusts in his book *Explaining the Constructive Trust*.[57] This is a not a book which has attracted much support – not least because it fell in line neither with the restitutionary scholarship nor with the traditional equitable case law: consequently, neither the Oxford School nor the Chancery judges and commentators would find much in it which they could support. However, Elias's work is valuable, not least because it highlights another line in the equity scholarship: the consequentialist line. This book has presented much of the debate about equity as being a debate under the surface between common lawyers and equity specialists, between restitution scholars and equity scholars, between positivists and natural lawyers. However, there is another species of scholar who considers equity – the consequentialist – who erects an understanding of what 'unconscionability' might mean as a technical question by means of analysing the case law and categorising the various cases according to features they have in common or in disagreement.

Elias explains the three aims of constructive trusts as being: perfection, restitution and reparation.[58] The constructive trust discussed by Elias is one that explicitly speaks in the language of gifts and which is of less use in a commercial context.[59] The 'perfection aim' is identified most clearly in *Re Rose*,[60] on the basis

---

[57] G. Elias, *Explaining the Constructive Trust* (Clarendon Press, 1990).
[58] Ibid, 4.
[59] Ibid, 14.
[60] [1952] Ch 499.

that the <u>settlor's intentions should be given effect to</u>. The perfection aim concentrates on using the constructive trust as a means of perfecting the choices and contracts which individuals had sought to make but which have been found to be ineffective.[61] In Elias's view, the restitution aim is inherently less 'harsh' than the perfection aim and the reparation aim, because the restitution aim does no more than 'remove superfluities in the defendant's hands' by transferring them back to their more justified owner.[62]

### Categorising unconscionability

As was mentioned in the discussion in Chapters 1 and 2 of this book, while equity is often presented as being simply a discretionary doctrine with no rules, in truth, trusts law and most of the equitable remedies have hardened in practice into doctrines which obey the doctrine of precedent closely and which have developed rules on certainties and so forth. In consequence, much of the trusts law scholarship in particular presents close analyses of the cases and of the rules which are presented in them. As with all case law codes of law, there are cases at the edges which may take a maverick point of view. There are also cases which have developed doctrines like proprietary estoppel and the law on trusts of homes into ways of using high-level principles which are similar to family law; but that is because they often involve families and their homes. They are still not entirely discretionary; instead, they use precedent in their own ways.

If the common law is supposed to be a beacon of good order then we might question why the judges and the commentators on the tort of negligence cannot come to a decision as to whether standards of 'fair, just and reasonable' are part of that tort or not, and so forth. The law of tort is in a more confused condition than the law on express trusts ever was. Listening to common lawyers complain about the perceived disorderliness of equity is like listening to a man who has just left a noisy tavern brawl, covered in his own blood and the blood of others, trying to tell you that you should be ashamed because you have not got your jacket on straight.

## UNCONSCIONABILITY AS OBSERVED BY EQUITY SCHOLARS

### Mapping unconscionability without the need for ideology or theory first

It would be perfectly possible (as was acknowledged in Chapters 1 and 2 of this book) to decide, on the basis of much of the published scholarship, that I had blundered in explaining the debates in equity and trusts as beginning with an abstract notion: 'What is a conscience?' As was made plain in Chapter 1, equity could be understood as being deontological (in the sense of having a central, high-level principle of conscience which must be understood in the abstract before any further analysis can proceed), or it could be understood as being consequentialist (in the sense that the concept of conscience does not need to be understood in

---

[61] Elias, above n 57, 9, fn 2.
[62] Ibid, 75.

theoretical terms first but should be understood instead as being the amalgamation of the cases which have demonstrated, defined and delineated what it means to act 'unconscionably' and so give rise to constructive trusts). This important section considers the approach of two important scholars in this area: Professor Nicholas Hopkins and Dr Martin Dixon.

### Finding the unconscionability in *Rochefoucauld v Boustead*

Nicholas Hopkins has written a series of articles on the concepts of 'conscience' and 'unconscionability' which have focused on how those concepts have actually been used in the case law, and what we can learn from their usage so as to define what they mean in practice. So, in 2006, Hopkins considered, inter alia, the *Rochefoucauld v Boustead*[63] form of equitable doctrine, which is now understood in the case law as being a form of constructive trust.[64] The argument which is advanced there is that it would be possible to find that there had been unconscionability and then to give the courts a discretion to decide what form of remedy should follow; whereas, at present, the House of Lords in *Westdeutsche Landesbank v Islington*[65] was clear that English trusts were institutional in that they arose automatically, and that the nature of the trust was a proprietary right fixed over the property which had been treated unconscionably or its traceable proceeds. Methodologically, however, Hopkins does not retreat into a moral base to justify the courts in any finding they wish; instead that article is a careful analysis of how *Rochefoucauld v Boustead* worked, how it may be understood as a constructive trust (as opposed simply to the ancient principle that statute cannot be used as an engine of fraud by someone who promised to sell land to X then realised that a statutory formality had not been performed and so sought to sell the land to Y instead). Importantly, Hopkins begins by identifying much of the traditional theorising about the nature of equity, before drilling down into the case law and finding much more of interest in the precise dicta delivered by the judges and by the different schools of commentators.

A similar approach is taken by Hopkins in an essay published in 2007[66] which models the way in which unconscionability is used in *Rochefoucauld v Boustead* and similar cases. What looms large behind this essay is an idea expressed by Parkinson (and quoted by Hopkins) in the following way: '[T]he conscience of equity must not be given a life of its own, independent of the specific doctrines through which it finds expression.'[67] For Australian lawyers like Parkinson, however, the remedial constructive trust (in which Australian courts may fix whatever remedy is appropriate to the finding of unconscionability, a little like the English proprietary

---

[63] [1897] 1 Ch 196.

[64] N. Hopkins, 'Conscience, discretion and the creation of property rights' (2006) 26 *LS* 475.

[65] [1996] AC 669.

[66] N. Hopkins, 'How should we respond to unconscionability?' in M. Dixon and G. Griffiths (eds), *Contemporary Perspectives on Property, Equity and Trusts Law* (Oxford University Press, 2007), 3.

[67] P. Parkinson, 'The Conscience of Equity' in P. Parkinson (ed.), *The Principles of Equity*, 2nd edn (Law Book Co., 2003), 53.

estoppel in that limited sense) perhaps creates a greater risk of its acquiring 'a life of its own'. So, Hopkins distinguishes between cases where a person reneges on a pre-contractual agreement (what he calls a 'subject to' situation), as opposed to other situations such as proprietary estoppel which are predicated on different notions of unconscionability (and in many cases not even unconscionability at all). There is also a difference identified between two-party cases and three-party cases, and so on. His purpose is to differentiate between the qualitative levels of unconscionability in different types of cases, and the nature of the constructive trust that arises. This is different from debating what a conscience means theoretically on a deontological basis.

## Unconscionability in land law

Martin Dixon specialises in land law and in equity (and also in international law). His perspective is therefore often on the overlap between land law and equity, especially in relation to ownership of the home and equitable devices which are used to circumvent the land registration requirements on occasion. The overlap here is different from that explored by the Oxford School. The restitution specialists have spent little time on the ancient abstractions (e.g. the law on prescription, 'lost modern grant', fee simple absolute in possession and so forth) and the necessary formal rules which attend the ownership and use of land. Land law has always sought formality, even before the Statute of Frauds in 1677. Therefore, Dixon's perspectives on equitable doctrines like proprietary estoppel and land law are always illuminating, in a series of articles, his textbooks on land law and his contributions to *Megarry and Wade's Law of Real Property*. In one article in particular,[68] Dixon sets himself the task of trying to stake out (appropriately enough for a land lawyer) the topography of unconscionability as it is used in cases of proprietary estoppel.

The principal question which is addressed in Dixon's article, as he explains it also was in the House of Lords in *Cobbe v Yeoman's Row*,[69] is as follows:[70]

'To what extent should we allow estoppel to create property rights through the back door when there is a clear public policy, expressed in statute, that generally property rights should be created with a certain degree of formality?'

The backdrop to this article was the House of Lords decision in *Cobbe*, in which Lord Scott cajoled the House into limiting proprietary estoppel in cases in which pre-contractual negotiations and representations had induced one person to suffer great personal detriment, only for the contract to fail to materialise. Even Lord Walker, who had used the idea of unconscionability so well in cases like *Jennings v Rice*,[71] was induced to turn from the old equitable religion.[72] Later in *Thorner v*

---

[68] M. Dixon, 'Confining and defining proprietary estoppel: the role of unconscionabilty' (2010) 30 *LS* 408.
[69] [2008] UKHL 55.
[70] (2010) 30 LS 408, 410.
[71] *Jennings v Rice* [2003] 1 P & CR 100, [2002] EWCA Civ 159.
[72] That reads like a Star Wars reference in which a Jedi is turned to the dark side: and for that reason it stays in the text.

*Major*,[73] Lord Walker (without Lord Scott present) felt emboldened to return to the traditional idea that proprietary estoppel could operate so as to prevent unconscionability. In that case it went so far as to find a representation in a situation in which two men barely spoke to one another!

In his analysis, Dixon surveys the case law, seeking out the circumstances in which unconscionability has and has not been decisive either in the finding of the estoppel or in the shaping of the remedy, as well as divining the meanings which could be ascribed to the idea of unconscionability on this consequentialist basis. Admirably, Dixon nails his colours to mast when he tells us that he believes 'it is possible to anchor proprietary estoppel with a discretionary framework in a way that is principled and which explains why it can operate to create proprietary rights'.[74] That is, the uses of unconscionability in the proprietary estoppel case law can be explained and ordered by analysis of the existing case law (of which there is a lot), without losing any of their genuinely equitable features. His conclusion, based on a careful winnowing[75] of the case law, is that unconscionability in this context means 'going back on an assurance about formality, in conjunction with a "rights assurance" that is "certain enough" and detrimental reliance'.[76]

## Creating taxonomy by scholarship not by ideology

The order in Dixon's work is not introduced by ideology but rather by observation. This is akin to the work of a biologist: the biologist does not manufacture plants and insects to conform to particular patterns. Rather, the biologist observes the patterns and groupings that exist in nature, and uses them to generate a taxonomy which explains how the natural world is ordered (and thus facilitates an understanding of how the natural world changes over time through evolution and environmental degradation). This is unlike the Oxford School taxonomy which seeks to impose the ordering on ideological grounds in advance of the observation. The sort of work which Dixon does is important within the ecology of equity. Like a bee carrying pollen from flower to flower, scholars like Dixon, Hopkins and (it is hoped) Hudson help the judges and the practitioners by observing the flora and fauna, by explaining their nature and how they are changing, and by suggesting ways of understanding and developing them. The judges generate so many judgments which are now available online in a way that was simply not available more than 10 years ago,[77] that it is only because there are scholars who devote their time to reading all of that case law and presenting it back to the judges and the practitioners that it is possible to understand how equity actually

---

[73] [2009] 1 WLR 776.

[74] Dixon, above n 68, 413.

[75] See how we use agricultural metaphors to talk about land law.

[76] Dixon, above n 68, 419.

[77] Before websites like www.bailii.org did their vital work of making all these judgments available online for free, the only law we knew about were the cases that were actually reported in the hard-copy law reports.

functions. This is a very different form of equity from an equity which begins from a high-level principle or from ideology and works outwards. This is more akin to fieldwork botany, or to fieldwork sociology in which the raw material is acquired and then analysed by social scientists.

## CONCLUSION

When all is said and done, *Rochefoucauld v Boustead*[78] rests on the simple idea that it was wrong for the defendant to have promised to do one thing and then to have done another on realising that the claimant had failed to acquire the formal protection of a statutory procedure. The defendant was clearly exploiting a situation in an unconscionable way. Clearly, we would all be uncomfortable if judges simply delivered judgment in the following terms: 'I don't know why, but I know I don't like that. Order accordingly.' We would not like the judiciary to decide cases on a whim. We want to know why they have decided as they do, so that we can understand how the law is developing. More importantly, in very many ways of course, the litigants themselves want to know why the judges have decided as they have. However, at root, the court in *Rochefoucauld* could spot an unconscionable exploitation of a technicality which would cause detriment to the claimant; and one of the oldest equitable principles, from the time of Aristotle, was that equity exists so as to achieve justice in circumstances in which a statutory rule would otherwise cause injustice if it was applied unthinkingly, because the legislator had not anticipated this particular eventuality.

Importantly, judges will always want to be able to reach what they consider to be the 'right' result, regardless of the law. On occasion, they will observe that the law binds them and that, with regret, there is nothing they can do: but that can only be in situations in which their regret does not outweigh their discomfort with the outcome. For a judge like Lord Denning, every injustice was a call to arms. His use of judicial discretion, detailed so clearly in his many volumes of memoirs such as *The Due Process of Law*,[79] which explained his judgments in relation to ownership of the home (considered in the next chapter), led to the sort of judicial creativity-through-equity which so disturbs the Oxford School.

However, the Browne-Wilkinson, Templeman and Goff generation of judges never went in for naked judicial creativity in equity. Progressive judgments like *Reid* and *Tinsley v Milligan* (analysed in detail in the previous chapter), and the decision in *Westdeutsche* which reminded us of ancient principles, were all based on careful property law logic, a close analysis of the earlier case law and a seasoning of high-level principle to ensure that the outcomes were always morally defensible. That is not naked judicial discretion. Instead, it is principled judgment. And that is something we must want from our judges. When we live in a confusing,

---

[78] [1897] 1 Ch 196.
[79] A. Denning, *The Due Process of Law* (Butterworths, 1980).

ever-changing, surprising world, we need to remember our moral principles so that we can meet the challenges presented by that world with a clear head. That is not an absence of thought nor an absence of principle. Synthesised with a system of clear rules, that sort of equity is necessary to meet the challenges of the modern world.

# 9

## TRUSTS OF HOMES

## INTRODUCTION

The law relating to the ownership of the home, and the debates that surround it, are among the most intellectually rewarding in equity and trusts. They enable you to go to the heart of debates about British society, debates about the central organising principles of equity and trusts, and debates about the nature of law itself in its social context. The issues considered in this chapter relate to the ownership of the home in every situation except for the allocation of rights in the home after divorce.[1] Whereas many of the issues relating to express trusts can appear to be technical and abstract, the issues relating to ownership of the home are easy to understand and vital (even if some of the legal models used to address them are not).

Land is centrally important to human beings. There is nothing more important to a nation than its land. Equally, there is nothing more important to a human being than their home. However, the home is something more than just land and buildings. It is something spiritual, emotional and deeply significant to each individual. Disputes over the home are therefore deeply emotionally charged for each individual involved. Similarly, disputes as to the ownership of the home are central to our popular culture: most soap operas, as well as many novels and movies, revolve around the breakdown of relationships and the treatment of the home. We all understand those disputes intuitively. The human dimension of every legal dispute considered in this chapter must always be borne in mind.

What the various legal models for recognising rights in the home expose are attitudinal differences between the various judges and commentators as to the sorts of issues that are important when allocating rights in the home: for example, whether rights should depend entirely upon financial contributions, or whether other factors, like caring for the children of a relationship, are of equal importance; and whether rights should be concretised from the outset or made capable of change throughout a relationship.

---

[1] The law considered in this chapter is implacably bourgeois: that is, it relates to home ownership and not to renting or other modes of occupation.

This chapter identifies some of the more vital debates in this area from the broad literature. The legal principles are outlined in the next section before the debates are laid out. The first debate relates to the central concept of 'common intention' in the case law, and whether or not that is a useful test in this context. The common intention test was the 'big bang' in this area when it was first introduced in the 1970s, but as an example taken from the TV show *The Big Bang Theory* illustrates, it may not be the most suitable approach in the modern world. The second debate considers the sorts of 'real life' scenarios and the types of relationship which may or may not involve acquiring rights in the property, in part by reference to the TV show *Sex in the City*, where the main character wins the right to leave a hairdryer in her boyfriend's apartment but thereby probably denies herself any rights in his home. The third debate asks why the equitable test of unconscionability has disappeared from this area of law, and what the concept of 'fairness' in the cases could mean. The last debate sets out a comparison of English law with the very different tests adopted elsewhere in the Commonwealth in reaction to the perceived inadequacies of the English common intention test.

## THE LAW RELATING TO OWNERSHIP OF THE HOME

### THE PRINCIPLES IN OUTLINE

The law in this area underwent a significant change in 1970. Previously, ownership of the home had been covered by the Married Women's Property Act 1882, which provided a scheme for allocating rights to married women in particular circumstances. In the House of Lords in *Pettitt v Pettitt*[2] in 1970, the first impression came that change was in the air (in part in the discussion of the judgment of Diplock LJ in the Court of Appeal). The changes in British society during the 1960s had been profound, with the crumbling of a lot of the pre-war social order. It was not until 1973 that the institution of marriage was regularised by means of the Matrimonial Disputes Act, which made divorce less medieval than the sort of farcical arrangements which were so memorably illustrated in Evelyn Waugh's novel *A Handful of Dust*.

In 1971, in the House of Lords in *Gissing v Gissing*,[3] Lord Diplock established the concept of 'common intention' in English law, whereby the court would allocate rights in the home in accordance with the common intention of the parties to the relationship. This approach supposed that the parties would be in the sort of stable relationship (like an idealised form of marriage) in which they might have established their common intention in relation to their property rights from the outset of their relationship.

---

[2] [1970] AC 777.
[3] [1971] AC 886.

This concept was allowed to grow in later cases. However, it splintered into incoherence as different cases took different approaches to the idea of what a common intention might involve. For example, in *Cowcher v Cowcher*,[4] Bagnall J identified that some judges had taken the approach that the common intention related to an agreement about the amount of money each of the parties would contribute, whereas other judges had focused on an agreement as to the size of the interest each of them would acquire. In cases like *Grant v Edwards*,[5] Browne-Wilkinson V-C identified the principle as turning on the equitable treatment of the various parties to the relationship.

By contrast, in the House of Lords decision in *Lloyds Bank v Rosset*,[6] it was held that there were two ways of acquiring rights in property based on the seemingly composite concept of 'constructive trust or proprietary estoppel'.[7] First, prior to the date of acquisition of the property there must be some agreement, arrangement or understanding between the parties as to their rights in the property, in tandem with some detriment being suffered by the claimant. Secondly, in the alternative, rights would be acquired by anyone who had contributed to the purchase price or to the mortgage instalments, but 'it is at least extremely doubtful whether anything less will do'. The judgment of Lord Bridge in *Rosset* was criticised roundly by many commentators and was ignored by many judges in later cases (in spite of the fact that it was the unanimous decision of the House of Lords). Hudson made the following criticism of that judgment:[8]

'What Lord Bridge appeared to forget is that people fall in love. And that when they fall in love they sometimes move in together, or get married, or have children. Or sometimes they don't fall in love but they have children and so have to move in together. And so on and so on. Hundreds of years of novels, plays and (latterly) films have shown us the perfidies of the human heart. Similarly, they have shown us (to quote Shakespeare's *King Lear*) that fate deals with us cruelly: "as flies to wanton boys are we to the gods / they use us for their sport." It is not possible to create a strict test like that in *Rosset* and expect either that people will always sit down calmly in those glorious early days of a relationship and decide who is to have what equitable interest in the home, or that people will be able to form a common intention at the start of their relationship which will work perfectly throughout it without anyone becoming ill, being made redundant, falling out of love, or whatever else. Life is just not like that. It is suggested that it is contrary to the very core of equity's flexible ability to do right on a case-by-case basis to use concepts like that in *Rosset* to attempt to fetter and bind the ability of the courts to see the right result in any particular case and ... to isolate the best possible outcome.'

---

[4] [1972] 1 WLR 425.

[5] [1986] Ch 638.

[6] [1991] 1 AC 107.

[7] As is discussed below, a synthesis of these principles is impossible unless one or other of them is radically changed.

[8] Alastair Hudson, *Equity & Trusts*, 15.4.4.

The response to this clear (if unsatisfactory) tidying of the law by the House of Lords in *Rosset* was a period of extensive judicial disobedience towards the doctrine of precedent: judges rarely followed *Rosset*. For example, in *Springette v Defoe*[9] and in *Huntingford v Hobbs*,[10] the Court of Appeal held that allocation of rights in the home was dependent on resulting trust principles (an approach not even mentioned in *Rosset*). In *Huntingford* it was held that whereas resulting trusts ordinarily took effect at the date of acquisition, the resulting trust could be altered so as to accommodate the cost of constructing a conservatory on a property after the date of acquisition.

In *Midland Bank v Cooke*,[11] significantly, Waite LJ held that it was open to the court 'to undertake a survey of the entire course of dealing between the parties'. That included a wife's role in looking after the children, taking temporary work when times were hard, paying for grocery and other shopping, and so forth. All of these forms of contribution had been ruled inadmissible in cases such as *Lloyds Bank v Rosset* and *Burns v Burns*.[12] Nevertheless, this new direction in *Cooke* was accepted by the Court of Appeal in *Oxley v Hiscock*[13] and the House of Lords in *Stack v Dowden*.[14]

In the meantime there had been other cases which had operated by reference to a principle of unconscionability. So, in *Cox v Jones*,[15] Mann J took the approach of considering all of the factors in play between the parties (an unmarried pair of barristers) and allocating proprietary rights in such a way that he could ensure that neither party was treated unconscionably. In that case, the younger woman (who had not paid directly for the properties but who had contributed in other ways) was entitled to ownership of a flat and a share of a house the alteration of which she had overseen. Interestingly, allowing a right in part on the basis of supervising building work was exactly the activity which had been rejected in *Lloyds Bank v Rosset* as founding no equitable proprietary rights. In *Jennings v Rice*,[16] the Court of Appeal awarded rights in property on the basis of many years attending the owner of property, so as to avoid any unconscionability.

The link with unconscionability has arisen in cases involving proprietary estoppel. Ordinarily, proprietary estoppel arises on basis of a representation being made by the defendant to the claimant,[17] in reliance on which the claimant acted to her detriment. Once the estoppel has been made out, a separate question arises as to the appropriate remedy, and the motivation for that remedy. In some cases, the motivation for the remedy has been the enforcement of the promise (for example,

---

[9] [1992] 2 FLR 388.
[10] [1993] 1 FLR 736.
[11] [1995] 4 All ER 562.
[12] [1984] Ch 317.
[13] [2004] 3 All ER 703.
[14] [2007] 2 WLR 831.
[15] [2004] 3 FCR 693.
[16] [2003] 1 P&CR 100.
[17] The representation must be meaningful and cannot simply be part of ordinary conversation or flirting: as in *Lissimore v Downing* [2003] 2 FLR 308.

by awarding a freehold in property which the claimant had been promised she would receive in the defendant's will),[18] or the avoidance of detriment being uncompensated (which may lead to a mere award of money if the detriment was comparatively limited)[19] or the avoidance of the claimant being treated unconscionably.[20] The remedy relating to proprietary estoppel may therefore range from a purely personal award of compensation at one end of the spectrum, through to the award of a proprietary right, such as ownership of the freehold of the property, at the other end of the spectrum. In some cases there has been an award which granted proprietary rights (over a cottage on farmland, and a field making up part of a farm, on which the claimant had worked) as well as compensation.[21] In one remarkable decision, a divorced first wife and the second wife of a deceased owner of property were ordered to cohabit in the deceased's former property.[22]

The impression as a result of this must clearly be that the law is a mosaic of different doctrines. In keeping with one of the central themes of this book, this form of law-making makes it difficult to know with certainty what the law is, although it does mean that individual judges can come to appropriate conclusions on the precise facts in front of them. When the House of Lords gave judgment in *Stack v Dowden*,[23] Baroness Hale gave a careful judgment which was influenced, it is suggested, by her own career as a leading academic and Law Commissioner in the field of family law. Her Ladyship hoped that the formalities of conveying land to couples would lead to a regularisation of this area. While few specific rules were overruled, there was a preference implied for undertaking a survey of the entire course of dealing between the parties over the approach in *Rosset*. Unfortunately, *Stack* and the Privy Council decision in *Abbott v Abbott*[24] failed to redirect the law.

It was only in the Supreme Court decision in *Jones v Kernott*[25] (see further below) that the *Stack* decision was explained and a restatement of the core principles set out by Lady Hale and Lord Walker. These principles offer to usher in a new age, in which the courts may seek to do 'fairness' between the parties if their 'common intention' cannot be identified. Interestingly, in *Stack v Dowden*, Lord Neuberger proposed a powerful dissenting judgment which returned to traditional concepts: his Lordship suggested that the court should begin with a resulting trust, looking at the parties' cash contributions to the property, and then use constructive trust principles to account for subsequent activities.

One of the debates remains a debate between strict traditional models and open-textured newer models. In that sense, this is part of the core debates which have run throughout this book.

---

[18] *Re Basham* [1986] 1 WLR 1498.
[19] *Campbell v Griffin* [2001] WTLR 981.
[20] *Jennings v Rice* [2002] EWCA Civ 159.
[21] *Gillett v Holt* [2000] 2 All ER 289.
[22] *Porntip Stallion v Stallion Holdings* [2010] 1 FCR 145.
[23] [2007] UKHL17, [2007] 2 WLR 831.
[24] [2008] 1 FLR 1451.
[25] [2011] UKSC 53, [2011] 3 WLR 1121.

## THE DECISION OF THE SUPREME COURT IN *JONES v KERNOTT*

The decision of the Supreme Court in *Jones v Kernott*[26] attempted to clarify the judgment in *Stack v Dowden*, and in so doing the judges sought to straighten out the relevant principles. So, Lord Walker and Lady Hale delivered a joint judgment; and Lord Kerr attempted to identify the principles which were agreed between the members of the Supreme Court.[27] Those principles are the following. First, the Court began by examining who was identified as being the owner of the property on its legal title:

> '(i) In joint names cases [i.e. where both litigants are entered on the legal title as being the owner of the property], the starting point is that equity follows the law. [Thus, the equitable interest would be divided in the same way as the legal title.] One begins the search for the proper allocation of shares in the property with the presumption that the parties are joint tenants and are thus entitled to equal shares.'[28]

This means that where the legal title in the property has been put in the joint names of the parties then it is presumed that parties are to be joint tenants in equity. Alternatively, where only one person is identified as being the owner of the property, the presumption is that that person is the sole owner of the equitable interest over the property. As with all presumptions in equity, that presumption may be rebutted by showing that the facts were intended to be something different from that presumption.

Significantly, the Supreme Court then set out the position if this presumption could be rebutted, in the following fashion:

> '(ii) That presumption can be displaced by showing (a) that the parties had a different common intention at the time when they acquired the home or (b) that they later formed the common intention that their respective shares would change ...'[29]

The rebuttal of the presumption may take effect either before purchase or at a later date.[30] What is unclear here, significantly, is *what sort* of common intention would be required to rebut this presumption after the purchase, especially given that the parties are likely to present different evidence at trial if equitable ownership is contested between them. The question then is as to the way in which the common intention is to be identified. (Deciding what is meant by a common intention is something which will require a reference back to the older cases which have not been overruled by the Supreme Court. Some guidance is given, however.) As it was put in the Supreme Court:

---

[26] Ibid.
[27] Ibid, [68].
[28] Ibid.
[29] Ibid.
[30] Resulting trusts focused on the parties' financial contributions are relegated below.

'(iii) The common intention, if it can be inferred, is to be deduced objectively from the parties' conduct ...'[31]

This complex idea means that a subjective intention is impossible to prove definitively, and therefore the court must rely on objective evidence such as documentation, proof of any discussion the parties had as to their equitable rights (whether through e-mail, text or evidence of personal conversations), much of which will be contested between the witnesses, and so forth. Moreover, the ways in which the parties conduct themselves, what each party pays for (including the mortgage and other household outgoings), how the parties organise their living arrangements, etc. will all be conduct suggesting their intentions as to the equitable ownership of the property. In that sense, what the parties must have intended is deduced objectively from the parties' conduct.

In many cases where the evidence is inconclusive, the court will have recourse to the final principle of fairness:

'(iv) Where the intention as to the division of the property cannot be inferred, each is entitled to that share which the court considers fair. In considering the question of what is fair the court should have regard to the whole course of dealing between the parties.'[32]

Thus, ultimately, the court will have to have recourse to what is 'fair' between the parties. This will require, it is suggested, that the courts will potentially have recourse to all of the earlier authorities considered in this chapter in deciding what constitutes and effects fairness between the parties.

## ISSUES FLOWING FROM THE DECISIONS IN *JONES v KERNOTT* AND *STACK v DOWDEN*

### Issues with the meaning of words

The persistent issue with the English approach to the acquisition of rights in the home is in the continuance of the idea of 'common intention' at the heart of this area of law. The difficulty with the decision of the Court of Appeal in *Oxley v Hiscock*[33] was that Chadwick LJ considered that the court could 'supply' the parties' common intention if that intention could not be otherwise identified. This meant that it would be the court which would be telling the parties what their intention was, as opposed to finding the parties' (possibly unknowable) common intention. This awkward idea continued in the Supreme Court with the idea that the parties' common intention might be objectively ascertained, as opposed to being proved to have been the parties' own, actual intention. The common intention concept is considered further below.

---

[31] *Jones v Kernott* [2011] UKSC 53, [2011] 3 WLR 1121, [68].
[32] Ibid.
[33] [2004] 3 All ER 703.

A further issue relates to the concept of 'fairness'. If a common intention cannot be identified, the courts may turn (according to the Supreme Court) to making an order for what is 'fair'. However, the courts have given no guidance as to what fairness might involve. Instead, it is treated impliedly as being an open-ended concept. It may be that tying the concept more closely to family law would be preferable, or else the concept of fairness must be explained. Otherwise the concept of fairness must develop consequentially on a case-by-case basis. This idea is considered further below, by reference to concepts of fairness in the philosophical literature.

## That there has been no progress in practice

The purpose behind the change in the law away from *Rosset* to the new approach in *Jones v Kernott* was to move away from a straightforward obsession with identifying which person had contributed how much money to the purchase price of the property, and towards a broader range of factors drawn from undertaking a survey of the entire course of dealing between the parties. However, this masks the fact that the courts have singularly failed to make any practical difference at all: Mrs Rosset failed to acquire any rights in her home because she had contributed no money to the purchase price or to the mortgage instalments; Ms Stack, of *Stack v Dowden* fame, had contributed approximately 60 per cent of the purchase price and mortgage instalments in relation to her home, and therefore she acquired 60 per cent of the equitable interest; Ms Jones, of *Jones v Kernott* fame, had contributed approximately 90 per cent of the purchase price and mortgage instalments in relation to her home, and therefore she acquired 90 per cent of the equitable interest; the same was true of *Oxley v Hiscock*.

In essence, in all of the leading cases, the equitable interest which was awarded eventually was exactly the same as the parties would have been awarded if those rights had been awarded solely on the basis of how much the parties had contributed to the purchase price of the property, as under resulting trust principles. The new direction in the law has not made any meaningful change to the outcome of the cases as yet.

I ask you to read the previous paragraph again. Have you done that? What it means is the following thing. The upshot of the new approach in the recent leading authorities (such as *Stack v Dowden* and *Jones v Kernott*) in this jurisdiction has been that there is no meaningful change in practice. Rights in the home are allocated in practice on the basis of the amount of money contributed to the property. As yet, it is not clear from the judgments themselves what other outcomes would *actually* be deployed by the senior courts so as to disturb the proportions which would be allocated by a resulting trust approach.

There are only two contexts in which the courts have actually done anything different from simply awarding proprietary rights in accordance with the parties' financial contributions to the purchase price of the property. First, the decision of Waite LJ in *Midland Bank v Cooke*[34] found that Mrs Cooke should be entitled to a

[34] [1995] 4 All ER 562.

half share in the property, even though she had contributed significantly less than half of the purchase price. His Lordship was concerned, in effect, to find that a heterosexual married couple (who had in effect thrown in their lot together as a married couple might) was entitled to resist a claim for repossession from Midland Bank on the basis that the wife had a substantial right in the home which could resist the bank's rights.

Secondly, the cases on proprietary estoppel permit the courts to award a range of remedies beyond property rights in accordance with the size of the parties' cash contribution to the property. So, in *Porntip Stallion v Stallion Holdings*,[35] the judge ordered that the deceased's first wife and his second wife should cohabit in their[36] former matrimonial home. In other cases, the courts have felt themselves at liberty to identify whatever remedy they think appropriate. Thus, in the enlightened decision in *Burns v Burns*,[37] the Court of Appeal was asked to decide as to the property rights of a frail, elderly man who had sold his home so as to contribute to the purchase of a house with his son and daughter-in-law, before their cohabitation proved impossible. Their plan had been for the two younger people to care for the older man. Whereas the court could have ordered that the man should receive a proportion of that house on resulting trust principles, it actually ordered that he should receive an annuity from his cohabitants sufficient to pay for sheltered accommodation for the rest of his life. That elderly man had no need of property rights by this stage because he was old and infirm. Therefore, the Court generated the remedy that he needed, as opposed to the remedy which he was entitled to receive. That is the power of proprietary estoppel: it empowers the court to sculpt judgments which are appropriate to the context, instead of simply recognising preexisting property rights.

# Debate 1

## Is 'common intention' a meaningful concept?

### THE LIMITATIONS OF COMMON INTENTION

The concept of a common intention between cohabitants has been criticised roundly by the courts of other Commonwealth countries, as is discussed in Debate 4 below. In short, that is because the notion of a common intention is such a limited and unsuitable one in practical terms. While in theory it may seem possible for a judge like Lord Diplock to talk of the common intention of a married couple like Mr and Mrs Gissing, setting out in life together in the wake of the 1939–45 war, it seems a much more difficult thing to expect that there will necessarily be a common intention between cohabitants in the twenty-first century, that

---

[35] [2010] 1 FCR 145.
[36] Yes, it had been the former matrimonial home of both wives. During the second marriage, the three of them had cohabited.
[37] [1984] Ch 317.

such a common intention would remain constant throughout the term of their cohabitation and that it would be capable of proof at the end of their relationship after they had descended into litigation over their home.

## EVERYDAY LIFE AND EVERYDAY DISAGREEMENTS

The shortcomings with the law in this area – and indeed the near impossibility of creating satisfactory legal rules in this area – spring to life when we begin to think about practical examples of real cohabiting relationships. Let us suppose that two people decide to live together as a romantic couple, and let us put aside the possibility that any two or more cohabitants might not be a romantic couple at all. Let us further suppose that our romantic couple decide to buy a house or flat together after a year or more of their relationship, and put aside the possibility that one cohabitant might be moving into a home which is already owned by the other cohabitant. Let us suppose that they agree that they will contribute half each to the mortgage and that the property will be in their joint names, and put aside the possibility that one of them will earn more money than the other and that one of them might therefore seek an advantage on the legal title. Even by narrowing down our example in this way, that still does not mean that the cohabitants will have a common intention as to all aspects of their relationship which might have an effect on their own intentions for their joint occupation of this home. One of them might want children while the other does not; one of them might already be carrying the seeds of a debilitating disease, which will put strain on their relationship and lead to their partner having to assume all of the mortgage repayments when they are no longer able to work; or one of them may be so violent and alcohol-dependent that they are ruled unsuitable to care for any child that they may have in the future. Should these factors affect their common intention in legal terms? They would clearly come to affect their separate understandings of how their relationship functions, and how their home is used and maintained.

Whereas the neatness of their ownership of the legal title suggests that they are deciding everything in tandem, it does not reach very deeply into their relationship. If the partner who was originally chosen to pay the mortgage becomes ill in later years, then to deny the partner who actually pays for the mortgage in the future any enlarged rights in the home seems unfair, particularly if you think that the principal deciding factor is to be the amount of cash that is contributed to the property. If they are not in agreement about whether or not they want children (and therefore whether their home is to be a family home, or simply their shared residence while they are together as an unmarried couple in a sexual relationship) suggests that there is a disagreement about many of the factors which were important in cases like *Midland Bank v Cooke*, where the nature of family unit so impressed Waite LJ that he awarded the wife a half share of the house even though she had paid very little towards it in cash.

It does not cater for the situation in which one of them might be too fearful of confrontation to voice their concerns about their relationship for fear of jeopardising that relationship. The very idea of a *common* intention suggests that there is a clear discussion of their intentions, or at least some meeting of minds. That there is a failure by one of them to initiate an awkward discussion may mean that the couple never discuss their feelings properly, and in consequence that they never form a meaningful common intention about their relationship. Alternatively, they may be a couple who discuss their feelings regularly and who therefore change their common intention frequently over time: as the years pass, people's ambitions, feelings and circumstances change to a greater or lesser extent. If the couple is childless then their intentions in their late thirties (if they decide that it is too late in life for a child) may be very different from their intentions in their late twenties (when they might have expected that they would have a child at some point). Consequently, the home may become a source of capital to them (with which they can buy another, trendier home, or against which they could raise a loan to fund a carefree, childless life), as opposed to being a practical, family home. Or, alternatively, an unexpected pregnancy when a female partner is 39 years old might introduce such a radical change to their circumstances that they have never discussed this possibility and what it might mean for them now that they need a bigger home with another bedroom. In times of emergency or stress, it is more likely that the couple will deal with the emergency than that they will sit down to discuss ownership of their home. When one of them falls seriously ill, the illness takes priority over a discussion of who will now be the owner of the home when the other partner necessarily assumes responsibility for the mortgage.

In any of these cases, the common intention may be illusory, or it may be something real but changeable. This raises two different problems. If there was no actual common intention, should the court fabricate a common intention for convenience to satisfy the test (and if so, from what materials)? If there was a shifting common intention, which formulation of that common intention should be taken to be the legally decisive one: the one at the start of their relationship, the one at some arbitrary point in the middle of their relationship, the one they actually discussed out-loud on one occasion or the one immediately before the litigation when things were presumably going wrong? And once the parties end up in the witness-box in court, it is even less likely that they will present entirely honest and impartial accounts of what their intentions used to be when they started living together.

There have been decided cases in which one party has lied to the other party, or misled them, or been unfaithful to them:[38] how should this affect their supposed common intention? Is the wronged party to be assumed to be in possession of the rights which they would have acquired but for the deceit? Although, if the deceitful party was deceitful, presumably they had no intention on agreeing to a middle course of action to which the other party would have agreed (in which case we would be punishing them for their deceit, rather than awarding property rights according to their common intention). There have been several cases in which

---

[38] *Eves v Eves* [1975] 1 WLR 1338.

married couples have simply lapsed into a pattern of caring for the children and earning money as seems most appropriate to them; and cases in which unmarried couples have done things which judges have found peculiar (such as maintaining separate bank accounts for their separate earnings in spite of decades in a relationship together). Should we indulge the parties' own oddities, or should we impose onto them an objective idea of what they should have intended?

Indeed, it is the self-employed, the artistic and the quixotic who pose the greatest challenge to the idea of common intention, precisely because they are less likely to form rational common intentions (which can be proven later in court) than the Gissings might have been in the late 1940s. It is also more difficult for a court to impose a likely common intention on them without subjecting their bohemian lives to the normalising influence of a bourgeois court ordering what the court considers to be the most appealing outcome, while pretending that that had been the parties' common intention at some time in real life. The court would be 'normalising' in this context, in the sense that it would imposing its own morality and conception of the good life on the litigants, rather than accommodating the litigants' own intentions as to their own lives. Clearly, accepting the autonomy of the parties themselves to choose their own lifestyle is preferable – and the very idea of a common intention test accepts that the parties should be free to create their own way of living. However, in practice, when people have not created a common intention which can be proved in court, then the court has to identify some way of resolving the question as to how the home is to be owned in property law terms.[39]

Moreover, the law on common intention in the ownership of the home no longer applies to married couples (whose affairs, except in relation to mortgage possession proceedings, are likely to be decided by the statutory principles governing divorce). Instead, this area of law applies to the unmarried, the homosexual, the non-traditional, the volatile (as in *Cox v Jones*[40]), the counter-cultural, the marginalised (but private property-owning) and so on: in short, the fun people in any society. With the waning of the institution of marriage and the waning of the myth that people lead identical, ordered lives without skeletons in their closets or dreams of freedom in their hearts, it is less and less likely that these people will live lives which are characterised by an easily identifiable set of assumptions about their private lives.

So what is the law to do when trying to allocate people rights in their homes on separation, bankruptcy or mortgage repossession? The answer, it is suggested, should involve greater honesty in the jurisprudence than claiming to effect the

---

[39] It may be difficult to prove these things in court when the parties have separated and so begin to misremember – or to lie – about the events that took place much earlier in their relationship when they were in love. *Cox v Jones* [2004] 3 FCR 693 is an interesting case study of the sort of biased, unconvincing evidence which parties to a failed romantic relationship are likely to give in court, as Mann J informs us, even when they are themselves barristers (and so, one might have thought, professionally qualified to act as good witnesses in their own interests).
[40] [2004] 3 FCR 693.

couple's common intentions while actually imposing a normalised conception of what the court thinks they should have intended onto them. The peculiarity of the very idea of a common intention formed at the start of a relationship is considered in the next section.

## THE LIMITATIONS OF THE IDEA OF COMMON INTENTION IN PRACTICE

In an episode of the TV show *The Big Bang Theory*, the uber-geek[41] Sheldon Cooper improbably finds a girlfriend: the differently geeky Amy Farrah Fowler. The characters' combination of oddness and intelligence is the heart of the programme's comic conceit. Sheldon Cooper in particular is the poster boy for hyper-intelligence and social stupidity being contained in one awkward body. Amy was introduced in later series to develop the Sheldon character. When Sheldon and Amy decided to formalise their interaction as being some form of boyfriend–girlfriend relationship, Sheldon produced a hard copy of 'The Relationship Agreement' which was intended to codify in legally-binding, contractual form their rights and responsibilities in relation to the minutiae of their future relationship.[42] (This continued a long-running joke in the show, whereby Sheldon regularly produced a signed copy of 'The Roommate Agreement' which is used to control and to punish his roommate Leonard for slight infractions of Sheldon's extremely odd and taxonomic life.) Even more peculiarly, perhaps, Amy entered into negotiations with Sheldon over the contents of the Relationship Agreement rather than dismissing the idea out of hand.

The humour is located in the fact that Sheldon's behaviour in codifying the precise details of their putative relationship is instantly recognisable to the audience as being aberrant. That is a very important point. Sheldon does not fall in love: instead he codifies the common intention which he wants them to agree to have. And everyone in the audience laughs because this seems so strange. The central comic conceit here is that only a person as odd as Sheldon could possibly treat another person in this way. Only an oddball could possibly want to agree in quasi-contractual form how long a boyfriend should be expected to comfort a girlfriend for different types of upset, when a girlfriend should be expected to provide first aid to her boyfriend and so forth. Only an oddball would want to agree in advance all of the minutiae of their putative, fledgling romantic relationship with another person. And yet this particular oddness is exactly what the concept of common intention expects us all to do in real life to establish our respective rights in our homes.

The idea of a common intention expects that at the outset of their relationship two people will agree all of the issues surrounding the ownership of their home which may arise in the future. All of this is to be decided at the time when a relationship is so fragile. Do the courts really expect that we will all act like Sheldon Cooper when we begin cohabiting with someone? The definitive weirdo in our popular culture is apparently the model for our relationships in property law.

---

[41] Geek is not a term of abuse in this context. Geek is good.
[42] 'The Flaming Spittoon Acquisition', Season 5, Episode 10, 2011.

The idea is so implausible that the only possible interpretation of the common intention idea is that the courts expect that they will assemble their own view of what the parties could be taken to have intended at the date of trial. The problem with that approach is that a court creating the parties' intention is self-evidently not the same as the parties forming their own common intention. Therefore the entire concept behind the test is an illusion. Indeed, it has been described by some courts elsewhere in the Commonwealth as being a 'phantom' and a fiction, as is considered in Debate 4 below.

## Debate 2

## How does the law match up to the reality of modern relationships?

### FROM TOOTHBRUSH TO ENTITLEMENT

An example of the 'normal chaos' of people's private lives is the mawkish, consumer Gomorrah that is presented in the television series *Sex and the City*. This programme was set in Manhattan during the boom years of the 1990s and the early 2000s, during which Americans lived in a consumer dream before the financial crash of 2008. It followed the lives and loves of four women. The central character, Carrie Bradshaw, wrote a newspaper column which inquired into the mores of dating and relationships among Manhattanites. This device enabled her character to act as narrator to the show as she and her friends lived out the issues in her column. Carrie had an on/off relationship with a rich banker known as 'Big'. One particular theme which runs through the episodes in Season 2 is whether or not Carrie can elicit any sense of commitment from Big, or whether their relationship is purely sexual. So, among other issues, Carrie wants to be allowed to feel at home in Big's apartment as a signal of the evolving nature of their relationship. However, Carrie does not begin to move into Big's minimalist, masculine New York apartment by talking things over with her lover. Instead she moves in chattel by chattel.

What distinguishes human beings from the animals is our ability to use language to resolve complex issues; but nevertheless it is often in the most crucial issues about our relationships and our lives that we tend to use that faculty least, often simply out of fear about whether or not we might cause irrevocable harm to ourselves. This is an often unacknowledged problem with the common intention test: people will frequently not want to express a common intention out loud for fear of risking the relationship in the early days.

An issue running through a few episodes of *Sex and the City* centres around a toothbrush and a hairdryer.[43] If Carrie could leave a toothbrush or a hairdryer in

---

[43] The issue began with a hairdryer in *Sex and the City*, 'Evolution', Season 2, Episode 23, (Home Box Office, 999), written by Darren Star.

Big's apartment then she feels that that would be a core marker in the transition of their relationship from casual lovers to committed lovers, and then possibly in time to cohabitees.[44] The premise of those episodes is that the intentions, desires and expectations of each of the characters are treated as though they are unknowable and unspeakable. It is one of the more irritating facets of the programme: the characters are inherently childlike (in a pejorative sense) in that they often seek to indulge their basic desires but are generally incapable of discussing any of the things that truly bother them. In short, they spend money instead of growing up. The programme's central conceit is that Carrie can only analyse these sorts of issues through a series of seemingly unanswerable questions which she poses at the beginning of her lightweight, ironic newspaper columns. The scriptwriter's device is to allow us to hear her discuss them as her love life plays itself out for our entertainment while she composes her columns.

In the event, Carrie is not allowed to move her own toothbrush into Big's apartment. Instead, he presents her with a spare toothbrush head for his own electric toothbrush which becomes 'hers'. Symbolically, in relationship terms, she feels that this has given her an emotional right to live with a (spurious) degree of permanence in his home. Symbolically in legal terms perhaps we must accept that she was not allowed to move her own chattel into his property but rather she was given permission to use one of his chattels whenever she was in temporary occupation. For her, emotionally, a significant line towards cohabitation had been crossed; for we property lawyers, however, there is almost a clear denial of any right in property in that same action, in favour of an easily terminable licence. It is precisely because Big makes the gesture of permitting Carrie to use one of his toothbrush heads that we know he is limiting any entitlement she may otherwise feel she has to occupy *his* home and use *his* chattels.

Leaving the glossy, magazine patina of Carrie Bradshaw's fictional life aside for a moment, this particular plot twist presents us with an axiomatic demonstration of why either positivist approaches to the law on trusts of homes like *Rosset* or commonsensical approaches like that of Baroness Hale in *Stack v Dowden*, will either fail to produce a workable legal rule or will fail to deal *successfully*[45] with all cases even if they do. There is no external logic to the lives of Carrie and Big: rather, they can only make sense within the bubble of their own relationship. There is no moment at which their relationship alters in a way which the law could ever identify as establishing Carrie with some rights in the home which previously belonged solely to Big; nor in another series would such rights in the apartment, which had previously belonged solely to Carrie, necessarily transfer to her other great love, Aden. Instead, the law is required to deal

---

[44] I will not spoil the plot by revealing how their relationship ultimately pans out.

[45] For present purposes, at this stage, a 'successful' disposal of the issues would involve addressing the justice of an individual case and dealing with all of the factual issues without simply applying a rigid rule unthinkingly so as, in part, to fail to deal with all of the issues and claims arising between the parties.

with abstract issues relating to the particular peculiarities of one particular relationship at a time. As we consider these questions, our nation is teeming with lovers wondering what their partners are really thinking, while secreting hairdryers and razor blades into the crevices of their lovers' bathrooms like stealthy emotional assassins.

## WHY SEX AND THE CITY MATTER

Sex matters. It matters an enormous amount to the people who are having it. (Possibly it matters even more to people who are not.) As anyone who has looked outside their bedroom window (or even through their computer's Windows) will have noticed, people are doing it all sorts of different ways. People are often led by their sexuality into situations which they would not choose when in their right minds. However, sex is one of the great motivating factors, as advertisers have long known. And it is entirely irrational.

Modern love is not always about hearts and flowers in the way we might have associated with a Shakespeare sonnet. As Arctic Monkeys put it in their song 'I bet that you look good on the dancefloor', there are no Montagues or Capulets (as in Shakespeare's *Romeo and Juliet*). Instead the background to young romance in British town centres on Friday nights is likely to be 'banging tunes in DJs' sets' playing on 'dirty dancefloors' while the lovers live out their 'dreams of naughtiness'. (I particularly like the reference to 'naughtiness', which brings a little of the slapstick back into modern love-making.)

That is how many modern, 'romantic' relationships start. They start with a raised heartbeat and a quickening pulse. Hormones race. The first meeting may echo to the sound of Kylie Minogue's 'I can't get you out of my head', or the evening after that first meeting may exhibit that very phenomenon of not being able to get the other person out of your head. The language we use to describe love also indicates being slightly, temporarily deranged. For example, the expression 'being fond of someone' in its modern usage describes liking that person. In its older usage, however, the word 'fond' refers to madness. King Lear describes himself in the Shakespeare play as a 'foolish, fond old man'. My grandmother used to refer to football hooligans in the 1980s as 'fond young things' without a hint of warmth. Even in its modern sense, to be fond of someone is to be slightly unhinged, irrational and emotional. This is not the sort of mindset in which people can calmly negotiate the terms on which they will live together forever, nor even just for a little while. When we become fond of someone, and we decide to live with them, we are supposed to form a sensible common intention in spite of our temporary madness.

Cohabitation may flow some months after that initial, animal passion, or it may begin unintentionally a short time afterwards if one of the couple starts to stay over at the other person's place and then neglects to leave. The parties may not notice they are 'in a relationship' for some time – possibly not until they have their first argument, or decide to go on holiday together, or buy a new bed suitable for them both. But none of the things that two human beings will do on, under or near that bed will be born out of cold logic. Their common intention is an artificial construct which can only ever approximate to the complex play of emotions and ideas that inhabit their early days in a relationship.

Some relationships do begin with cold logic, of course. An older couple may decide to get together precisely because they are both in their mid-thirties, both know they want children and so both advertise on the Internet for a partner. When they meet, they realise that they are sufficiently compatible in many of the things that seem to matter to them (solvency, social class, expectations of life and so forth), and they may very well turn their minds to the practicalities of which home that is available to them (his, hers or a new one they will have to buy) will best suit their life project. In arranged marriages (a different situation because they will be governed by divorce law most likely), there is a logic to the proceedings. The couple may very well be more likely to stay together because their attitudes and expectations may well have been born out of the culture which led to their union being arranged by cautious, sensible parents. Of course, there is nothing more British than an arranged marriage: for centuries, the monarchy and the aristocracy were very careful to arrange suitable marriages for their offspring. In P.G. Wodehouse's novels, Bertie Wooster was constantly being assailed by interfering aunts who sought to arrange marriages for him with ghastly, 'corn-fed' young women, one of whom had a laugh so jarring that it reminded Bertie of a troop of cavalry charging over a tin bridge. However, such a carefully arranged union is in itself an exception which tends to prove the point that no rigid style of law-making will quite suit the enormous variations of circumstance which apply to modern love. Our cities abound with people living out their very individual life projects. Our countryside teems with them too. Every successfully contented person exhibits their own legitimate strangeness. The expectation that they will conform to the tidiness which is expected of them by the common intention principle is perhaps a little optimistic.

The point is that it is impossible to have a one-size-fits-all approach to the law in this area. By the same token, the parties are unlikely to form a sensible, provable common intention in the early days of a relationship. What is going on the parties' minds – about hairdryers, toothbrushes and the discomfort of a bed designed only for one person being occupied by two people – may well have nothing to do with their common intention.

## Debate 3

### What is the future for unconscionability and fairness in trusts of homes?

This section considers what might be meant by the concept of 'fairness' and what has happened to the idea of unconscionability in the English law on trusts of homes.

## FAIRNESS

The concept of fairness which is at play in *Jones v Kernott*[46] is unclear. There is a model in New Zealand, considered below, which deals with fairness in the sense of granting the courts a wide discretion to anticipate the reasonable expectations of the parties and to achieve fairness between them. What is 'fair' on that model is what the parties could reasonably have expected to receive given the nature of their relationship, their conversations with one another, and so forth. Nevertheless, the meaning of fairness here remains unclear in the abstract.

Is fairness limited to the parties' financial contributions? Well, the policy underpinning the recent case law was to begin a movement away from the older cases which had focused solely on financial contributions. The intention was therefore to take into account factors other than financial contributions.[47] However, is fairness to take into account the entire course of dealing between the parties, including the care of children, maintenance of the home, taking career breaks, and so forth? And, if so, how does that differ from broader cases on common intention like *Midland Bank v Cooke*?[48]

The philosopher John Rawls developed a concept of fairness in his book *A Theory of Justice*.[49] In essence, Rawls was asking the reader to accept that egalitarianism (that is, an increase in equality in society) was a socially just means of organising society. To do so, Rawls asked us to imagine that our society was being recommenced from scratch. We were all to be held behind a 'veil of ignorance', where we would not know what our station or position would be in this new society. In this situation, Rawls argued that everyone would consequently agree that the only sound basis on which to start the new society would be on the idea that we would all be equal. Rawls argued that that would be fair. Modern society, in essence, permits inequality due to its history and the entrenched advantages of some people who are currently wealthy. So, Rawls argued that if we started over again then we would all choose to be equal.[50] For Rawls, in consequence, 'fairness' meant 'equality'.

Therefore, we might argue that the equality found in *Midland Bank v Cooke* and the ancient principle that 'equality is equity' might underpin this idea of fairness. In that case, Waite LJ considered the authorities before him to be 'mystifying' due

---

[46] [2011] UKSC 53, [2011] 3 WLR 1121.
[47] *Abbott v Abbott* [2008] 1 FLR 1451.
[48] [1995] 4 All ER 562.
[49] J. Rawls, *Theory of Justice* (Oxford University Press, 1971).
[50] Many commentators objected to Rawls's theory on the basis that many people prefer to take the risk of being rich or poor, as opposed to being equal; and that people would prefer a society in which there was the freedom to become rich. This is a basic argument between left and right in politics. Rawls was in truth arguing tendentiously for equality as someone from the left of the political spectrum, and to justify that he was imagining a utopia in which the entirety of society was being reorganised from scratch and in which we would necessarily choose (so Rawls believed) to be equal in such a situation. Rawls therefore wanted to make the point that we should work for more equality in our own society because that is fair.

to their different conceptual underpinnings. In undertaking a survey of the entire course of dealing between the parties, his lordship decided that the fairest approach was to award Mrs Cooke an equal share in the matrimonial home so that the Cookes together could resist the claim for repossession that was brought by their mortgagees. Interestingly, he did so in reliance on the idea that 'equality is equity', even though that had been resisted in *Pettitt v Pettitt*.

Unless the concept of fairness is connected to a philosophy, it is simply an empty word.

## THE PRINCIPLE OF UNCONSCIONABILITY

On one view, equity is predicated deontologically on the idea of conscience. The idea of the conscience of the defendant is the moral centre around which all equitable doctrines revolve: trusts implied by law, injunctions for breach of confidence and so forth. The particular nature of this deontology is problematic because our understanding of the moral core (the idea of conscience) is itself informed by individual cases, and therefore this equity is also consequentialist (i.e. based on cases and not simply on a central moral standard). This was discussed in Chapter 2. Nevertheless, the basis of equity is morality, even if its methodology is complex.

In the law on trusts of homes, the idea of the conscience has disappeared in England and Wales. There was a line of cases (including *Jennings v Rice*[51] and *Cox v Jones*[52]) which prioritised the idea of conscience. The decisions in *Oates v Stimson*[53] and *Van Laetham v Brooker*[54] not only began with the idea of conscience, but they also linked the constructive trust in trusts of homes to the mainstream constructive trust. In that sense, the constructive trust used in *Westdeutsche Landesbank v Islington*[55] came to have a parallel with the previously closed area of common intention constructive trusts. Collins LJ consciously drew this link in *Oates v Stimson*. The benefit of using the idea of conscience in this way is that it draws on a well-spring of trusts law jurisprudence, that it is based on firmer ground in terms of precedent than the idea of 'fairness' in property law, that it operates in parallel with the law in other Commonwealth jurisdictions and that it provides a moral centre for the law. The idea of unconscionability has been developed in several other Commonwealth jurisdictions, as is considered next.

---

[51] [2002] EWCA Civ 159.
[52] [2004] 3 FCR 693.
[53] [2006] EWCA Civ 548.
[54] [2005] EWHC 1478 (Ch), [2006] 2 FLR 495.
[55] [1996] AC 669.

# Debate 4

## How did other Commonwealth jurisdictions deal with the common intention concept?

### INTRODUCTION

The common intention concept sent the countries of the Commonwealth off in search of their own legal tests to allocate rights in the home. Each of them decided that there were shortcomings in the concept: that it was insufficiently flexible; that it resembled a contractual bargain too closely; that it did not suit the cultures of their own countries. It was a profound moment: countries such as Australia, New Zealand and Canada detached themselves culturally from England in a very significant part of their social lives. This section considers the debates which each of those three Commonwealth jurisdictions initiated with England and Wales in their jurisprudence about the unsuitability of the common intention concept. We shall focus on the early cases which saw the initial break from England, and the reasons for so doing.

### CANADA AND 'UNJUST ENRICHMENT'

#### The roots of the Canadian approach

The Canadian jurisdiction has developed its own principle of unjust enrichment (i.e. one that differs completely from the Oxford Restitution School concept of unjust enrichment that was discussed in Chapter 3) to decide disputes in relation to the ownership of the family home. It should be recalled that Lord Reid rejected the suggestion in *Pettit v Pettit*[56] that the English law should adopt a principle of unjust enrichment in its own treatment of rights in the home. His Lordship's reasoning was that unjust enrichment would found a remedy only in money and not any proprietary right. This section considers the Canadian attitude to allocating rights in the home and will uncover two points: first, that a constructive trust will be imposed only in circumstances in which a money judgment would not satisfy the parties; and, secondly, that work in the home will qualify a claimant for some remedy, whether personal or proprietary.

The Canadian approach is based, in large part, on the US Restatement of Restitution, which identifies the need to reverse unjust enrichment as the underpinning of the law: one should not under-estimate the dialectic which inhabits Canadian jurisprudence between English law precedent on the one hand and a North American culture shared with the USA on the other hand. As the operation of the constructive trust is stated in the US treatise *Scott on Trusts*:[57]

> '[A] constructive trust is imposed where a person holding title to property is subject to an equitable duty to convey it to another on the ground that he would be injustly enriched if he were permitted to retain it.'

---

[56] [1970] AC 777.
[57] A.W. Scott and W.F. Fratcher, *Scott on Trusts*, 3rd edn (1967), vol 5, 3215.

As shall emerge, the Canadian approach to restitution of unjust enrichment varies slightly, but significantly, from the notion of restitution advanced in England by the Oxford School, principally in that the Canadian law considers that the term 'unjust' relates to a general concept of right and wrong, fair and unfair. It also offers a defence of some 'juristic purpose' for the enrichment. This is the antithesis of the taxonomy of Professor Birks and Lord Goff and Professor Jones, as discussed in Chapter 3.

The Canadian cases grasp the nettle of the following dilemma: merely focusing on financial contributions and disallowing other contributions ignores the broad range of transactions, arrangements and compromises which are typically reached in families. Rather, there is a broader policy decision to be made as to whether equity should take into account the value of contributions to the property other than those made in cash.

### The test for unjust enrichment

The Canadian courts had accepted the decision in *Gissing v Gissing*[58] when it was first passed down in 1971.[59] Before the unjust enrichment principle emerged, the Canadian Supreme Court in *Rathwell v Rathwell*[60] continued to prefer resulting trusts analyses. Although it did contain a strong dissenting judgment of Dickson J which advanced a test based on unjust enrichment, the change to unjust enrichment was yet to come.

The gloriously Canadian element in the emerging unjust enrichment principle was the sort of activity which would be taken into account as constituting unjust behaviour. So, in *Peter v Beblow*,[61] a decision of the Canadian Supreme Court, it was found as a fact at the termination of a relationship that the respondent male partner had received the services of a housekeeper, homemaker and stepmother to his children from the appellant without any compensation having been paid to her. Therefore, he had been enriched at her expense. However, it was found that while the defendant had benefited from this enrichment by receipt of labour and services, the appellant had not suffered deprivation because she had occupied the property rent-free. The core of the Canadian approach is the imposition of a proprietary constructive trust, 'where a person who holds title to property is subject to an equitable duty to convey it to another on the ground that he would be unjustly enriched if he were permitted to retain it'.[62]

The sea-change in the Canadian case law came in *Pettkus v Becker*[63] in the leading judgment of Dickson J. The parties were an unmarried couple who had lived together for 19 years. The property at issue was the farm in which they had both

---

[58] [1971] AC 886.
[59] See the decision of the majority in the Supreme Court case of *Murdoch v Murdoch* (1974) 41 DLR (3d) 367.
[60] [1978] 2 SCR 436.
[61] (1993) 101 DLR (4th) 621, 642–53.
[62] Ibid, 629.
[63] (1980) 117 DLR (3d) 257.

lived, and a bee-keeping business which had been established through their joint efforts. The woman claimed an entitlement to half of the business and to the land. The court was unanimous in holding that she should be entitled to a constructive trust to prevent any unjust enrichment on the part of her former partner. Dickson J set out the general underpinnings of the Canadian approach:

'[W]here one person in a relationship tantamount to spousal prejudices herself in the reasonable expectation of receiving an interest in property and the other person in the relationship freely accepts benefits conferred by the first person in circumstances where he knows or ought to have known of that reasonable expectation, it would be unjust to allow the recipient of the benefit to retain it.'[64]

In the later case of *Peter v Beblow*[65] the test is more clearly stated. For there to be an unjust enrichment in the Canadian law relating to equitable rights in the home, it was held that three conditions must be satisfied:

'(1) there has been an enrichment; (2) a corresponding deprivation has been suffered by the person who supplied the enrichment; and (3) there is an absence of any juristic reason for the enrichment itself.'[66]

The effect of this test is said to be the creation of a presumption that the 'performance of domestic services will give rise to a claim for unjust enrichment'.[67] The principal driver away from the English common intention constructive trust was that, in the words of Dickson J, the courts were involved in the 'meaningless ritual' of searching for a 'fugitive common intention'.[68] On the facts of *Pettkus*, no common intention had been formed but the court wished to provide the claimant with a remedy. It was considered that a judgment in money by way of equitable compensation would have been inappropriate to prevent that unjust enrichment, and the court therefore made an order for a constructive trust over the property at issue. That constructive trust was completely contrary to the approach to constructive trusts taken in England, as set out in Chapter 8.

## AUSTRALIA AND 'UNCONSCIONABILITY'

A significant turn in the Australian law away from the common intention concept was demonstrated by the decision of the High Court of Australia in *Baumgartner v Baumgartner*.[69] The plaintiff and defendant had lived together, sharing all household and other expenses, for a period of four years. They had not married, although the plaintiff had changed her name by deed poll so that it was the same as that of her partner. The couple had one child during this time. The couple sold

---

[64] Ibid, 274.
[65] (1993) 101 DLR (4th) 621.
[66] Ibid, 630, *per* Cory J.
[67] J. Mee, *The Property Rights of Cohabitees* (Hart Publishing, 1999), 192.
[68] (1980) 117 DLR (3d) 257, 269.
[69] (1988) 62 ALJR 29.

a home which had been wholly owned by the defendant, and sought to construct another one with the sale proceeds of the first and a mortgage taken out in the man's name. The plaintiff worked throughout the relationship and passed her wage packets to her partner each time she was paid, on the basis that he looked after their financial affairs. The plaintiff eventually left her partner with their child, and claimed an equitable interest in the property.

It was found that while the parties had not formed a common intention, that would nevertheless not dispose of the matter. The court wanted to provide for a means of acquiring rights in the home which went beyond straightforward financial contribution to the acquisition cost of the home. The court held that a proprietary interest by way of constructive trust would be ordered where failure to do so would have been 'so contrary to justice and good conscience' that it could not have been permitted. This approach is best explained as a test based on the issue whether or not the trustee's retention of the beneficial interest would be 'unconscionable'. On these facts it was held that it would be unconscionable for the plaintiff to deny any beneficial interest to the defendant.

This test of unconscionability allows the court, in effect, to impute motives and to judge the justice of the case objectively – that is, without the need to pretend to be able to read the minds of the protagonists in the way that the English common intention constructive trust pretends to do (in cases such as *Oxley v Hiscock*[70]). The approach in Australia has therefore been to return to the notion of unconscionable behaviour as a general yardstick for measuring the suitability of an order in favour of the award of an equitable interest in land in any case.

### Forms of unconscionability granting rights in the home

Direct contributions to the purchase price and to the mortgage instalments still count towards an interest in the property.[71] Similarly, work done in repairing the property will afford some equitable interest.[72] Other contributions will also be recognised. Facilitating the payment of the mortgage by paying for other expenses will lead to the acquisition of an equitable interest in the home.[73] More extensively, working unpaid in the family business will allow a party to acquire rights in the home.[74] An important explanation of the principles was added in *Bryson v Bryant*[75] by Kirby P:

> 'It is important that the "brave new world of unconscionability" should not lead the court back to family property law of twenty years ago by the back door of a preoccupation with contributions, particularly financial contributions ... Nor should those who have provided "women's work" over their adult lifetime ... be told

---

[70] [2004] 3 All ER 703.
[71] *Atkinson v Burt* (1989) 12 Fam LR 800.
[72] *Miller v Sutherland* (1991) 14 Fam LR 416, 424.
[73] *Baumgartner v Baumgartner* (1987) 164 CLR 137.
[74] *Lipman v Lipman* (1989) 13 Fam LR 1.
[75] (1992) 29 NSWLR 188.

condescendingly, by a mostly male judiciary, that their services must be regarded as "freely given labour" only or, catalogued as attributable solely to a rather one-way and quaintly described "love and affection", when property interests come to be distributed.'

The question which follows is precisely how far this notion of unconscionability is intended to stretch. Clearly it will encompass things otherwise dismissed by *Rosset* and other English cases as merely 'women's work'.[76] What is less clear is the extent to which unconscionability will bind third parties. It is evident that it can bind the couple themselves as to their own agreements, situation and expectations, but that does not necessarily translate in the same way to third-party creditors and so forth.

## NEW ZEALAND – 'REASONABLE EXPECTATIONS' AND 'FAIRNESS'

A further approach has been developed in New Zealand which is focused on the recognition of the expectations which the parties could be intended to have formed in the context of their relationship. This approach is the most conceptually broadly based of the four jurisdictions considered here. The New Zealand cases deliberately eschew the conceptual tightness of other jurisdictions, such as England's formalist 'common intention constructive trust', Canada's purposive 'unjust enrichment compensation or constructive trust' and Australia's 'unconscionability based on a joint venture'.[77] The courts in New Zealand have sought instead to generate a means of allocating rights between the parties which achieves 'fairness' in general terms.[78]

The New Zealand courts initially applied the decision in *Gissing v Gissing*,[79] but they would not accept the *Lloyds Bank v Rosset*[80] approach. The new model constructive trust was flirted with in a few cases[81] before the reasonable expectations test was finally developed.[82] The unjust enrichment approach was not adopted,[83] although Cooke P was concerned that the law should develop so as to account for 'the reasonable dictates of social facts' in the same way that Canada and Australia had sought to recognise rights in the home as being based on more than simply financial contribution.[84] In short, the practical problem facing the court was how to provide a remedy where a 'reasonable person in the shoes of the

---

[76] M. Bryan, 'The conscience of equity in Australia' (1990) 106 *LQR* 25.

[77] Cooke P praised 'Lord Denning's frank reliance on justice, good conscience and fairness': *Phillips v Phillips* [1993] 3 NZLR 159, 168.

[78] As one judge has put it, 'Expressions such as "the formless void of individual moral opinion" may be quaint but like many legal metaphors [such as common intention] they do little to clarify': McMullin J in *Pasi v Kamana* [1986] NZLR 603, 607.

[79] *Gough v Fraser* [1977] 1 NZLR 279; *Brown v Stokes* (1980) 1 NZCPR 209.

[80] [1991] 1 AC 107.

[81] *Carly v Farrelly* [1975] 1 NZLR 356 – drawing on cases like *Hussey v Palmer* [1975] 1 WLR 1338.

[82] *Phillips v Phillips* (1993) 3 NZLR 159; after comments in *Pasi v Kamana* [1986] 1 NZLR 603.

[83] *Wayward v Giordani* [1983] NZLR 140.

[84] Ibid, 148.

claimant would have understood that their efforts would naturally result in an interest in the property'.[85]

New Zealand recognises a category of relationships called 'de facto unions', after *Gillies v Keogh*,[86] which includes any form of relationship in which the parties intend to be treated as a unit. In such a situation where a couple are living in a de facto union, the court will consider the 'reasonable expectations' of the parties in relation to their home. In assessing reasonable expectations the court would consider:

1. the degree of sacrifice by the claimant;
2. the value of the contributions of the claimant compared to the value of the benefits received; and
3. any property arrangements which the parties have made themselves.

On the facts of *Gillies v Keogh*, the defendant had made it clear throughout her relationship with the claimant that she considered the money with which she bought the house (derived from a previous settlement made solely in her favour) to be entirely sacrosanct. Therefore, she had bought a house solely with her own money, and the proceeds of sale of that house were subsequently used to buy a house in which both parties would live. The couple pooled their earnings, and the claimant had done some work on clearing the second house when it had been acquired. However, the court dismissed the claimant's argument that he be declared to be entitled to a 40 per cent share of the house, on the basis that the defendant had made it clear from the outset that the property was to have been entirely her own. It is suggested that the same conclusion could have been reached on the basis of a common intention constructive trust (on the basis that the claimant was clearly entitled to nothing after express discussions), but the court was adamant that it wished to create its own test based on the reasonable expectations of the parties: here, that the claimant had no reasonable expectation of any rights in the home.

It was held that a constructive trust can be imposed in the absence of a common intention. Instead, general notions of reasonableness and fairness were considered to have formed part of the traditional concept of unconscionability leading to a constructive trust. The court will consider two further aspects in 'grey area' cases. First, 'sacrifice' made in relation to other opportunities in life,[87] such as foregoing employment or alternative accommodation. Secondly, the value of 'broadly measurable contributions' to the relationship as compared to the 'broadly measurable benefits received' in return for those contributions – thus accounting not only for money expended but also the benefits of, for example, rent-free occupation which were received. This general approach is to be compared to the strictures introduced in the English law by *Rosset*, where a rigid, bright-line test has been created. The

---

[85] *Pasi v Kamana* [1986] 1 NZLR 603, 605, *per* Cooke P.

[86] [1989] 2 NZLR 327.

[87] Cf *Grant v Edwards* [1986] Ch 638 and *Greasley v Cooke* [1980] 1 WLR 1306 in relation to detriment evidenced by personal lifestyle choices.

New Zealand approach is concerned to do justice between the parties in a general sense without the formalist approaches of English law.

In *Phillips v Phillips*,[88] proprietary estoppel was dismissed as being an 'indirect and abstruse way of creating rights'. Like the similarly dismissed common intention constructive trust, 'the notion of an implied representation or acquiescence and an acting upon it has a fictional quality reminiscent of common intention ... and it would be difficult to stretch to justify monetary relief'.[89] The English common intention constructive trust is compared to 'chasing phantoms' by Cooke P, as it was in Canada. What is significant is that these jurisdictions have decided to reject the doctrines of constructive trust and proprietary estoppel for being too artificial to provide an adequate form of resolution to disputes relating to the family home.

What this discussion demonstrates is that there are many other models for the organisation of the ownership of the home. The debates about the ownership of the home, and the basis on which that ownership should be decided, are pleasantly never-ending.

---

[88] (1993) 3 NZLR 159, 167–71.
[89] Ibid, 168.

# 10

## BREACH OF TRUST AND STRANGERS

## INTRODUCTION

This chapter considers the debates about the liability of strangers in connection with breaches of trust. The primary liability for a breach of trust rests with the trustees, i.e. when there is a breach of trust, the beneficiaries are required to sue the trustees first. The liability of the trustees is considered below. There is then a secondary liability for so-called 'strangers' who are not express trustees but who are nevertheless taken to be responsible for that breach of trust, either because they assisted that breach or because they received property as a result of the breach of trust. In either case, liability typically turns on whether or not the defendant can be shown, respectively, to have been dishonest or to have acted unconscionably with knowledge of the breach. In either case, the stranger will be liable for the entirety of the defendants' loss. Given that many trusts involve enormous sums of money – such as pension funds – the liabilities which may be faced by the strangers are potentially enormous too. Consequently, the scope of these liabilities is much contested. That is the subject of this chapter.

### THE SEVERAL AVENUES OF REDRESS OPEN TO BENEFICIARIES IN CASES OF BREACH OF TRUST

The law on breach of trust demonstrates very clearly how significant trusts were in the eighteenth and nineteenth centuries. The beneficiaries of a trust were accorded an extraordinary range of defences so as to protect them against the possibility of a loss being caused by a breach of trust. So, beneficiaries may proceed against the trustees for recovery of the trust property, for reinstatement of the value of the trust fund, and for equitable compensation. Beneficiaries do not, strictly, need to worry about recovering their losses from elsewhere because the trustees are required to act on behalf of the trust; therefore, the beneficiaries merely need to commence legal proceedings against the trustees, and then the trustees will sue any likely third parties who may be responsible for the loss. So in practice, it will be the trustees who will conduct most of the litigation by joining those third parties as defendants to the litigation. It is common in practice for the trustees to be acting de facto as though they were the claimants, even though they are formally the first defendant: that is because the trustees acknowledge their prima facie liability to the beneficiaries (under *Target Holdings v Redferns*[1]), and then the trustees will seek to recover as much of the compensation owing to the beneficiaries, or any of the trust property which has been lost from the second, third and fourth defendants. The question is: Against whom may those trustees seek to impose liability for the loss to the trust?

In practice, if the trustees themselves have few resources then it may be necessary to find third parties who can bear the loss to the trust. If the trustees had the benefit of an exclusion of liability clause in the trust instrument (as was considered in Chapter 6) then it would be impossible for the beneficiaries to recover their loss against the trustees unless the trustees had acted dishonestly (as was held by the Court of Appeal in *Armitage v Nurse*[2]). This is a real hindrance to enforcing liability for breach of fiduciary duties in the real world against professional advisers under the terms of a written trust instrument, because limitation of liability language will usually be included in such a trust instrument. For example, if the trust had been invested unsuccessfully and in breach of the terms of the trust instrument, but if the trustees had the benefit of an exclusion of liability clause in that trust instrument, then the beneficiaries would have to seek to recover their loss from any third party, such as professional investment advisers who had tendered investment advice to the trustees or any bank which had received the trust money in breach of trust. It is exactly those sorts of third parties – solicitors firms, accountancy firms and financial institutions – who are likely to have sufficient wealth to recoup the trustees' loss which will be the target of an action for breach of trust. Those professionals may be liable under the tort of negligence, or they may be liable in equity as 'strangers'.

The trustees may also proceed against any third parties as 'strangers' if they have dishonestly assisted a breach of trust (so-called 'dishonest assistance'), or alternatively if they have unconscionably received trust property further to a breach of trust with knowledge of that breach of trust (so-called 'unconscionable receipt'). In either case, the remedy is the imposition of a personal liability to account to the beneficiaries for the whole of the loss caused by the breach of trust on those strangers as though they had been trustees (that is, they are said to be made liable as 'constructive trustees').

Alternatively, there are proprietary liabilities of the sort which are discussed in the next chapter. So, the trustees may seek to recover the very property which was taken from the trust in breach of trust, by means of a 'following' claim. Therefore, if a vintage sports car was held on trust, then the trustees may use a following claim to recover that specific sports car from whoever has it in their possession. However, if that property has been substituted for other property without any

---

[1] [1996] AC 421.
[2] [1998] Ch 241.

mixing of property, then an action based on tracing at common law would entitle a right to be brought against that substitute property (so-called 'common law tracing'). So, if the sports car had been sold and if the sales proceeds had been used to buy shares, then the trustees might use a common law tracing claim to take those shares. Alternatively, if the property had been mixed with other property (so that the original property could not longer be separated out) then a tracing action in equity would be necessary (so-called 'equitable tracing'). Thus, if the sale proceeds from a sale of the sports car had been paid into a bank account which already contained other money, then recovering proprietary rights in the money would require an equitable tracing action. Tracing actions are considered in Chapter 11.

The impression we should form of the law on breach of trust at this stage is that the beneficiaries have several avenues for seeking redress for any loss suffered as a result of the breach of trust. Compared to the common law liabilities of damages for breach of contract or the commission of a tort, this range of equitable liabilities is self-evidently considerably broader. This perpetuates the stereotype considered in Chapter 1, to the effect that equity is more imaginative in its development of new doctrines than the common law with its principal focus on damages.[3] Another point we can take from this initial survey of the breadth of the remedies for breach of trust, is that one of the self-appointed missions of trusts law is to protect the beneficiaries of trusts, under the umbrella of the trustees' fiduciary duties, against any wrongful loss of property and of value to the trust fund.

## THE NATURE OF LIABILITY FOR BREACH OF TRUST

Liability for breach of trust, as it was established by the House of Lords in *Target Holdings v Redferns*,[4] created the requirement that there must be some causal connection between the breach of trust and the loss. In that case, solicitors had committed a technical breach of trust in misusing client money. That client money was supposed to have been held on trust by the solicitors for the claimant until a mortgage was taken over land, as part of a larger land transaction in which the claimant was making a loan which was being secured over that land. The solicitors used the trust money for their own purposes before replacing the equivalent cash amount which should have been held on trust. Meanwhile, third parties had caused a loss to the trust by fraudulently over-valuing the property which was to have provided the mortgage security to the claimant. Later, the claimant sought to exercise its security over the land when the loan was not repaid: at that time, the claimant realised that the land had been fraudulently over-valued and therefore that it would not be able to recover its loss by selling the land. It was held that

---

[3] Remember, other remedies for breach of contract, such as specific performance, rescission and rectification, all arise in equity, not common law.
[4] [1996] AC 421.

when the claimant had suffered this loss, that was the result of over-valuation by the third-party valuers and had not been caused by the solicitors' breach of trust. Consequently, the solicitors were not liable to compensate the claimant, because their technical breach of trust had not caused the claimant's loss, even though they had committed a breach of trust. The previous state of the law would have imposed something akin to strict liability on the solicitors. In consequence, the chances of a trustee escaping liability for breach of trust have increased if the trustee can demonstrate that, in spite of having committed a technical breach of trust, the loss was caused by some other factor.

The heads of liability against the trustee are threefold. First, a proprietary liability on the trustee to replace the precise property which had previously been held on trust. If that is not possible then, secondly, to reconstitute in cash the value of the trust fund. This second head of liability is a personal liability. Thirdly, another personal liability, to compensate the beneficiaries in general terms for any loss resulting from the breach of trust. The remainder of this chapter considers how liability may be attached to third parties beyond the trustees.

## THE LAW ON DISHONEST ASSISTANCE

A defendant will be personally liable to account to beneficiaries for any loss caused by a breach of trust if that defendant dishonestly assisted that breach of trust.[5] Therefore, the defendant must be shown to have been dishonest. The question considered below is what the concept of dishonesty should mean. The concept of assistance is little considered in the cases and appears to be very broadly drawn. The defendant is referred to as a 'constructive trustee' in the sense that the defendant is construed to be a trustee and made liable for the loss caused by the breach of trust as though an express trustee.

## THE LAW ON UNCONSCIONABLE RECEIPT

A defendant will be personally liable to account to beneficiaries for any loss caused by a breach of trust if that defendant received trust property with knowledge of the breach of trust, and provided that the defendant was found to have acted unconscionably.[6] Therefore, the defendant must be shown to have had knowledge of the breach of trust. Knowledge in this context refers to actual knowledge, or constructive knowledge in the sense of knowledge which she would have had but for wilfully shutting her eyes to the obvious, or knowledge which she would have had but for wilfully and recklessly failing to make the inquiries which an honest and reasonable person would have made.[7]

The concept of 'receipt' has been treated differently in different cases: it has been taken either to mean the ownership which would have been sufficient to

---

[5] *Royal Brunei Airlines v Tan* [1995] 2 AC 378.
[6] *Bank of Credit and Commerce International (Overseas) Ltd v Akindele* [2000] 4 All ER 221.
[7] *Re Montagu* [1987] Ch 264.

found a tracing action,[8] or having control or possession of trust property.[9] More recent cases have added the requirement that the defendant must also have acted unconscionably.[10] This means that it is not sufficient, as was the case previously, that the defendant had knowledge of the breach of trust; rather, she must also have acted unconscionably in a situation in which she had constructive knowledge.

## Debate  1

## Is 'dishonesty' objective or subjective?

### THE SCOPE OF THE DEBATE

The principal debate within the law on dishonest assistance is as to the nature of the concept of 'dishonesty'. There are three general positions: first, that the concept of dishonesty should be entirely objective; secondly, that the concept of dishonesty should be subjective to some extent; and, thirdly, that the concept of dishonesty should be broadly objective but that it should take into account some subjective factors. Each of these positions is considered in turn. What emerges is that the courts have shown determination to introduce some subjectivity into the law, even though it is accepted that the test is supposed to be primarily objective.

### (1) The 'pure' objective model of dishonest assistance

It was the judgment of Lord Nicholls in the Privy Council in *Royal Brunei Airlines v Tan*[11] which introduced the concept of 'dishonesty' to this head of liability, whereas the test had previously been one which asked whether or not the defendant had had knowledge of the trust. In that instance, it was not a requirement that the trustee could be proven to have acted dishonestly. Instead it was sufficient that the defendant had assisted a breach of trust in circumstances in which the defendant had had (in that case) actual knowledge that there was a breach of trust when the trustee, which was a travel agency company, used the trust money for its own purposes.

Importantly, Lord Nicholls held that the defendant must be shown to have assisted the breach of trust and also that the defendant had acted dishonestly in so doing. As Lord Nicholls put it:[12]

> 'Whatever may be the position in some criminal or other contexts (see, for instance, *Reg v Ghosh*[13]), in the context of the accessory liability principle acting dishonestly, or with a lack of probity, which is synonymous, means simply not acting as an honest person would in the circumstances. This is an objective standard.'

---

[8] *El Ajou v Dollar Land Holdings plc* [1993] 3 All ER 717; app'd [1994] 2 All ER 685.
[9] *Macmillan v Bishopsgate* [1995] 1 WLR 978.
[10] *Bank of Credit and Commerce International (Overseas) Ltd v Akindele* [2000] 4 All ER 221.
[11] [1995] 2 AC 378.
[12] Ibid, 389.
[13] [1982] QB 1053.

Therefore, his Lordship intended that the test was to be an objective test, i.e. it would be sufficient for the defendant to be liable if the defendant had not acted as an honest and reasonable person would have acted in those circumstances. Therefore, one should look at the circumstances, and ask what an honest and reasonable person would have done in those circumstances, and then ask whether or not the defendant behaved in that way.

It is important to recognise that Lord Nicholls considered whether or not the concept of dishonesty should include any subjectivity. To this end, his Lordship continued from the passage quoted immediately above:[14]

> 'This is an objective standard. At first sight this may seem surprising. Honesty has a connotation of subjectivity, as distinct from the objectivity of negligence. Honesty, indeed, does have a strong subjective element in that it is a description of a type of conduct assessed in the light of what a person actually knew at the time, as distinct from what a reasonable person would have known or appreciated. Further, honesty and its counterpart dishonesty are mostly concerned with advertent conduct, not inadvertent conduct. Carelessness is not dishonesty. Thus for the most part dishonesty is to be equated with conscious impropriety. However, these subjective characteristics of honesty do not mean that individuals are free to set their own standards of honesty in particular circumstances. The standard of what constitutes honest conduct is not subjective. Honesty is not an optional scale, with higher or lower values according to the moral standards of each individual. If a person knowingly appropriates another's property, he will not escape a finding of dishonesty simply because he sees nothing wrong in such behaviour.'

This passage is important. Lord Nicholls acknowledges that people might ordinarily consider dishonesty to be subjective, but note that important use of the word 'However'; his Lordship was clear that that was *not* the approach that was being taken in this area: 'The standard of what constitutes honest conduct is not subjective.' That much could not be clearer. Therefore it is a shame that, later in his judgment, Lord Nicholls held as follows:[15]

> '[W]hen called upon to decide whether a person was acting honestly, a court will look at all the circumstances known to the third party at the time. The court will also have regard to personal attributes of the third party such as his experience and intelligence, and the reason why he acted as he did.'

It is this short sentence-and-a-half which has been seized upon by several judges (as considered in the third approach below) as permitting some subjectivity to be taken into account. Taking into account the personal attributes of the defendant (such as 'experience and intelligence') means that the court is not simply asking what an honest and reasonable person would have done; instead, it may be asking what a person as stupid or dishonest as the defendant would have done.

---

[14] [1995] AC 375, 389.
[15] [1995] 2 AC 378, 391.

## (2) The 'hybrid' subjective model of dishonest assistance

*The hybrid subjective–objective model in the House of Lords*
A different approach was taken in the House of Lords in *Twinsectra v Yardley*.[16] In that case, the defendant solicitor had taken on responsibility for a formal solicitor's undertaking which had previously been given by another solicitor to a lender, to the effect that he would only allow loan moneys to be used in a specified way by his client. The solicitor has succumbed to pressure from his client to hand the moneys over to the client, at which point the client misused them. The solicitor contended that he had not dishonestly assisted in a breach of these duties relating to the loan moneys because he had not subjectively understood the terms of the solicitor's undertaking. Lord Hutton gave a speech which held that while *Tan* was to be followed in the sense that dishonesty was required before liability for assistance in a breach of fiduciary duty could be imposed, and while it was necessary to ask what an honest person would have done in the circumstances, it was *also* necessary to ask whether or not that particular defendant had realised that honest and reasonable people would have considered his behaviour to have been dishonest.

Lord Hutton was a criminal lawyer who was more used to the criminal standard of dishonesty which requires subjective dishonesty; therefore, it was unsurprising that that instinct took over in his judgment in holding that it would be a grave finding that a solicitor had been dishonest and therefore that subjective dishonesty would need to be found so as to justify that outcome. Nevertheless, Lord Hoffmann agreed with him. Therefore, the House of Lords asserted that a defendant would need to be both objectively dishonest by the standards of honest people, and also that the defendant would have to realise that honest people would consider her behaviour to have been dishonest.

In the later Privy Council decision in *Barlow Clowes v Eurotrust*,[17] the court (in an unanimous judgment delivered by Lord Hoffmann) held that the test should be an objective one. The court attempted – somewhat disingenuously – to reinterpret the decision in *Twinsectra* so that it should not be read as having created a subjective standard for dishonesty. In *Eurotrust*, the defendant had assisted rogues to funnel investors' money out of the fraudulently-operated investment empire they ran, through the Isle of Man and into the banking system where it was difficult to locate. In essence, the trial judge found that the defendant must have realised what was going on, and moreover that he had been dishonest when he assisted those activities. The defendant had argued – in reliance on Lord Hutton's judgment in *Twinsectra v Yardley* – that his personal motto was, in effect, that one should always do whatever one's clients wanted without question, and consequently he argued that he had not appreciated that other people would consider his behaviour to have been dishonest. This prompted the Privy Council to revert to an objective test

[16] [2002] 2 AC 164.
[17] [2005] UKPC 37.

for dishonesty, because it would clearly be unacceptable to allow defendants to escape liability simply by arguing that their warped morals should excuse them from living up to the standards of ordinary society.

### Why an objective approach is better

The most convincing argument for an objective test is a pragmatic one. In cases involving dishonesty or an allegation that the defendant must have known that such and such was the case, it is likely that the defendant may simply lie or at the very least claim an innocence which is simply not credible. The case of *Barlow Clowes v Eurotrust*[18] is a perfect example of why subjective tests will typically not work in practice. After the decision of Lord Hutton in *Twinsectra v Yardley*, it was clearly open to a defendant to argue that her own, personal moral code meant that she was not consciously aware that other people would consider that her actions had been dishonest. If the test requires both a breach of the objective standards and also a subjective awareness that those standards had been breached, then the defendant has only to assert that she had not been subjectively aware of the matters which are alleged against her.

And so it was that the defendant in *Eurotrust* argued that it was contrary to his personal moral code to question any instruction given to him by a client. In consequence, he argued that he had not thought at all about the proprieties of assisting two shysters to commit a series of breaches of fiduciary duty in taking large amounts of money out of investment funds under their control. Clearly the judge at first instance and the Privy Council considered that this defence was simply disingenuous. It is clear from reading the judgments that none of those judges was prepared to accept the defendant's audacious plea that he did not think he was doing wrong by allowing money to be laundered through his organisation. Two things happened as a result. First, rather than argue that the defendant should not be believed on the basis of a subjective test, the Privy Council instead sought to re-explain what had been decided in *Twinsectra v Yardley*. Secondly, by reverting to a purely objective test, the Privy Council found that the defendant had been dishonest and was therefore liable for dishonest assistance. Therefore, it is suggested that whenever a defendant seeks to maintain a defence based on a subjective test, the judge will always be considering the credibility of the defence when measured against what the judge believes an objective or reasonable person would have done in those circumstances.

An objective test requires a judge to enunciate the nature and content of the objective standards against which the defendant is being measured. This will lead to a clear development of the law, because the judge in each circumstance will have enunciated both the standards against which the defendant was being measured (thus providing sufficient material for an appeal) and also the factors which demonstrated a failure to live up to those standards. A subjective test requires the judge to assess the credibility of a defendant's claim that she did not know that

---

[18] Ibid.

such and such was the case, and so forth: this has the effect of limiting the development of the law to a series of assessments of the credibility of individual defendants from case to case. It would not necessarily, however, generate clear statements of the underlying legal principles which were being applied, in that while the judge might recognise that the test involved a demonstration that the defendant was aware that she had acted consciously dishonestly, all that would be learned was that in a courtroom on a given day, a given defendant failed to mount a credible defence of her own honesty.

### (3) The 'impure' objective model: taking some subjective factors into account

One might have thought that the law had therefore reverted simply to a *Tan*-model of objective dishonesty. However, later High Court and Court of Appeal decisions[19] have focused on the following passage in the judgment of Lord Nicholls (quoted above), so as to permit them to take into account the subjective beliefs of the defendant in the case in front of them:

> '[W]hen called upon to decide whether a person was acting honestly, a court will look at all the circumstances known to the third party at the time. The court will also have regard to personal attributes of the third party such as his experience and intelligence, and the reason why he acted as he did.'[20]

This is an 'impure' model of objective dishonesty in the sense that these High Court judges always acknowledge that they must follow the decisions in *Tan* and in *Eurotrust*, but in so doing they highlight these few words (in a judgment of thousands of words) to justify looking into some of the defendant's 'personal attributes' (i.e. her subjective attributes). Thus, the courts will now consider what an honest person would have done in those circumstances if she had had the personal attributes of the defendant. Once the personal attributes of the defendant (and not simply her actions in the circumstances in which she acted) are taken into account, the test has become a subjective one, at least in part.

The confused state of the current law is set out in the following form by Morgan J in a good summary of the authorities, but one which mixes objective and some subjective elements:[21]

> 'The test as to dishonesty ... is as follows. Dishonesty is synonymous with a lack of probity. It means not acting as an honest person would in the circumstances. The standard is an objective one. The application of the standard requires one to put oneself in the shoes of the defendant to the extent that his conduct is to be assessed in the light of what he knew at the relevant time, as distinct from what a reasonable person would have known or appreciated. For the most part dishonesty is to be equated with conscious impropriety. But a person is not free to set his own standard

[19] *Starglade v Nash* [2010] EWCA Civ 1314; *Fiona Trust & Holding Corporation v Privalov* [2010] EWHC 3199 (Comm).

[20] [1995] 2 AC 378, 391.

[21] *Aerostar Maintenance International Ltd v Wilson* [2010] EWHC 2032 (Ch).

of honesty. This is what is meant by saying that the standard is objective. If by ordinary objective standards, the defendant's mental state would be judged to be dishonest, it is irrelevant that the defendant has adopted a different standard or can see nothing wrong in his behaviour.'

The subjective elements creep in when one must put oneself in the shoes of the defendant and when one must look for 'conscious impropriety', as opposed to considering solely what an honest person would do in the circumstances.

## Debate 2

## What does it mean to have knowledge in unconscionable receipt?

The concept of knowledge remains central to liability for the 'receipt-based' doctrine, even after the concept of 'unconscionability' was added to it by the decision in *Bank of Credit and Commerce International (Overseas) Ltd v Akindele*.[22] The state of the law at present is best defined by Carnwath LJ in the Court of Appeal in *Charter plc v City Index Ltd*,[23] when he held that 'liability for "knowing receipt" depends on the defendant having sufficient knowledge of the circumstances of the payment to make it "unconscionable" for him to retain the benefit or pay it away for his own purposes'. Therefore, the current state of the law is that there must both be knowledge of the breach of trust and unconscionability on the part of the defendant.

### THE CONCEPT OF KNOWLEDGE

The concept of knowledge was delineated first by Peter Gibson J in *Baden v Société Générale*,[24] borrowing a five-fold categorisation which was suggested in argument by Leolin Price QC, which outlined the categories of knowledge in the following way:

'(a) actual knowledge;
(b) wilfully shutting one's eyes to the obvious;
(c) wilfully and recklessly failing to make inquiries which an honest person would have made;
(d) knowledge of circumstances which would indicate the facts to an honest and reasonable man;
(e) knowledge of circumstances which would put an honest and reasonable man on inquiry.'

The fourth and fifth categories are the most interesting, given that they are potentially the broadest. A person would be deemed to have knowledge of a breach of trust simply if he did have knowledge of some factor which, put crudely, would have made a reasonable person suspicious.

---

[22] [2000] 4 All ER 221.
[23] [2008] 2 WLR 950.
[24] [1993] 1 WLR 509.

It was the judgment of Sir Robert Megarry V-C in *In re Montagu's Settlement Trusts*[25] which removed the last two of the *Baden* categories of knowledge. The facts and circumstances of *Montagu* are, in many senses, shameful. The Duke of Manchester had been the life tenant of a settlement which held a number of very valuable heir-looms, including paintings by great masters and even Katherine of Aragon's travel-ling trunk. The Duke had been life tenant, but was therefore not absolutely entitled to the property: that is, he was not entitled to treat the property as though it was his. And yet the Duke took it upon himself to sell many of these items of property even though they were not his to sell. It appears that the trustees were too deferen-tial to prevent him from doing this. The question was whether or not the Duke had had knowledge of the breach of trust: at some point in time he had had knowledge of circumstances which should have put him on inquiry, because the terms of the trust had been explained to him. However, Megarry V-C was determined not to find him liable. The way in which this was achieved was by restricting the categories of knowledge to the first three on the basis, it was said, that liability should arise only where the defendant had acted wilfully. Therefore, because the Duke had forgotten about the terms of the trust, he was taken not to have had knowledge of it at the time of selling the trust property.

It is worth asking, just for a moment, whether a member of the public who was not a Duke would have been offered the same largesse by the Chancery Division of the High Court. Who else could have sold artworks and bric-a-brac worth millions of pounds at auction and have argued credibly that they had forgotten that that property did not belong to them? Answer: no one.

## THE REQUIREMENT OF UNCONSCIONABILITY

In *Charter plc v City Index Ltd*, Carnwath LJ held that[26] 'liability for "knowing receipt" depends on the defendant having sufficient knowledge of the circumstances of the payment to make it "unconscionable" for him to retain the benefit or pay it away for his own purposes'. The approach set out in *BCCI v Akindele*[27] was that the court should first consider whether or not the defendant had the appropriate knowledge, and then ask whether the defendant had also acted unconscionably. In that case, the defendant had been a very high-profile client of a bank which had been oper-ated fraudulently by its staff: those staff members had paid the defendant more money than he had been entitled to from his investments so as to keep his business with the bank.[28] It was held that while the client had information which should have put him on inquiry about the overpayments which were being made to him, he had not solicited those overpayments and therefore he could not be shown to

---

[25] [1987] Ch 264, 273.

[26] *Charter plc v City Index Ltd* [2008] 2 WLR 950.

[27] [2000] 4 All ER 221.

[28] Think about it: people buy underwear because David Beckham wears it, or wear perfume because Victoria Beckham wears it, so it is not hard to imagine people deciding to invest with a bank because a well-known figure from their community banks there.

have acted unconscionably. So the addition of the standard of unconscionability will tend to absolve people from liability who would otherwise have been liable for knowing receipt on the basis that they knew about circumstances which should have put them on inquiry.

The net effect in this area of the law has been a dilution of liability. Whereas people would once have been expected to make inquiries once something suspicious came to mind, now the law will not hold them liable if they fail to make any such inquiries. That tells us a lot about the lowering standards in our law. The courts of equity are permitting people to get away with lower moral standards than before. At the same time, however, commercial regulation is becoming more intense. For example, the Money Laundering Regulations 2007 impose obligations on deposit-takers to make active inquiries in relation to any 'suspicious' activity, and ss. 327 and 328 of the Proceeds of Crime Act 2002 require banks specifically to make reports to the authorities of any suspicious activity. It is peculiar that banks acting as trustees may be required to make money-laundering reports when trusts law does not require that of them.

# Debate 3

## What does is mean to be dishonest?

### PHILOSOPHICAL QUESTIONS AROUND DISHONESTY

The question of what constitutes dishonesty interests philosophers as much as anyone.

Ask yourself the following question: What *is* an honest person? Who among your family, friends and acquaintances is 'an objectively honest person'? Do they live a perfect life? Do they never tell lies, not even 'little white lies' to make their friends feel better? Did they never lie as a child? Do they never claim to be busy on a lazy day off when they are accosted in the street by a charity worker with a clipboard? Are there likely to be any secrets in their Internet browsing history? What are the attributes of this perfect citizen? Do they act honestly in every aspect of their life: for example, how do they eat their sandwiches honestly? How does the objectively 'honest person' differ from someone who is a 'reasonable person'? Our suspicion might be that the standard of the 'honest person' which the judges would use would resemble very closely the attitudes of each individual judge.

### QUESTIONS ABOUT LYING AND DECEPTION POSED BY PHILOSOPHERS

One question which is currently interesting many philosophers is the following one: What is lying and what is deception? This is an important question for private law in relation to the tort of deceit (i.e. fraud) and in relation to concepts like dishonest assistance. Of course, the concept of dishonesty need not be coterminous with the concept of lying, nor with the concept of deception. One can deceive oneself by believing something which one wants to be true (that a pet will survive an operation, that a friend did not commit a crime), but that does not mean that one is necessarily dishonest. However, the models of lying and of deception which have been posited by the philosophers are useful because they throw into relief both what is unique to the legal models of dishonesty and what is problematic about trying to erect an objective standard of what is an honest person in equity or a reasonable person at common law.

### Carson's definition of lying, and its relation to fraud and dishonesty in law and equity

Thomas Carson, in his book *Lying and Deception*, posits the following definition of lying.[29] A person tells a lie if:

- that person makes a false statement;
- that person either believes that statement to be false or probably false, or does not believe that it is true; and
- that person in some way warrants the truth of that statement.

One key difference between this statement and the common law concept of fraud in the tort of deceit is that it is sufficient for the tort of deceit that the defendant was reckless, or even just careless, as to whether their statement was true or false.[30] Carson wants the liar consciously not to believe it is true; whereas common law liability is met if that person induces another person to rely on the statement in a situation in which they might not know whether the statement is true or not. Thus, legal liability effectively imposes a positive obligation on the makers of such statements not to be careless about the content of their statements, on pain of compensating their listeners for reasonably relying on their inducements. For Carson, there need not necessarily be an inducement to do anything: rather, the lie exists in itself.

The key difference between Carson's model and dishonest assistance is that the model in dishonest assistance is the behaviour of an objectively honest person in such a situation. Dishonest assistance is therefore not limited to lying but rather covers any act which is different from what an honest person would have done in the circumstances. While dishonest assistance would encompass lying on the model set out by Carson, it extends much further than that. As with the test of knowledge in unconscionable receipt, it is suggested that dishonesty in dishonest assistance includes failing to make the inquiries which an honest and reasonable person would have made to establish the true facts, and so is not limited to a belief that the statement is untrue. Again, the law is impliedly imposing an obligation on people to make reasonable inquiries into the facts on pain of bearing the loss that another person suffers by means of a breach of trust. Therefore, stranger liability in general terms is involved in a normative project (which requires people to act in particular ways so as to evade liability) which is not present in the philosophers' models of what constitutes dishonesty.

---

[29] T. Carson, *Lying and Deception* (Oxford University Press, 2010), 24.
[30] *Peek v Gurney* (1873) LR 6 HL 377.

## Lying, 'bullshit' and law

The philosophers' models of deceit are passive in the sense that they do not seek to impose obligations on ordinary citizens like the law does. This is unsurprising, because law is necessarily concerned with allocating liabilities for suffering or having to compensate losses, and thus for creating standards of good behaviour at the same time. However, the philosophers do also consider actions, and where the lines should be drawn between different types of actions and their honesty. So, Carson's definition of lying differs from Frankfurt's concept of 'bullshitting' from his book *On Bullshit*.[31] For Frankfurt, the important thing about bullshit is that the person making the statement does not care whether the statement is true or false. Instead, the bullshitter is simply attempting to convince his listeners to agree with him.[32] Frankfurt's model of bullshit comprises three things:

1. an intention to deceive;
2. not necessarily lying; and
3. being unconcerned with the truth of what is said.

Frankfurt considers that bullshitters are different from liars in that liars must be concerned with the truth of what they are saying (and therefore are consciously saying something they believe to be untrue), whereas bullshitters are concerned only with the outcome of getting other people to believe whatever they say. So, a politician may make a speech which seeks to convince us about the correctness of a military intervention in another country on the (mistaken) basis that that other country has weapons of mass destruction which can be used against us: Frankfurt would consider that that politician is primarily concerned with convincing us about the need for military intervention, but is not necessarily concerned with whether or not there are such weapons in existence, and therefore is not a liar because he is uninterested in the weapons.

There are two problems with this approach. First, the politician is probably actually very concerned about the presence of the weapons, and is operating on the basis of a mistaken perception of the risks which has caused that politician and the people around them to ratchet up their rhetoric to a point where they can gain popular support to carry out the course of action which they consider to be necessary.[33]

---

[31] H. Frankfurt, *On Bullshit* (Princeton University Press, 2005).

[32] Interestingly, even though it is my practice to use the feminine form for hypothetical pronouns (she, her, etc), I have immediately, unconsciously lapsed into referring to bullshitters as being male.

[33] It is unlikely that an elected politician would bomb another country for fun. However, it is likely that an elected politician (especially one with no experience of war nor of security services) would defer to all of the incorrect, over-excited misinformation being provided to him by the security services, with the result that he comes genuinely to believe that there is a threat (because people who know about these things tell him that they think there is a threat) and therefore seeks to convince everyone else of the course of action which he has come to believe is necessary. It was on exactly this basis that the Hutton Inquiry decided that Tony Blair genuinely believed that the invasion of Iraq was necessary in 2003, that he consequently urged an invasion of Iraq on the British people, and that he was later shown to have been mistaken about the reasons for war which he gave at the outset. It was a case of negligence and error on such a terrible scale that it caused much popular opinion to think that it must have been deceit.

Bullshit and rhetoric are similar here because both are designed to convince the listener of the correctness of a particular course of action. The second problem is that carelessness about the content of what is said is so similar to lying consciously as to be the moral equivalent of conscious deceit. This is why the laws on dishonest assistance, on unconscionable receipt and on fraud all encompass situations in which a person has failed to ascertain the facts or to understand the circumstances (within reasonable limits) before causing or allowing others to suffer loss.

### A worked example of the difficulties with dishonesty, bullshit and the reasonable person

Let us take an example of the questions we have considered so far in this chapter. Suppose that the Chief Executive Officer ('CEO') of an investment bank tells the Press that the news that his bank has suffered a loss of $100 million, as a result of a disastrous series of speculations conducted by a poorly supervised trader, is merely 'a blip, because this bank can absorb a loss of $100 million without any problem'. Was he being dishonest if the total losses caused by this trading activity eventually reach more than $6,000 million?[34] These are all the facts that we have for this hypothetical example: when the CEO spoke, the losses were known publicly to be $100 million, but only a couple of months later the true size of those losses would transpire to be $6,000 million (or, $6 billion). Suppose, for the purposes of this hypothetical example, that it is impossible to prove whether or not the CEO had been informed that the losses which the bank stood to suffer were much greater than $100 million.[35] By making that fact unknown, we can explore what we want the law to be in this area, and what might cause us to decide one way or another if the facts turn out to be different. So, was the CEO being dishonest (in a legal and in a non-legal sense) when he spoke to the Press about losses that were known publicly to be at $100 million as being merely a blip, when they would reach $6 billion in a few weeks? Or was the CEO 'bullshitting' when he dismissed the initial losses as being merely a blip: that is, was the CEO consciously misleading the public, or was he unconcerned about the truth of his statement?

If the CEO's intention when he spoke to the Press was to calm the markets, to calm investors in the bank and also to ensure that customers kept their money with his bank, was he simply attempting to create good public relations by minimising the risk to the bank? And, if so, does good public relations involve deceit or bullshitting? After all, as we know from the collapse of US investment bank Lehman

---

[34] This hypothetical example is only very loosely based on the JP Morgan Chase losses of US$6.2 billion on the so-called 'London Whale' trades. Losses were initially put at a few hundreds of millions of dollars but quickly rose to the much larger figure of US$6.2 billion. JP Morgan Chase was disciplined by its regulators for having failed to inform the regulators when it realised the true scale of its losses. During this mini-crisis, the bank's CEO dismissed the problem as being merely 'a tempest in a teacup'.

[35] This is a sensible approach for us to take as lawyers. Once a trial judge has found what the facts *are* then debate is closed off in many senses. The more interesting debates about the nature of the law require us to struggle without the luxury of a definitive statement of what actually happened. Instead we need to test where the boundary lines should be placed.

Brothers in September 2008, if a bank loses the confidence of the marketplace and its investors, then that bank may see its capital erode very quickly and other banks may refuse to deal with it, thus causing it to nose-dive into insolvency. Therefore, was the CEO trying to fend off that sort of market reaction? In his own mind, was the CEO determined above all else to protect his bank from this short-term crisis in confidence in his bank? If so, he may have been bullshitting in that instance because he wanted to convince the markets of something untrue – that the losses were comparatively small and could be absorbed easily by the bank – in a situation in which he did not care about the truth. All he cared about was the outcome: investors continuing to invest and other banks continuing to deal with his bank. Perhaps there were people working away in his bank while he was speaking, trying both to calculate the potential size of the losses in the future and to minimise those losses.

Of course, much would depend on what the CEO actually knew at the time he made the statement. If the bank was so badly managed that no one in senior management actually knew how large the losses would become, then we might say that the CEO was both negligent (in making a public statement without knowing what the true position was) and nevertheless bullshitting (because he made the statement with the sole objective of achieving a positive outcome for his bank without actually knowing the truth). In defence of the CEO, it might be said that he had asked all the questions he needed to ask internally and that no one could have foreseen the losses which resulted. In such a situation, it could be said that the CEO was misinformed or self-deluding about the profitability of his bank, but not lying because he himself had no reason to believe the losses would have grown beyond $100 million.

If the CEO thereby caused a pension fund (a trust) to invest in his bank, that might cause the trust to suffer a loss when the shares in his bank fall in value when the true extent of the losses are published. If that triggered a breach of terms of pension fund's trust instrument,[36] would the CEO be personally liable for dishonesty? It might be argued that he assisted the breach of trust by inducing the trustees to invest in his bank by under-estimating the impact of those losses; alternatively, it might be argued that his remarks in the Press were too remote from the trustees' decision to invest. Significantly, if the CEO was making those statements precisely to encourage investment, we might argue that he should bear a direct liability to all investors. The question would be as to his dishonesty here. What would an honest person have done in the circumstances?

The more serious suggestion would be whether the CEO was motivated, regardless of the truth, to encourage investors to invest new money with his bank (in the form of buying shares) or other customers to enter into large, new transactions with the bank, as well as convincing existing investors and customers to maintain

---

[36] E.g., the pension fund's trust instrument may impose a requirement on the trustees as to the credit worth or 'suitability' of any bank or other company in which they invest, something which might be harmed by the revelation of the true size of these losses.

their existing transactions. In that situation it could be said that the CEO was committing fraud where, careless of the truth of his statement, he was seeking to induce large numbers of investors and new customers to deal with his bank regardless of the unfolding story. It could be argued more convincingly that there was a direct link between those new transactions and his purpose in making the statement: one which an objectively honest person might not have made.

All of this discussion leads us is into a difficult set of questions, from the perspective of the law on dishonest assistance, as to what is meant by 'dishonesty'. What would an honest person do in these circumstances? That would be the *Tan* model of this test; but later cases (as discussed above) have emphasised the need to consider the question in the circumstances of the defendant. The question is almost more difficult if it is changed to be: What would an honest person in the circumstances of the CEO (needing to protect his bank from falling in the markets) with his knowledge and experience (and a mindset which convinced him to put the short-term interests of the bank first) do? There are very few bank CEOs in the world. They are not like ordinary people – not least because of their personal wealth, their power within their multinational organisations and beyond those organisations, and their shared belief in free markets with as little financial regulation as possible. If all of those circumstances are to be taken into account then it is more likely that we would excuse a CEO who wishes to protect his bank, because our objectively honest person becomes an objectively honest person whose role is to maintain the viability and profitability of a multinational investment bank, and who is a person whose experience has also led him to believe that those markets should be free from moral and regulatory constraints. Alternatively, we might take the view that this last set of 'experiences' shades into a purely subjective mindset and so ought to be ignored for the purposes of this test.

There is another possible approach which is based on a utilitarian attitude[37] to the need for markets and banks to remain operational, even at the expense of a little transparency all the way. Such an objectively honest person might take the view that fending off questions from journalists with a little bullshit is entirely reasonable if it will keep the bank solvent and allow business to continue. The CEO may have a genuine belief in the virtues of maintaining the good standing of his bank so that its failure will not cause the sort of impact which the failure of Lehman Brothers caused to the world economy in 2008 when it collapsed. This might seem to us to be objectively more acceptable than a mere desire to avoid the bank suffering short-term losses: if the CEO was simply trying to keep the bank afloat so that he could receive a personal bonus, then that would appear to us to be unacceptable and possibly even corrupt; whereas a desire simply to maintain order in the financial markets, and so to avoid the sort of harm that is caused by a crash, would appear to be more laudable. What is interesting is that the impact of the statements made in the Press remains the same: investors, regulators and

---

[37] Utilitarians generally accept a little harm to individuals if the larger benefits to society as a whole justify it.

customers have been misled. What is at stake is whether or not the CEO's personal motivations for saying what he said should make him liable for any losses that resulted.

Alternatively, if all of these circumstances were seen through the eyes of 'the man on the Clapham omnibus'[38] then it might be more likely that we would not accept the probity of the CEO's subjective concerns about keeping his bank in profit, and we might focus instead on his failure to establish all of the facts before he spoke, his underlying desire to keep his business profitable before anything else and so forth. Through those eyes, the CEO might appear to have been self-interested, and therefore wilfully blind to true facts and the harm that might result. We might think that the CEO was taking a risk in the hope that his personal objectives would be achieved.

In 2014, an ordinary member of the public might be less sympathetic to the CEO's actions, particularly at a time when banks are blamed for the economic aftermath of the financial crisis which they caused. For example, the Parliamentary Commission on Banking Standards reported only in 2013 on the many failures of business probity which it had found in banks, so those concerns are not irrational because that was only one report among many to come to the same conclusions.[39] Which raises another question: Is the honest or reasonable person supposed to be divorced from the short-term prejudices of much of the population? Or should the objectively honest person stand outside short-term popular opinions, and thus stand outside time and outside society? If bankers are believed to be selfish, greedy and untrustworthy because of the well-publicised actions of some of them, then should that prejudice be taken into account in deciding what an honest person thinks ought to have been done?

If the honest person has no knowledge of complex investment banking, is that person's mindset the appropriate starting point for measuring the actions of investment bankers? Alternatively, if the benchmark for the honesty of investment bankers is taken to be other investment bankers, then that simply has the effect of closing investment banking off from the ethics and morals of the rest of society, which is clearly undesirable because it prevents the ethics of banking from being connected to any general ethical system, and it may also lead to an entirely separate area of law being created for bankers with different norms from the rest of the law.[40]

Another approach, in relation specifically to banking, would be to look at the regulatory codes (drawn from statute) which apply to banking and use them as part of the objective yardstick. For example, the Financial Conduct Authority's *Principles for Businesses* rulebook in the UK, which sets out the 'high-level' principles by reference to which all regulated persons are to be regulated, requires that

---

[38] Which is the standard usually used in contract law for identifying the reasonable person.

[39] See Alastair Hudson, *The Law of Finance*, 2nd edn (Sweet & Maxwell, 2013), Ch. 45 generally.

[40] Of course, some would argue that this happens already as lawyers with different specialities split into camps servicing different clients, with different judges and different academics falling into different fields which mirror those in practice. Are commercial lawyers really using the same legal norms as family lawyers, for example?

all such people act 'with integrity', in the best interests of their clients and so forth. By comparison with dishonest assistance in equity, we might say that this principle of 'integrity' could be read in parallel with the equitable requirement that people act in good 'conscience'. Consequently, the contents of the detailed financial rulebooks could be used to establish a code of objective rules governing the activities of bankers. So, where those regulations provide that 'all communications with the public must be fair, clear and not misleading', that might embolden us to say that the CEO was misleading when he sought to encourage us all to believe that his bank had suffered only small losses which were a fraction of the size of the total losses which would materialise in the future. This is more so when the rulebooks also place a personal obligation on that CEO to ensure that there are robust and effective management systems within the bank to identify losses, to supervise employees and so forth. If the CEO had a regulatory obligation to ensure that these sorts of trades were monitored properly, would it be acceptable for him to claim to have had no knowledge of the true position at the time when he made his statements to the Press?

So, one of the real problems in relation to the concept of dishonesty is knowing who the honest person is; just as the problem for the common law is knowing who the reasonable person is. Instead, it will commonly be the case that the judge will simply end up asking whether or not they thought that the defendant acted in a way which the judge considers to have been honest.

# 11

# TRACING

## INTRODUCTION

The law on tracing is problematic from its very core. Using tracing, property rights in one item of property may be transferred into different items of property, and even translated into entirely different sorts of proprietary and non-proprietary rights in the form of charges, liens and constructive trusts by way of remedy.[1] Consequently, the claimant can acquire ownership rights against items of property in which the claimant had never previously had any rights. Clearly this form of action achieves justice for claimants who have had property taken from them by fraudsters and other wrongdoers; it also provides a different quality of justice for those who have had property taken from them without their consent in other ways.

What is clear from the case law, in cases such as *Re Diplock*,[2] is that wrongdoing is not a necessary prerequisite for tracing to take place. In that case, trustees mistakenly paid money to a charity; it transpired later that the relevant clause in the trust instrument was ineffective. The beneficiaries were entitled to trace in the wake of the property which had been passed to the charity. The charity was innocent, but the beneficiaries were still entitled to trace so as to protect their original property rights. At that level, it appears that even equitable tracing is not concerned with right and wrong. There are questions as to whether or not constructive trusts imposed as a result of tracing actions are really dependent on demonstrating unconscionability, or whether they are imposed solely to vindicate the claimant's original property rights.

The particular strength of English law tracing is that it permits claimants such as the victims of theft from their electronic bank accounts to pursue their lost funds into the sorts of mixed bank accounts into which criminals usually pay funds of this sort so as to distance them from their original source. At this point many civil code jurisdictions forgo any proprietary rights against the thieves in favour of personal claims akin to tort. The problem with a personal claim in this

---

[1] For further details on the relevant principles in this area, see A.S. Hudson, *Equity & Trusts*, (Routledge, 2014) Ch. 19.
[2] [1948] Ch 465.

context is that the thieves will usually have paid the money through front companies which will have been wound up, and they will have salted any assets away so that they personally appear to have no assets against which the victims could proceed.

The underlying issue with tracing is as to the basis on which property rights in item $x$ may be translated into item $y$ when the claimant has never previously owned $y$.[3] For example, if the claimant was the sole beneficiary under a trust over shares, how do we justify those equitable property rights being translated into land which was acquired with the sale proceeds of those shares, after they were paid into a mixed bank account which had been held on trust for another person?

In the background there is a constant sense that there is something *just* or *equitable* about that beneficiary being entitled to take rights in the land if it was bought with money which was taken unlawfully from their trust fund. It just seems *right* to an English lawyer somehow that the claimant is able to get something. However, as will emerge below, the courts have been clear that tracing does not operate on the basis of 'justice'; rather, the House of Lords was clear that tracing operates on the basis of hard-and-fast property law.[4] The vindication of property rights, ultimately, must be the justification for tracing actions. Without a lawful reason for using the trust fund in this way – for example, if the trustees had been entitled to sell the shares, or if the recipients of the funds had given full consideration for them or had changed their circumstances in reasonable reliance on receipt of that property – there is something satisfying in permitting the beneficiary to recover either their original property or, if that is impossible in practice, any property which can be demonstrated to have been substituted for that property.

The principal issue remains whether that tracing action is predicated on the wrong which was committed by the first defendant (typically the trustee) in taking the claimant's property unlawfully, or whether there is a qualitatively different type of wrong in a second defendant retaining that property or whether it has another basis. The difficulty with basing tracing on the first defendant's wrong is that the claimant would only have a personal claim against the defendant. Such a personal claim would be limited in practice by any exclusion of liability in a clause in the trust instrument, which would be decisive if the trustee was merely negligent in the management of the trust: that is, the trustee benefiting from such a provision would be able to resist any personal claim. A personal claim against any other defendants would be difficult to maintain unless they had been fraudulent or negligent themselves in inducing a breach of trust (as was discussed in the previous chapter). Moreover, a personal claim will work only if the defendants are solvent and have assets in a jurisdiction against which the tracing action can be enforced.

[3] A. Burrows (2001) 117 *LQR* 412.
[4] *Foskett v McKeown* [2001] 1 AC 102.

Wrong = personal claim → vuln to exclu + solvent

If the basis for the action is not a wrong committed by the first defendant or any other person, then the explanation must lie in another area of law. The explanation that is advanced in relation to unjust enrichment, as is explained below, is that a tracing action reverses any unjust enrichment which the recipient of the property may have taken at the claimant's expense, subject to a defence that if the recipient had changed their position in such a way then it would be unjust to require that the property is given up to the claimant. This approach has complications in relation to the establishment of the extent to which the defendant has been enriched and whether that matches the loss to the claimant. The further problem is that the law has historically not been based on unjust enrichment.[5] Rather, the law has been based on property law and the need to protect the property rights of the owners of property against non-consensual abuse by others. The concept that has been used is that of 'vindication' of those property rights, as is considered below. The line between equity and unjust enrichment thinking is explored below. First, we consider the ways in which equity permits tracing into mixed funds that discussion segues into a second debate about the nature of the remedies which equity permits. Then the ground is set for a consideration of equity and unjust enrichment to round off this chapter.

## Debate 1

## Which methodology of equitable tracing is better?

Our first debate within the law of tracing concerns the appropriate methodology for carrying out the tracing process in equity. (The other debates tend to revolve around theoretical questions as to the categorisation of tracing within private law, as is considered below.) Tracing is a process in which a claimant seeks to identify property which is a substitute for their own property and against which they will seek to bring a claim in place of their original property.[6] The precise remedy which is sought is a separate question from the property against which the legal action is commenced, as is discussed below.

When the claimant's original property (or its traceable proceed) has been mixed with other property, then that target property can only be traced in equity (and not common law). Equitable tracing is only available under the law as it is currently organised if the claimant's original property had been held on trust, or if there was some similar equitable proprietary right which would call the equitable jurisdiction into play. The debate which is considered here is whether the methodology should proceed under the old 'first-in/first-out' approach, or a newer, proportionate share approach.

---

[5] See the House of Lords decisions in *Westdeutsche Landesbank v Islington* [1996] AC 669 and *Foskett v McKeown* [2001] 1 AC 102.
[6] Ibid.

The old approach was established in *Clayton's Case* in the early nineteenth century.[7] In essence, *Clayton's Case* held that when tracing of money held in current bank accounts was being conducted into a mixture, then the property in that mixed fund would be deemed to be allocated in accordance with the order in which the claimants contributed to that mixture: the first people to put property into the mixture would be deemed to be the first people to take property out of that fund, the second contributor to that account would be the second to take property from that account, and so on. This approach is based, it is suggested, on older models of property law which were concerned with tangible property, even though *Clayton's Case* itself was concerned specifically with money in current bank accounts. This approach makes sense in relation to soft fruit warehouses, for example. If you were storing oranges in a wholesale warehouse, then you would ship out the oldest oranges in the warehouse when an order arrived because that would prevent those oranges from spoiling; whereas, if the most recent oranges were shipped out first, then the old oranges would continue to moulder at the back of the warehouse. The first oranges into the warehouse would be the first oranges to go out of the warehouse.

The alternative approach has been used in Canada.[8] In essence, when there is a mixture of property, the contributors to that fund take rights against that mixture (and any property acquired from that mixed fund) in proportion to their contribution to it. So, a claimant who had contributed £20 to a fund of £100 (i.e. one-fifth of that fund) would be entitled to take one-fifth of any property which resulted from that mixture. So, if the £100 was invested in shares which increased in value to £200, then that claimant would be entitled to one-fifth of those shares which are now worth £200.

The Canadian approach has not yet displaced *Clayton's Case* in England and Wales, even though there has clearly been a drift in the English cases towards the Canadian approach. The problem has been that the majority of cases have been decided in the High Court, and therefore the *Clayton's Case* approach has not been able to be overruled. However, the only Court of Appeal decision on point, in *Barlow Clowes v Vaughan*,[9] was not able to apply the proportionate share approach to its own facts.[10] In that case, Woolf LJ delivered a judgment in which he clearly suggested a preference for the proportionate share approach, identified the *Clayton's Case* approach as being merely a fiction and suggested that fictional doctrines like *Clayton's Case* should not be used when their results would be 'irrational or arbitrary'.

[7] (1817) 1 Mer 572.

[8] *Re Ontario Securities* (1988) 52 DLR (4th) 767.

[9] [1992] 4 All ER 22.

[10] In that case, the government was seeking to recover assets taken from investors by a fraudulently operated financial institution. The government was standing in the shoes of the investors, because the government had already bailed the investors out and was attempting to recover the bail-out money. The large number of investors and investments meant that the Court of Appeal had decided it would be impossible to identify the proportions which were attributable to each investor, and in any event it was unnecessary because the government was simply tracing into the whole of the lost investments.

As a result, later High Court decisions have refused to follow *Clayton's Case* on the basis that its application would have been irrational and arbitrary on their particular facts, thus following Woolf LJ to the letter.

The question, then, is which is the better approach? The first-in/first-out approach has the following problem: if two people contribute equally to a mixture on different days, and half of the mixture is used to buy profitable shares on one day and then unprofitable shares are bought with the other half on another day, then the first contributor would take all of the profitable shares and the second contributor would be left with all of the unprofitable shares. Given that the two contributors in this example have contributed equal amounts to the fund, it is irrational and arbitrary for the first contributor to take all of the profits when the second contributor acquires less valuable shares. The argument accepted in Canada is that the fairer approach is to share the profitable and the unprofitable shares equally between them, because there is no reason to benefit one contributor over the other. Things might be different if the first contributor's trust had been created originally to acquire those specific shares, in which case allocating them to the person who was intended to acquire them all along would be neither irrational nor arbitrary.

## Debate 2

### Why does a proprietary doctrine use non-proprietary remedies?

The House of Lords in *Foskett v McKeown* (above) confirmed that tracing is part of property law; and yet several of the remedies which follow on from a tracing action are not proprietary remedies strictly so-called. There are four principal remedies available in relation to tracing actions: liens, charges, constructive trusts and subrogation. There is no definitive, comprehensive judicial guidance as to which remedy should be used in which circumstances, once a right to trace into identified property has been established. There are some judgments which comment on the utility of this or that remedy in a particular context, but there is no *comprehensive* discussion of this phenomenon. If we confine ourselves for the moment to equitable tracing, we can see the difficulties in selecting the appropriate remedy from the following introductory discussion.

Take, for example, the equitable lien which is used in many tracing cases. Tracing is a proprietary process in which a claimant seeks to establish proprietary rights over identified property, which flow from some equitable interest in some other property, which has been traced into that identified property which constitutes the subject matter of the claim. If, however, the claimant is seeking to trace her proprietary rights in the original property into the property held by the defendant, then why is she forced to rely in some cases on a merely *possessory* remedy such as the equitable lien to provide her remedy?

A lien, in the strict sense, does not grant the claimant a proprietary remedy. A lien merely grants a right of possession over property, so that the claimant can detain that property until the defendant pays her whatever sum of money may represent the loss to her of her original property. The holder of that right must apply to the court before the possessory right granted by a lien entitles the rightholder to treat the property as though she has ownership rights in it by selling it. Similarly, a charge does not, strictly speaking, grant a property right to the rightholder; whereas a mortgage (i.e. a charge by way of legal mortgage) does grant a property right to the mortgagee, which can be registered at the Land Registry if it relates to land. Thus, a chargeholder must petition the court to be allowed to sell the charged property. In both cases, a right which requires the permission of the court to exercise that right cannot be a complete right in that property.

There is nothing objectionable in using these sorts of doctrines to provide remedies after the tracing process has been completed, because they provide pragmatic responses to tracing (and have done for centuries). Nevertheless, it is odd that they are not strictly proprietary. By contrast, the constructive trust does grant equitable proprietary rights to the beneficiary, and as such may be a preferable form of right if the claimant wants to take ownership of the property. If the claimant would prefer to acquire a right in money then a lien or a charge will provide her with sufficient security to do so.

## Debate 3
### Is tracing concerned with property or unjust enrichment?

The Oxford Restitution School, particularly in the work of Professor Lionel Smith,[11] has argued that the law of tracing should be considered to be a part of unjust enrichment law as opposed to being a part of property law. The argument is predicated on the idea that when property is taken from a person (for example, a beneficiary under a trust) and passed to another person, that other person has been enriched at the expense of the previous owner of the property. The question would be as to the remedy to be applied. The original model of restitution, as examined in Chapter 3, considered that it would be a resulting trust which reversed the unjust enrichment by subtracting the enrichment from the defendant. That model of resulting trust was ruled out by the House of Lords in *Westdeutsche Landesbank v Islington*.[12]

The competing approach is that the law of tracing should be considered to be a part of property law, and that it has nothing to do with reversing unjust enrichment at all. A masterly summary of the arguments has been presented by Graham Virgo.[13] In the House of Lords in *Foskett v McKeown*,[14] Lord Millett ruled

[11] L. Smith, *The Law of Tracing* (Clarendon Press, 1995).
[12] [1996] AC 669.
[13] G. Virgo, 'Vindicating vindication: *Foskett v McKeown* reviewed' in A.S. Hudson (ed.), *New Perspectives on Property Law, Obligations and Restitution* (Cavendish Publishing, 2004), 203.
[14] [2001] 1 AC 102.

definitively that tracing is a part of property law as opposed to being a part of unjust enrichment:[15]

> 'The transmission of a claimant's property rights from one asset to its traceable proceeds is part of our law of property, not of the law of unjust enrichment. There is no "unjust factor" to justify restitution (unless "want of title" be one, which makes the point). The claimant succeeds if at all by virtue of his own title, not to reverse unjust enrichment. Property rights are determined by fixed rules and settled principles. They are not discretionary. They do not depend upon ideas of what is "fair, just and reasonable". Such concepts, which in reality mask decisions of legal policy, have no place in the law of property.'

It is suggested that this approach captures the purpose of the law of tracing. The law of tracing takes the approach that if a claimant loses item of property A, and if A is sold and the proceeds are used to buy item of property B, then the claimant should be entitled to trace her rights from A into B, thus grounding a right of some sort against B. The objective of tracing law is therefore to 'vindicate' the claimant's property rights which were originally in item of property A. Those property rights are traced from one item of property to another. Therefore, it is a proprietary doctrine. It is not limited to situations in which the unjust factors which are required by unjust enrichment law are present. Unjust enrichment law would require that there was a mistake or some similar factor; however, that is not the purpose of tracing law. Tracing law exists to protect the value expressed by the original property rights by tracing through different forms of property.

*Foskett v McKeown* was a perfect factual scenario to raise questions about the nature of tracing. In a slightly simplified form, the facts of that case were as follows. A father had taken out a life assurance policy over his own life in favour of his children and his wife. The policy would pay out approximately £1 million. There were five premiums to be paid for the insurance policy in amounts of approximately £10,000. The father was also a trustee of a trust, from which he took amounts of money in breach of trust to pay the fourth and fifth premium payments. The father later committed suicide, thus triggering a pay-out under the policy. The question was whether the insurance pay-out should go to the children, subject to an obligation to repay the £20,000 to the trust, or whether the beneficiaries of the trust should be entitled to trace their trust moneys into the last two premium payments on the life assurance policy and thus be able to establish rights in two-fifths of the total pay-out of £1 million. It was held that the beneficiaries were entitled to a proportionate share in the insurance pay-out.

Lord Browne-Wilkinson considered whether this area of law was concerned with wrongs or with a general discretion in the court to award whatever is considered fair, or whether it was a part of property law:[16]

---

[15] Ibid, 127.
[16] Ibid, 109.

'It is a fundamental error to think that, because certain property rights are equitable rather than legal, such rights are in some way discretionary. This case does not depend on whether it is fair, just and reasonable to give the purchasers an interest as a result of which the court in its discretion provides a remedy. It is a case of hard-nosed property rights.'

Thus, tracing is allocated clearly by the House of Lords to property law. It is neither a zone for pure equitable discretion, nor is it a part of unjust enrichment. However, the choice of remedies available to the parties is part of the general equitable ability to match an appropriate outcome to the facts, as was discussed above.

## THE UTILITY OF TRACING

One of the more useful applications of tracing law, and one of the reasons why the English jurisdiction is so popular among banking lawyers, is its ability to recover money which has been laundered through successive bank accounts, misapplied by fraudsters, or treated similarly. Unlike civil code jurisdictions, in which these sorts of events could only be remedied by payment of damages in essence, English law enables a claimant to bring a proprietary claim. The advantage of the proprietary claim in relation to a money laundering or similarly criminal scheme is that the criminals will never leave any entity in the chain with enough money to pay damages; therefore, being able to identify the ultimate destination of the traced property means that the claimant will be able to recover its loss in a form which will defeat an insolvency and most criminal schemes.

## VINDICATION OF PROPERTY RIGHTS

Among the many ideas which teem in tracing law, an important concept which has been advanced within the unjust enrichment scholarship has been the idea of tracing being used in the 'vindication of property rights', in the writings of Graham Virgo.[17] The aim of this mooted head of restitution provides a basis for tracing which recognises that the claimant had rights in property before the unjust or wrongful act of the defendant which led to the defendant taking possession of that property. Lord Millett used this idea in *Foskett v McKeown*[18] to bolster his explanation that tracing is part of property law in that it vindicates the original property rights of the claimant by pursuing them into substitute property.

The etymology of the word 'vindicate' is interesting. While it has a happy coincidence with the Roman action of *vindicatio*, the word 'vindication' culled from that Latin root also has a sense of 'avenging' as well as 'restoring'. In common with what has already been said about restitution for wrongdoing in the preceding section, the notion of vindicating property rights would tally with a sense of

---

[17] G. Virgo, *The Law of Restitution* (Oxford, 1999), 656.
[18] [2001] 1 AC 102.

punishment in the treatment of those who have wrongfully taken possession of another's property.[19]

## Counter-arguments

Birks objected to the idea of vindication in tracing law on the basis that it described a motivation for permitting tracing but does not tell us what has triggered the tracing process. Unjust enrichment specialists prefer that something like mistake or undue influence has triggered the tracing process.[20] The concept of vindication tells us why we might want to trace, but not the legal basis for the action. The counter-argument would be that it hardly matters, because vindication tells us that it is any non-consensual interference with the claimant's property rights which entitles the claimant to pursue her property through a tracing or following process. This is predicated on a high-level principle of the need to protect property rights, and not on the sort of detailed taxonomy on which Birks insists. The Oxford School has persisted with the idea that tracing should operate on a basis akin to civil code attitudes – i.e. that the precise basis for the claim must be demonstrated from a taxonomic list of claims – and on the basis that there must be a distinction between claims to the claimant's original property and claims to substitute property.[21] As to the second point, the distinction between following and tracing claims in *Foskett v McKeown* does recognise that distinction.

## WHETHER THERE SHOULD BE ONE FORM OF TRACING OR TWO

There is a strong argument to the effect that there is no need for one set of tracing principles at common law and another set of principles in equity. Lord Millett was clear in *Foskett v McKeown* that there is 'no sense in maintaining different rules for tracing at law and in equity'.[22] Given that tracing is a process which is distinct from the claim which may be brought against the traced property once it has been run successfully to ground, Lord Millett argued that it could not matter whether that detective work of identifying the target property was conducted under common law or equitable principles. His Lordship was clear, however, that his judgment was not to be read as merging the two doctrines, because that would be a matter which would require further consideration. In an essay titled 'We do this at common law and that in equity',[23] Professor Burrows has also criticised the persistence of the division between the two codes. Professor Birks has gone further,[24] pointing out that at least since the decision in *The Mecca* in 1897,[25] the rule in *Clayton's Case* has been used 'on both sides of Westminster Hall', i.e. it has

---

[19] P. Jaffey, *The Nature and Scope of Restitution* (Hart Publishing, 2000), 374.

[20] P. Birks, (1996) 26 *UWALR* 1; [2002] *CLP* 231.

[21] Burrows, above n 3.

[22] [2001] 1 AC 102, 128, citing P. Birks, 'The Necessity of a Unitary Law of Tracing' in R. Cranston (ed.), *Making Commercial Law* (Clarendon Press, 1997), 239; and Smith, above n 11, 120–30.

[23] Burrows, above n 3.

[24] P. Birks, 'Overview – Tracing' in P. Birks (ed.), *Laundering and Tracing* (Clarendon Press, 1995), 289 at 296.

[25] [1897] AC 286.

been used in common law tracing and in equitable tracing. This point is used by Birks as part of a broader argument that there are in many senses no real distinctions between common law tracing and equitable tracing, and in consequence that the two can be brought together in a unitary law of tracing.[26]

Traditionalists prefer that the division between the two codes of tracing is maintained.[27] Historically, the case law has taken the approach that tracing into a mixture could only be conducted in equity, and only if the claimant had some pre-existing equitable interest in the target property. For a traditionalist, no equitable doctrine should be prayed in aid unless the claimant had a right which justified the use of the equitable jurisdiction: so, parties to a contract had no right to access equity, but a beneficiary under a trust did. A part of the separation of these doctrines is founded on the idea that equity's breadth of remedies (when compared to the narrow range at common law) should only be used where an equitable interest is at issue.

The contrary approach to the traditional model is simply that there is nothing innate in this division between common law and equity. As the French philosopher Foucault suggests, law is simply the product of '*les choses dites*', that is, law is made up merely of things which are said, and therefore those things can be unsaid or said again differently. The current division between the two types of tracing is not innate; rather, it is simply the way in which the law has developed. Those rules could be restated in different ways. The modern approach is to suggest that the equitable tracing process which penetrates mixtures (something which common law tracing has never done) should be available to all sorts of tracing actions. The issue remains whether or not equitable remedies (such as charges, liens and even constructive trusts) could be available in circumstances in which there was no pre-existing equitable interest. It is suggested that the general conception of equity that was set out in Chapter 1 permits equitable doctrine to go anywhere that it is needed. It is the case, however, that doctrines like constructive trust could lose all coherence if they were made available in circumstances where there was no unconscionable conduct or in which there had not been any pre-existing equitable interest in the original property. Therefore, while the tracing process could be unified, the remedies which might flow from tracing would not all be easily applied across all forms of claim.

# Debated 4

## Do judges create property rights?

### WHY ARE JUDGES SO SENSITIVE ABOUT CREATING PROPRIETARY RIGHTS?

It is a feature of the English property law system that judges are reluctant to create property rights out of thin air. Instead, they prefer to recognise their existence or

---

[26] Ibid.
[27] For an account of the rules that are presented in the traditional approach, see D. Hayton, 'Equity's Identification Rules' in Birks (ed.), above n 24, 1; or indeed any textbook on trusts law.

to establish their creation on objective, rational grounds. So, in relation to constructive trusts, the institutional constructive trust in English law is established on such a complex basis precisely because the judges do not want to be seen to create those rights out of thin air. Consequently it is said that the constructive trust arises automatically on the defendant's conscience being affected, and therefore it is said that the property rights attached to it are not created by the judges.

Tracing is particularly interesting in this regard. Professor Craig Rotherham considered tracing as operating in the following way:[28]

> '[T]racing can only be regarded as a remedial process that gives rise to new property rights – an understanding which cannot be easily reconciled with traditional notions of property.'

That must be right. The point of an action based on tracing is that it acquires rights for the claimant in property which he had not previously owned. Rotherham's book[29] is a study of judges' reluctance to be seen to be *creating* property rights, as opposed simply to observing that they are already in existence. It is also a study of the ways in which many doctrines in our legal system do create property rights out of thin air. Clearly, the tracing process leads to property rights being created over new property in place of the property which the claimant formerly owned.

## THE EXAMPLE OF PROPRIETARY ESTOPPEL

What makes equity so difficult for the occasional visitor to it from other legal fields is that it is only really comprehensible as a complete whole. Taken as a whole, equity is built around the central idea that people must act in good conscience. More specifically, it is organised around the idea that equity will intervene to prevent a defendant from benefiting from any unconscionable act. On some occasions, this unconscionability is met by a proprietary response and on other occasions it is met by a merely personal right. Rotherham has explained that the English judiciary is uncomfortable with the idea of simply awarding proprietary rights ad hoc, and how in consequence the institutional constructive trust was developed so as to justify the award of proprietary rights to a claimant on the basis of some earlier unconscionable act on the part of the defendant.

The doctrine of proprietary estoppel is a particularly clear example of a pure equitable right in the sense that, once the entitlement to the estoppel has been made out,[30] the claimant may receive, at one end of the spectrum, almost any remedy, ranging from a personal right in money to compensate her detriment,[31] right through to the award of the largest proprietary right in land in the form of

---

[28] C. Rotherham, *Proprietary Remedies in Context – A Study in the Judicial Redistribution of Property Rights* (Hart Publishing, 2002), 89.

[29] Ibid.

[30] That is, on the basis of a representation made by the defendant which caused the claimant to act in reliance to her detriment.

[31] *Burns v Burns* [1984] Ch 317.

the fee simple absolute in possession at the other end of that spectrum[32] or anything in between.[33] The courts have commonly awarded a mixture of monetary compensation and a right to specific property to a single claimant.[34] In one remarkable case, the court required a previously divorced wife and the widow of a deceased man to cohabit in the same dwelling by way of a remedy for the divorced wife's claim in estoppel.[35] This remedy was in recognition of the divorced wife's purported rights in relation to that dwelling. Quite how the parties' entitlements would be unravelled if it transpired that they could not cohabit harmoniously together is something which remains at large. The remedy was intended to resolve the dispute between the parties and not to present a new paradigm in taxonomically pure property theory.

The doctrine of proprietary estoppel cannot be understood in taxonomic terms precisely because the judges have such a wide discretion available to them. Indeed, efforts at taxonomy in this field are doomed to failure precisely because the courts require flexibility in reaching judgments which are appropriate for specific circumstances.[36] The only successful accounts, such as that set out by Elizabeth Cooke in *The Modern Law of Estoppel*,[37] recognise that proprietary estoppel is part of a larger network of estoppels available in equity which are all ultimately co-ordinated around central principles of good conscience and the avoidance of uncompensated detriment (in circumstances in which the claimant had been relying on the defendant's representations) on the grounds of its unconscionability. The most successful accounts of proprietary estoppel in the case law have been in the clarity of the requirements of representation, reliance and detriment as set out by Edward Nugee QC (sitting in the High Court) in *Re Basham*,[38] and the identification of the underlying concept of dealing with 'unconscionability' at the heart of proprietary estoppel by Walker LJ in *Jennings v Rice*.[39] The doctrine of proprietary estoppel may look like a subject in need of order to an eager taxonomist, but this individual doctrine is entirely coherent when it is understood as being part of the matrix of equitable doctrines which seek to deal with unconscionable activity.

---

[32] *Pascoe v Turner* [1979] 2 All ER 945; *Re Basham* [1986] 1 WLR 1498; *Thorner v Major* [2009] 1 WLR 776.

[33] *Gillett v Holt* [2000] 2 All ER 289.

[34] Ibid.

[35] *Porntip Stallion v Albert Stallion Holdings Ltd* [2010] 1 FCR 145.

[36] See the forthcoming B. MacFarlane, *The Law of Proprietary Estoppel* – a title which in itself is doomed to misunderstand the nature of the subject matter.

[37] E. Cooke, *The Modern Law of Estoppel* (Clarendon Press, 2000).

[38] [1986] 1 WLR 1498.

[39] [2003] 1 P&CR 100.

# PART THREE

# OVERARCHING THEMES IN EQUITY AND TRUSTS

# 12

## WOMEN AND THE LAW
## OF TRUSTS

## INTRODUCTION

Equity has always had a complex relationship with women and with 'the feminine'. In its earliest incarnations, the role of trusts law was conceived of as being
a means of protecting women from the social mores of the time. Briefly put, a
settlor could settle property on trust in a way that would protect the rights of the
woman to use the trust property, whereas if the property had belonged entirely to
the woman then it would have passed to her husband when she married. The
trust offered protection for the woman. However, other commentators have questioned whether or not equity really did serve women so well, as is discussed
below.[1]

There are people who consider equity to be a 'feminine' way of thinking
because it is not obsessed with detailed rules and does not treat law-making
as being a sort of car maintenance which operates mechanically but rather
involves open-textured, sensitive decision-making which fits the context.
There is only so far one can get with that sort of nonsense: just imagine a
woman with a spanner or a man choosing furniture for his living-room,
and these stereotypes collapse. Not all men think alike and not all women
think alike. Nevertheless, there is the odd remark made by the philosopher
Immanuel Kant, that equity is 'a silent princess who never speaks', that persists
in the literature.

What is important in the consideration of trusts law is the need to understand
its social role, especially in the eighteenth century when its role was very important. That is where we shall begin.

---

[1] S. Scott-Hunt and H. Lim (eds), *Feminist Perspectives on Equity and Trusts* (Cavendish, 2001).

## Debate

## How were women treated by property law?

### TRUSTS IN THE NOVELS OF JANE AUSTEN

#### The Austen heroines at the whim of family settlements

The heroines of Jane Austen's novels were the victims of trusts. In *Sense and Sensibility* and in *Pride and Prejudice*, the female characters were all entering adulthood in strait-laced, bourgeois English society. The houses in which they lived, the sources of their money and all of the chattels which they used, were held on trust. At that time, complex family settlements were used to allocate rights to all forms of family property (houses, heirlooms, plate and other chattels) down the generations. Investments were slow-paced by modern standards: they were intended to bring in steady incomes over time.

The settlements in the Austen novels were generally organised on a 'fee tail' basis, whereby the property would pass to the next male heir. Austen heroines were always the children of a father who was the last man in his line. After their fathers died, their property would pass to a distant male relative. The result for the young heroines in the novels was that they would lose their homes and much of the property which they had used day-to-day. Therefore, Austen heroines were at risk of losing everything, because of the terms of the settlements which governed their lives. Much of the drama in Austen novels is therefore predicated on the obsessive need their mothers feel to marry their daughters off as quickly as possible to eligible husbands. The life of an upper middle-class woman in eighteenth-century England was precarious. It depended on her parents' ability to contract a successful marriage for her, or on the kindness of relatives taking her in.

#### The limited rights of married women to property and other things

It is easy to think of eighteenth- and nineteenth-century trusts law as being set in a distant time with distant concepts, but that would be to overlook something important about equity and trusts. It has sometimes been said that equity was the protector of women, and at one time there was some truth in this. For example, if you were to read the Jane Austen novel *Persuasion* then you would come to know that Anne Eliot was at risk from a fortune-hunting suitor who appeared to be wealthy and attentive at first. However, his goal was to marry her for her money, because at that time, when a couple married, all of the wife's property would become her husband's. The metaphor which was used at the time was that the wife became 'the shadow of her husband'. That seemingly innocuous idea in the Christian marriage concept that husband and wife become 'one flesh' takes on a very disturbing dimension when you realise that metaphorically the wife's flesh was taken to merge with her husband's, with the result that she effectively disappeared. The very fact that married women became merely the shadows of their husbands meant that they ceased to exist at all. Their property rights evaporated as soon as they married.

Even in a decision of the House of Lords in 1965 in *National Provincial Bank v Ainsworth*,[2] the rights of wives were described by Lord Wilberforce by beginning with the following, peculiarly old-fashioned concepts:[3]

> 'For though the wife had (apart from dower) no proprietary interest at law or in equity, in her husband's property, she had certain rights against her husband by virtue of her status of marriage ... [A] wife acquired the right to two things: the right of cohabitation with her husband and the right to support according to her husband's estate and condition. She could obtain against him, from the ecclesiastical courts, an order for restitution of conjugal rights which, in its usual form, ordered him to take her home and receive her as his wife and render conjugal rights – an order which could be enforced by attachment for non-obedience. ... [H]er rights were not rights *in rem*, nor were they related to any particular property; they were purely personal rights against her husband, enforceable by proceedings against his person, which he could satisfy by rendering her conjugal rights, i.e. by living with her and supporting her in a suitable home.'

The ecclesiastical courts would in essence order that a marriage be consummated, as well as that the wife be provided with an appropriate home. In *Scott v Scott*,[4] for example, a divorce was ordered on the basis that the wife was proved still to be a virgin after the marriage on the basis of a medical examination. Otherwise, conjugal rights were 'enforceable by proceedings against [the husband's] person', which sounds like a euphemism for something. The wife had no rights in property but only the earthier right to be 'received as a wife'. The significant point is that women were treated as being merely maternal, sexual vessels and property-less persons, who needed to be supported by their husbands.

Unfortunately, some of these attitudes were still present in the minds of some judges in the late twentieth century. Even though Lord Denning had developed the concept of the 'deserted wife's equity' in the 1960s, he still had the following to say in one volume of his memoirs, about the perceived differences between men and women:

> 'No matter how you may dispute and argue, you cannot alter the fact that women are different from men. The principal task in life of women is to bear and rear children: and it is a task which occupies the best years of their lives. The man's part in bringing up the children is no doubt as important as hers, but of necessity he cannot devote so much time to it. He is physically the stronger and she the weaker. He is temperamentally the more aggressive and she the more submissive. It is he who takes the initiative and she who responds ...'[5]

---

[2] [1965] AC 1175, [1965] 3 WLR 1, sub nom *National Provincial Bank v Hastings Car Mart Ltd* [1965] 2 All ER 472. The same case is referred to by different names in different law reports. In essence, the husband here used the company as a cypher for himself in an attempt to defeat his wife's claims to the family home.

[3] [1965] 3 WLR 1, 31.

[4] [1913] AC 417.

[5] A. Denning, *The Due Process of Law* (Butterworths, 1980), 194.

There really is nothing more to be said about these antediluvian attitudes. However, they explain the nature of pre-modern property law.

## THE SUPPOSED ROLE OF TRUSTS LAW IN PROTECTING WOMEN

The ancient rule, discussed above, that married women could not own their own property, meant that women were always at risk of losing property which had been theirs before marriage precisely because their husbands became, at law, the owners of their wives' property on marriage. The use of the trust was one way in which the rights of those women could be protected. Structuring the trust so that there was purportedly more than one beneficiary with rights to the trust property, meant that that property could be held on trust for that woman and also for other people as beneficiaries, with the result that the woman was not the outright beneficial owner of the property in question. The result was that this trust property did not pass to the woman's husband when she was married, precisely because the trust property was not entirely hers in equity. The husband could only become the owner of property which his wife owned outright; a well-structured trust would not be owned outright by the woman in equity. Therefore, a kindly father who wanted to protect his daughter against the possibility of her property being taken from her by an unkind husband, would settle that property on trust for his daughter in such a way that she did not have to lose it to her husband. In consequence, the trust appeared to be the defender of women in this context.

## TRUSTS AND THE LOWER CLASSES

It is important to point out one thing: all of the preceding discussion has related to the upper classes. The trust played no meaningful part in the lives of the working class. It is all too easy to consider trusts law as simply a parade of legal rules which are politically neutral. As Dicey put it: '[T]he daughters of the rich enjoyed for the most part the consideration and protection of equity; the daughters of the poor suffered under the severity and injustice of the common law.'[6] So, women in rich families could have the protection of family settlements. By contrast, women in poor families would not have the benefit of trusts at all, both because their families had no property to settle on trust and because they could not afford the advice of expensive trusts lawyers.[7]

## RIGHTS OF WOMEN TO THE HOME

The issues considered in Chapter 9 in relation to trusts of homes are significant in that they tended to demonstrate a particularly gendered approach to trusts law,

---

[6] A.V. Dicey, *Law and Opinion in England*, quoted in Crane, 1965, 254.
[7] E.M. Forster expressed a similar idea in *Howard's End*, to the effect that to trust is 'a luxury in which only the wealthy can indulge; the poor cannot afford it'.

until developments begun by Waite LJ in *Midland Bank v Cooke*[8] took a more nuanced view of the situation. Cases relating to the equitable ownership of the home between unmarried couples or home-sharers typically used to favour the breadwinner, who statistically would usually have been a man.[9] There were estoppel cases (such as *Pascoe v Turner*[10]) or equitable cases (such as *Midland Bank v Cooke* or *Cox v Jones*[11]) which saw value in women's contribution to the home other than the purely financial, and which therefore relied on 'undertaking a survey of the entire course of dealing between the parties' and avoiding unconscionability.

Things have begun to change, in no small part due to the flexibility offered by equity and trusts law. In more recent cases in front of the highest courts – in *Stack v Dowden*[12] and in *Jones v Kernott*[13] – it has been the women who have been the higher earners in the relationship. Lady Hale identified a need for a new generation to move away from the presumption in the old cases that if a man transferred property to his wife, then it was to be assumed that his intention was to make a gift to her because a man's role was to 'maintain' his wife. Significantly, the recent cases have been looking to the entire course of dealing between the parties, and taking into account non-financial contributions, instead of looking simply at the money that was contributed to the original purchase price. Perhaps now the position of women who are not able to contribute financially to the home is being recognised as a result of those recent decisions. A more significant effect, however, might be the more general inclusion of women in the workforce, which is both a patchy effect and one which has complex impacts on issues like childcare.

## RESIDUAL JUDICIAL ATTITUDES TO WOMEN

In spite of these developments, even in the twenty-first century, the conceptualisation of women by a mostly male judiciary can still be troubling on occasion. An otherwise unremarkable case (in that it tells us little about legal principle) is *Elithorn v Poulter*,[14] in which the female claimant is referred to as 'Madeline' by Rimer LJ throughout his judgment (even though she paid the entire purchase price for a couple's house), while the male defendant (who had paid nothing in cash) was referred to as 'Dr Elithorn' throughout that same judgment. By referring to her informally by her first name, this suggests a condescending attitude towards the female claimant; in comparison, the male defendant is referred to formally by both his surname and his highest university degree. Even more remarkably, it was held that the property should be deemed to be owned equally between them, in spite of the fact that she had paid the entire purchase price up-front.

---

[8] [1995] 4 All ER 562.
[9] See, e.g., the test set out by Lord Bridge in *Lloyds Bank v Rosset* [1991] 1 AC 107.
[10] [1979] 1 WLR 431.
[11] [2004] 3 FCR 693.
[12] [2007] UKHL 17, [2007] 2 WLR 831.
[13] [2011] UKSC 53, [2011] 3 WLR 1121.
[14] [2008] EWCA Civ 1364.

In many of the older cases on trusts of homes, there was a tendency to dismiss work which wives had performed in bringing up children and running the home as being simply the sort of work which was expected from women, and which could therefore be dismissed. These sorts of gendered attitudes must be exposed and criticised. There is still a large amount of work to be done on equity and trusts law in considering the sociology and the politics of that law as it functions in practice in the world.

# 13

# INJUNCTIONS

## INTRODUCTION

This chapter considers injunctions. Injunctions are often not studied on under-graduate equity and trusts law courses, which is a shame precisely because the law on injunctions tells us so much about equity. The study of injunctions illustrates commonality of principle between different areas of equity like trusts implied by law, proprietary estoppel and the law on injunctions itself.

## Debate 1

### Is the power to award injunctions really open-ended?

The court's jurisdiction to award injunctions has been described by Spry as operat-ing 'without limits, and can be exercised either in support of any legal right, or in the creation of a new equitable right, as the court thinks fits in the application of equitable principles'.[1] Lord Nicholls set out the breadth of the power of the courts to grant injunctions in the following terms in the House of Lords in *Mercedes Benz AG v Leiduck*, to the effect that:[2]

> 'the jurisdiction to grant an injunction, unfettered by statute, should not be rigidly confined to exclusive categories by judicial decision. The court may grant an injunc-tion against a party properly before it where this is required to avoid injustice ... The court habitually grants injunctions in respect of certain types of conduct. But that does not mean that the situations in which injunctions may be granted are now set in stone for all time. ... The exercise of the jurisdiction must be principled, but the criterion is injustice. Injustice is to be viewed and decided in the light of today's conditions and standards, not those of yester-year.'

Therefore, under statute and further to that decision of the House of Lords, the courts have a very broad, inherent power to grant injunctions in any sort of case in the interests of avoiding injustice. This is an axiomatic demonstration of equity

---

[1] I. Spry, *Equitable Remedies*, 6th edn (Law Book Co, 2001).
[2] [1996] AC 284, at 308.

in action: the courts have a general power to make any order which they consider necessary to avoid injustice in the particular circumstances of a case. Nevertheless, the courts have tended to develop strict principles governing the situations in which injunctions will be awarded in certain types of case (for example, interim injunctions granted before a full trial is held). That is, the judges have sought to limit their own discretion in practice. In a sense, that is typical of English equity in action, because the English judiciary are reluctant to award judgments on an entirely discretionary basis without reference to the rules which they feel ought to bind them. (The one exception to that principle might be family law where the law is deliberately mounted on general principles precisely so that judges can reach judgments in individual circumstances which are appropriate to the particular case.)

So, rather than having strict rules governing the grant of injunctions, those injunctions will tend to be predicated on broad principles to which the court will ordinarily be expected to have regard when awarding injunctions in particular types of case. The statutes have granted very wide powers to the judges to award injunctions. However, the judges have shown a tendency to limit their discretion in cases like *Jaggard v Sawyer*,[3] by setting out case law principles which judges must follow when using their ostensibly limitless statutory powers to award injunctions. This is a very typical trait of equity. For example, Sir Thomas Bingham MR considered the four probanda relevant for the grant of an injunction which had been set out in *Shelfer v City of London Electric Lighting Co*.[4] These are the four requirements which must be satisfied before a court will exercise its discretion to award damages instead of granting an injunction, in circumstances in which an injunction might otherwise be awarded:

> '(a) the harm suffered by the applicant must have been comparatively slight;
> (b) the harm suffered must be capable of being quantified in financial terms;
> (c) the harm suffered must be such that it can be compensated adequately by payment of damages; and
> (d) it must have been oppressive to the respondent to have granted the injunction sought.'[5]

Interestingly then, his Lordship was limiting the apparently open-ended power to award injunctions in that context by setting out the four things which the courts are required to consider when contemplating the award of such an injunction.

While this mixture of open-ended discretion and limiting rules may seem paradoxical, it has always been a part of equity. In Story's *Equity Jurisprudence*, published in the nineteenth century, Judge Story took the view that while a doctrine might revolve around the discretion of the court, it is nevertheless 'not of arbitrary or capricious discretion, dependent upon the mere pleasure of the Judge, but of that

---

[3] [1995] 1 WLR 269, [1995] 2 All ER 189.
[4] [1895] 1 Ch 287.
[5] Ibid, *per* A.L. Smith LJ.

sound, and reasonable discretion, which governs itself, as far as it may, by general rules and principles'.[6] So, as will emerge below in our second debate, the seemingly open-ended idea of protecting confidences by means of injunctions is actually circumscribed by more detailed equitable principles.

## Debate 2

## Does equity still have a role to play in the award of injunctions in privacy cases?

### INTRODUCTION

It is commonly assumed by common lawyers that the new tort of privacy has passed control of the law on privacy to the common law. In truth, however, equity has always had the ability to make orders in relation to cases involving confidential information and privacy; and in relation to modern privacy cases, the injunctions are always awarded on equitable principles. Most significantly, in recent years, the law on super-injunctions has developed rapidly in relation to attempts by footballers and others to keep their affairs secret, by enjoining both reporting of their activities and also reporting of the existence of an injunction to that effect.

### CONFIDENTIAL INFORMATION IN EQUITY AND IN TORT

Since at least the sixteenth century, equity has sought to protect confidences – such as commercial secrets, intellectual property, secrets contained in private correspondence, and even the notes of lectures which would defeat the lecturer's copyright in the lecture itself – generally by awarding injunctions to prevent the dissemination of confidential information. One of the leading cases in this area, *Prince Albert v Strange*,[7] involved Queen Victoria's husband, Prince Albert, suing Mr Strange when Strange had gained access to some etchings of paintings which Queen Victoria and her family had had made of their private life, their pets and so on. Strange had intended to exhibit those etchings to a paying public, and to publish a catalogue of the contents of that exhibition. It was held by the House of Lords that the contents of this catalogue (let alone the etchings themselves) were private information and that the publication of this private information would be prevented by a permanent injunction.

The principle which was set down by Lord Cottenham was that the court will enjoin the publication of confidential information where that would constitute a 'breach of trust, confidence, or contract'. Some of the most significant cases have involved the publication of information passed between husband and wife, which is necessarily considered to be private. So, in *Duke of Argyll v Duchess of Argyll*,[8] the

---

[6] J. Story, *Equity Jurisprudence*, vol. 2 (Little and Brown, 1839), 25–26.
[7] (1849) 41 ER 1171.
[8] [1967] Ch 302.

Duke of Argyll was enjoined from publishing information about his wife's attitudes to sexual morals and the sanctity of marriage in an article in *The People* newspaper.

The central principle which is used in the tort law cases was established in the equitable jurisdiction in *Coco v AN Clark (Engineering) Ltd*,[9] when Megarry J held that there are three prerequisites in this area: first, the information must be confidential or have arisen in a confidential context; second, the information must have been passed in a context which suggested it was confidential; and, third, the use of the information must be unauthorised and to the detriment of its owner. These principles were upheld in the Court of Appeal in *Imerman v Tchenguiz*,[10] when Lord Neuberger emphasised the difference between common law and equitable principles in this area. As his Lordship put it:[11]

> 'A claim based on confidentiality is an equitable claim. Accordingly, the normal equitable rules apply. Thus, while one would normally expect a court to grant the types of relief we have been discussing, it would have a discretion whether to refuse some or all such relief on familiar equitable principles. Equally, the precise nature of the relief which would be granted must depend on all aspects of the particular case: Equity fashions the appropriate relief to fit the rights of the parties, the facts of the case, and, at least sometimes, the wider merits.'

Here a husband was entitled to have his personal data, which had been stored on a server which he used in common with his brother-in-law, kept in confidence and not used in divorce proceedings. Importantly, the Court of Appeal held that these principles of confidence were based in equity.

Of course, the emerging law of tort is the controlling doctrine in relation specifically to privacy cases (except to the principles which underpin the injunctions themselves). So, Lord Nicholls explained in *Campbell v MGN*[12] how the traditional equitable doctrine was now giving way to a 'tort of the misuse of private information', which would both provide a remedy in damages and which would continue to provide a right to injunctions to prevent publication. Nevertheless, the general equitable principles relating to the protection of confidences remains, as was indicated by *Imerman v Tchenguiz*.

## THE LAW ON SUPER-INJUNCTIONS

### The public debate about super-injunctions

Super-injunctions were front-page news in 2010 and 2011. All super-injunctions are at root just interim injunctions. An interim injunction is an injunction which is awarded by a court before the trial is complete so as to protect the position of the parties before judgment. However, super-injunctions have the following added features, as they are defined by the *Report of the Committee on Super-Injunctions*,

---

[9] [1969] RPC 41.
[10] [2011] 2 WLR 592.
[11] Ibid, [74].
[12] [2004] 2 AC 457.

which was published in 2011 by the Master of the Rolls. It was explained that a super-injunction is:

> 'an interim injunction which restrains a person from:
> (i) publishing information which concerns the applicant and is said to be confidential or private; and,
> (ii) publicising or informing others of the existence of the order and the proceedings (the "super" element of the order) …'

Therefore, a super-injunction enjoins the defendant from publishing specified information and, moreover, it prevents the defendant or anyone else from publishing the fact that such an injunction exists. Therefore, for example, a footballer could enjoin a newspaper from publishing the fact that he has been having an extra-marital affair, and he could also enjoin any newspaper from publishing the fact that he had taken out such an injunction. The theory is that knowledge that such an injunction existed would in itself let the public know that the footballer had committed some sort of wrongdoing, and therefore that enjoining publication of any of that information before the court rules finally on whether or not the information is to be treated as being confidential permanently will protect the position of the footballer. This does mean, however, that the person with whom he had the affair is unable to speak in public about her own treatment, or to protect her position in public, or to profit from her experiences.

It is important that these are merely temporary injunctions pending a trial of the underlying issues. However, it is often argued by journalists that even a temporary delay in publication can, in effect, destroy a story by making it old news. It should be noted, however, that if the story does quickly become old news then it is unclear to what extent it was an important story in the first place.

The identity of the parties in these situations will also usually be kept anonymous. An 'anonymised injunction', where the parties' identities are kept secret, was defined as being:

> 'an interim injunction which restrains a person from publishing information which concerns the applicant and is said to be confidential or private where the names of either or both of the parties to the proceedings are not stated.'

It is common to have anonymised proceedings in criminal and in family law matters. Similarly, the principles governing interim injunctions generally apply to super-injunctions with the addition of certain principles considered below. However, it is in relation to the area of privacy in particular that super-injunctions have acquired their own peculiar lustre: after all, the media is never more excited than when talking about the media, as will emerge in the following section.

This tells us a lot about equity. First, the judges have broad powers to award injunctions when the circumstances require it. Those injunctions can have broad effects on freedom of speech for the Press as well as for the parties involved. Secondly, the judges can sculpt the conduct of litigation – including the award of injunctions to protect the position of the parties – so as to achieve justice on the facts of any given case. They may involve the pragmatic anonymisation of the parties to the litigation.

## The balancing act in relation to awards of injunctions for privacy

The law on super-injunctions and the law on other injunctions seeking to protect the applicant's privacy therefore run together. The principles of equity in relation to confidences have given way to the law of tort and, significantly, the principles of human rights law which were implemented into UK law by the Human Rights Act 1998. Applying those principles, in *Murray v Express Newspapers plc*,[13] Sir Anthony Clarke MR held that, in deciding whether or not to award an injunction to protect private information, the courts must balance the claimant's human right to respect for her private and family life under Article 8 of the European Convention on Human Rights, with the competing right to free expression of newspapers and others under Article 10 of the Convention. As Lord Steyn made clear in the House of Lords in *In re S (A Child) (Identification: Restrictions on Publication)*,[14] neither principle has supremacy over the other: instead the court must apply the concept of proportionality when deciding in any given context which of the two is to take priority in any given circumstances.

Consequently, that area of law would appear to be entirely a part of the common law, even though that would be at odds with the contemporaneous decision on the equitable duty of confidence in *Imerman v Tchenguiz* which was discussed above. This, however, is simply a prejudice of modern common lawyers. What they forget to examine is the deep root of this area of law in the notion of 'conscience' in equity. A root which still connects it to the equitable principles governing the award of injunctions.

## THE ANCIENT ROOTS OF THE DOCTRINE OF BREACH OF CONFIDENCE

So far we have considered the modern debates about privacy in the twenty-first century. However, all of this modernity has a tendency to mask the deep roots of the equitable principles from which the law on confidences and the law on injunctions have grown. The jurisdiction of equity to deal with breaches of confidence is beyond doubt. While the precise source of the equitable principles relating to the maintenance of 'confidences' is lost in the mists of equitable time, a judgment of the Lord Chancellor Sir Thomas More in the sixteenth century is often cited as the foundation of our understanding of the doctrine, and in particular the following idea: 'Three things are apt to be helpt in Conscience: Fraud, Accident and things of confidence'.[15]

Therefore, even in the sixteenth century, the protection of 'confidences' was a key part of equity. The most obvious examples of confidence in equity relate to particular categories of relationship of 'trust and confidence'. The clearest examples

---

[13] [2009] Ch 481.
[14] [2005] 1 AC 593.
[15] Quoted by Megarry J in *Coco v AN Clark (Engineers) Ltd* [1969] RPC 41, 46.

relate to fiduciaries duties such as trusteeship. The ancient rules against trustees permitting conflicts of interest (as considered in Chapter 12, for example in *Boardman v Phipps*[16]) are a clear example of the confidences which trustees were obliged to observe.[17] A modern expression of the law on confidences in equity is found in the judgment of Scott J in the *Spycatcher* litigation, in which he correctly identified that the law had always been concerned with 'obligations in conscience' not to breach confidences by publishing confidential information.

And so we come full circle: equity protects confidences through a series of open-textured principles which have hardened slightly into rules over time. This is the history of equity across the centuries. This area of law is in truth a constantly developing synthesis of general principles based on high-level ethical mores and strict rules which have been developed by the courts on a case-by-case basis.

---

[16] [1967] 2 AC 46.
[17] See A.S. Hudson, *Equity & Trusts*, section 12.7.

# 14

## CONCLUSION

### THE TROUBLE WITH PERFECTION

A successful legal system involves a synthesis of different types of legal thinking. More to the point, the register in which questions are asked will often dominate the answers which are generated. Thus, if a question is asked on the basis of economic efficiency, then the likely answer is that economic efficiency is the answer which maximises profits for businesses and involves the unthinking application of legal rules. If the questions are asked on the basis of morality, then equity is likely to have something to contribute.

The acme of the sort of questions which someone of a positivist, Oxford School turn of mind would like are mathematical questions. That is, questions with clear answers in which the question itself is clearly categorisable as a question about addition, or subtraction, or whatever. People of the opposite turn of mind simply do not believe that everything in the world can be reduced to neat mathematical formulae (some things, but not everything). A part of the problem with relying entirely on perfect taxonomies of law and on the rigid application of rigid rules is that we cannot even come up with perfect questions, let alone perfect answers. Consider the following typical question from an eight-year-old's maths class:

> Jimmy has a bath which has a volume of 100 litres. Each tap flows at a rate of 5 litres per minute. How long will it take for Jimmy to fill his bath?

Those of you who are of a mathematical turn of mind will have computed the answer in a fraction of a second, and will now be waiting impatiently to see where this discussion could possibly be going next. Alternatively, you may well be recoiling at the sudden introduction of mathematics into a book about law, and will now be reading on with a sense of queasiness. However, you may have seen this problem very differently. You may have seen the problem in the following way.

First, no one fills their bath completely. If you did, a lot of water would slop over the sides when you got in. So, immediately there is a question as to the extent to which Jimmy actually fills his bath. Secondly, no one fills their bath by turning both taps on full and leaving them there. As everyone knows, especially on a winter's morning, you fill the bath with a little cold water first and then add the hot water so as to minimise the amount of steam in the bathroom. If you are a clean-shaven man, this is important so that you can shave in an unmisted mirror while the bath fills. If you simply like to gaze at your reflection in your bathroom mirror, then the same point applies.

Moreover, there is the difficult business of the temperature of the bath. Unless you have a very clear routine in the morning, it is unlikely that you will get the water temperature right on your first try. If, for example, you know that in the two minutes it takes for your electric toothbrush to clean your teeth there will have been enough hot water added for you to begin immediately, then this may not be a problem. However, for most other people the time spent waiting for the bath to fill will be occupied by rummaging for underwear, or pottering about in the kitchen or staring blankly into the bathroom mirror waiting for death while the water pounds away in the background. Without a clear routine, self-evidently, you will have to return to the bath time and again to check on the level of the water and the temperature. You will most likely have to add hot and then cold until the temperature is right. There will probably be some swirling with your hands to mix hot and cold water better. If the phone rings or the toast burns or the postman calls, then it is likely that you will have to stop the taps altogether to avoid a flooded bathroom. Suddenly, the mathematics of water flow is only a part of the equation. Knowing the volume of the bath and the rate of water-flow is only a part of the question. The real questions are all about how individual human beings behave in practice in individual situations. Mathematics can only help so much. Aircraft could, reputedly, carry much less fuel if only mathematics could calculate turbulence and thus identify how much fuel would actually be required: but those calculations are too complex to be feasible. So, the rules of mathematics can only get us so far in some circumstances.

So what? Well, the rigidities of mathematics provide one certain answer to the question of how long it takes to fill this bath, but it will not answer the further question how long any given individual took to fill their bath on a given morning. To answer this second question we would need to know how full the bath needed to be, whether or not they stood in the bathroom watching the bath filling without losing concentration, how hot or cold they need their bath water to be, and so on. Therefore, the question may require us to inquire closely into the way in which that particular person filled their bath. In the same way, the common law may generate straightforward answers to straightforward questions, but there are situations in which the question must be answered differently by reference to the precise details of any given situation as equity does. Some situations can be addressed mathematically, others require more information; just as some situations can be addressed solely by common law rules, whereas others require equity.

If you are concerned with the messy reality of life, as opposed to an abstract theoretical model of an unlived life, then you will want a sort of rule-making which accommodates change, unexpected events and human nature. You are likely to prefer the 'real' reality of equity – one which anticipates how people actually draw their baths – to the well-meaning but slightly unreal rigidities of common law. Alternatively, if you are sensible, you will prefer a system which blends the predictability of common law with the flexibility of equity.

For the most part, these sorts of debates are really debates about which set of principles or which worldview should be used to resolve them: should we use economic efficiency, or predictability of outcome, or fairness to individual litigants, or the most advantageous outcome for business or some other standard as our central organising principle?

## A SUCCESSFUL SOCIETY IS A BLEND

A society works by blending different talents and points of view. Across a society, there will be different types of opportunities and threats in different contexts. What are needed are different people who can take appropriate advantage of those different opportunities and threats at different moments. The same is true of our law-making. While it may be thought that we are trying to create something which is called 'The Law' and which is sovereign over everyone, what we are doing in some situations is to create criminal law so as to deter or punish different types of activity (and notice how we punish or prosecute some more vigorously than others[1]); in other situations we are trying to resolve family breakdown with child law, divorce law and aspects of property law; in other situations we are offering up models to our citizens through trusts law, partnership law and company law, to use the concepts which the law has fashioned so as to facilitate their activities and to resolve disputes that may arise. So, in some cases the law is not meaningfully a sovereign; rather, it can often be a resource and a guiding hand. It may offer support in the way that a welfare state often offers structure and entitlement resulting from the right sorts of behaviour. It is not always exerting sovereign power in the form of the criminal law on murder, for example.

This book has not sought to argue that equity is better than common law. Instead, it has sought to resist the arguments that common law is necessarily better than equity, that equity is a bad form of law and that equity should therefore be removed from our juridical canon. It is not the primacy of one code over another which has been asserted here, but rather the need for a blend or synthesis of the two so as to create a rounded legal system. Clearly, there need to be rules. There need to be rules about the side of the road on which we should drive, who is entitled to dispense drugs in a hospital and what protection the state will give you through the courts if you create a trading company in accordance with the appropriate legislation. However, there will also be situations in which the 'letter of the

---

[1] E.g., we are likely to prosecute allegations of murder vigorously; but in relation to road traffic offences, the approach is often slack. In relation to white-collar crime, some complain that the financial crisis saw very few people prosecuted (one of the more high-profile being young Kweku Adoboli of Swiss bank UBS), and yet mystifyingly large numbers of careless executives escape without any sort of investigation into their affairs, let alone prosecution.

law' will not necessarily produce an ideal response, or worse, a positively unfair response. There will be situations in which people need some flexibility in which to create new models which will work better for them personally or better in unanticipated situations. One future for the UK economy is likely to be in the creative field and in the new frontiers of technology. By definition, an innovative economy may need innovative legal models (in terms of company law, tax law, intellectual property law and so forth) to maximise its success. Therefore, non-rigid ways of thinking will be important.

This book has sought to resist ideas of taxonomy and rigidity precisely because they offer only short-term solutions. Think of something rigid like a tarmac road. If left alone for a few years, the tarmac will begin to degrade and plants will begin to force their way through. Concrete buildings eventually subside. Mountains erode.[2] Eventually, over-rigidity leads to death. The clearest sign of death, of course, is rigor mortis. There is a line to be drawn between over-rigidity and a robust, civilised response to the inherent chaos of ordinary life. So, predictable rule-making is a sign of a civilised society only when it is accompanied by the ability to change and adapt when that becomes a necessity.

This book has not sought to present equity as being better than any other way of thinking. It has not even identified one single approach to equity. Instead, what has been suggested here, amidst all of the debates, is that a legal system needs a synthesis of strict rules (of the sort typified by statute and by common law) and mechanisms for achieving fair outcomes when the strict rules will not achieve that. To those of a tidy turn of mind, that may seem messy; but to those with a tidy turn of mind, the world probably seems messy already. We live in a world in which the banking system can collapse at any minute, in which terrorists fly aeroplanes into office buildings and in which there is always a war somewhere in the world. It would be foolhardy to suppose that we can design a scheme of strict rules in a world full of unexpected events. More to the point, there is something deeply humane about an equity which ensures that no one is treated unconscionably. It is a part of life. It is true that a well-ordered society needs strict rules and clear social conventions, but as the poet Emily Dickinson observed, if our only weather was sunshine, so that 'summer was an axiom', then 'what sorcery had snow'? A successful legal system is a synthesis of order and justice. A successful system of private law is a synthesis of common law and equity.

---

[2] Fact: the highest mountains are the youngest mountains in Earth's history. The older mountains have eroded. Given enough time, presumably all of the planet's mountains will be worn flat like Holland or East Anglia. Nothing is forever.

# INDEX